HOW TO THINK ABOUT

The
End
Time

MARVIN MOORE

Pacific Press® Publishing Association
Nampa, Idaho
Oshawa, Ontario, Canada

Edited by B. Russell Holt
Designed by Tim Larson
Cover photo by Butch Martin © Image Bank

Library of Congress Cataloging-in-Publication Data

Moore, Marvin, 1937-
    How to think about the end time / Marvin Moore.
        p. cm.
    Includes bibliographical references.
    ISBN 0-8163-1835-2
        1. Second Advent. 2. Seventh-day Adventists—Doctrines.
I. Title.

    BT886 .M645 2001
    236'.9—dc21   00-066571

01 02 03 04 05 · 5 4 3 2 1

Table of Contents

Introduction

In the late summer of 1999 I wrote an article for the *Signswatch*® news-letter[1] titled "How to Think About the End Time." The article had a dual focus: time setting and how to interpret signs of the end. You'll read about both of these issues in chapters 3 and 8 of this book.

Shortly after I'd written the article, it occurred to me that this topic would actually make a good book. I've thought a great deal about end-time issues during my career as an Adventist pastor and editor. I've especially had occasion to do this since becoming the editor of *Signs of the Times*® back in August 1994, because of the many letters and email messages I've received from people all over North America and various parts of the world with questions about the end time.

The majority of the time I find myself quite in agreement with the opinions and conclusions of my correspondents. However, sometimes I disagree, and usually my disagreement has as much to do with the process by which people reached their conclusions as it does with the conclusions themselves.

Thinking about the end time involves more than simply poring over the prophecies in the Bible and the writings of Ellen White and piecing together a scenario of end-time events. More often than not, this method will lead to erroneous conclusions. That's where the thinking *process* comes in.

Straight thinking about the end time involves a willingness to question every conclusion to be sure it's in harmony with the inspired evidence. And to do that, of course, we must study the evidence carefully to be sure we understand what it does and does not say. Straight thinking about any biblical topic requires that we use the right methods of Bible study, and this is especially true of Bible prophecy.

Adventists and other Christians who believe the end of the world is near naturally pay a great deal of attention to current events that appear to fulfill the Bible's end-time prophecies. Straight thinking about the end time requires a willingness to verify the factuality of data from noninspired sources to be sure it's accurate.

The King James Version of the Bible says that "no prophecy of the scripture is of any private interpretation" (2 Peter 1:20). Straight thinking about the end time requires a willingness to submit our views to others and to weigh their constructive criticism carefully. It means asking lots of questions, especially about our conclusions, and avoiding a rush to find the answers.

As I reflected on these issues, I realized that there are a number of areas in which there's confusion and disagreement among Adventists over the end time—enough to easily make a good book, so I wrote up a proposal and presented it to the book editors at Pacific Press. Their response was very positive. They asked me to proceed with the project. A year and a half later, the book you are now holding in your hand was a reality.

This brings me to a significant issue I had to deal with in the process of writing the book. Readers expect that a "how-to" book will instruct them how to *do* whatever the book is about: How to plant a garden, how to use a computer, how to bake a cake. But this book isn't about how to *do* anything. It's about how to *think*. And therein lies the problem, because I cannot tell you or anyone else how to think. The best I can do is tell you how *I* think about the end time, how *I* apply the principles of interpretation that I alluded to a few paragraphs back.[2]

I thought perhaps I should title the book "How *I* Think About the End Time," but that didn't seem quite right. So I proposed the title "Reflections on How to Think About the End Time by the Editor of *Signs of the Times*®," but the book editors didn't care for that. So we all ended up agreeing that *How to Think About the End Time* would be the best title, in spite of the fact that it appears to be telling you, the reader, how you should think.

So if you're tempted to say to yourself, "Who is Marvin Moore to tell *me* how to think?" please remember that I anticipated your response and tried to find a way around it. But in the end, *How to Think About the End Time* seemed to be the best title, with an explanation in the introduction that all I really want to do in this book is share with you how *I* think about the end time and hope my thoughts make sense to you.

With that caveat, I hope you'll reflect on my thoughts and make as many of them your own as seems appropriate to you.

Marvin Moore

---

1. *Signswatch*® is quarterly newsletter published by *Signs of the Times*® that discusses end-time issues of special interest to Seventh-day Adventists. For more information about *Signswatch*® or to subscribe, call 1-800-765-6955.

2. In a few places I have given specific advice on how to think about the end time where that advice is reflected in the inspired sources.

the
End Time

Shortly before Jesus returned to heaven, His disciples came to Him with an urgent question: " 'Lord, are you at this time going to restore the kingdom to Israel?' " (Acts 1:6).

That question is pregnant with meaning for every Seventh-day Adventist who is serious about his Church's foundational conviction—a conviction that has driven our movement's global outreach for more than 150 years now—that the return of Jesus is near. For you see, in Christ's time, as in our day, there was a widespread expectation that the time was near for the establishment of God's eternal kingdom.

Of course, the Jews' understanding of what that would entail was much different from ours. Indeed, we would think their view of the end time very strange. Nevertheless, let's take a few moments to sketch their beliefs and their expectations to see what lessons they may hold for us.

To start with, there were the promises of the Old Testament prophets about Israel's greatness. For example, Isaiah said:

> In the last days the mountain of the Lord's temple will be established as chief among the mountains; it will be raised above the hills, and all nations will stream to it. Many peoples will come and say, "Come, let us go up to the mountain of the Lord, to the house of the God of Jacob" (Isaiah 2:2, 3).

Israel will be the greatest among the nations! That's what the text says, isn't it? And that's what they believed. It may have seemed difficult to believe this when their nation was under Rome's thumb, but God's people have always been willing to believe the impossible when prophecy declares it. *They* couldn't conquer Rome, of course—though some tried awfully hard. But everyone knew that the Messiah, when He came, would lead the Jews to victory over all their oppressors. Didn't the prophecies declare that too? Didn't Isaiah predict that "the Lord has a day of vengeance, a year of retribution, to uphold Zion's cause" (Isaiah 34:8)? Didn't he declare that God was "angry with all nations," that His wrath was upon all their armies, and that He would totally destroy them (verse 2)? Didn't He foresee the day when, with vengeance in His heart, the Messiah would trample the nations in His anger (Isaiah 34:3, 4)?

And now for the best news of all: The day of the Messiah's appearance was at hand! Daniel's seventy-week prophecy, with its beginning in the middle of the fifth century B.C., was about to reach its conclusion in the first century A.D. Not only that, they could hasten His arrival! For, according to a common notion circulating in Palestine at the time, the Messiah would come when all Jews lived in perfect harmony with the law for just one day. Naturally, obedience to the law became very important to the most zealous among them. In fact, one extreme group at Christ's time was called the "Zealots" because of their zeal for strict observance of the law. Eventually, some of these people banded into a party to fight the Romans, and in this role they became fanatical opponents of the Roman domination of Judea to the point of assassinating anyone who opposed them!

You and I, looking at first-century Judaism through the lens of twenty-first-century Adventism may smile, but that's only because, with the benefit of 2,000 years of history, we understand that they failed to achieve God's most basic purpose for their existence.

That was *their* mindset. Now let's come back to our *Adventist* mindset about the end time. I suggest that, while there are many differences between their views and ours, there are several interesting similarities.

Chief among these is the great anticipation, based on our prophetic interpretation, that "the end" is near. Another significant similarity is the shared conviction that the failure to live our religious beliefs faithfully is a major cause of the delay in the return of Christ. And finally, there is the conviction that our group is special in God's eyes. We are His unique people. The Jews were "sons of Abraham." Our Church is "the remnant."

Jesus' disciples were steeped in these ideas. And given this background, imagine what it must have been like for them the day Jesus rode into Jerusalem on a donkey, the crowds shouting His praises and singing " 'Blessed is the king who comes in the name of the Lord!' " (Luke 19:38). The end was near! Jesus was about to establish His kingdom! All the prophecies pointing to Israel's greatness were about to reach their final fulfillment! The disciples' hopes soared to a fever pitch.

And each was assigning himself the role he would play in the coming kingdom. Of course, they each aspired to the coveted position of prime minister. And each probably assumed that Judas was the one to beat out of the job. In this competitive frame of mind, it's little wonder they came to the upper room so totally unprepared that Christ had to give them a living example of what it means to be a servant.

Please notice that *their confused thinking about the end time* combined with their innate human selfishness caused them to be spiritually unprepared for the institution of the preeminent sacrament of the next 2,000 years of Christian history.

A few hours later, a mob led by Judas came to arrest Jesus. Not to worry, though. Jesus was perfectly able to defend Himself. And at first that seemed to have happened. Ellen White says that "the angel who had lately ministered to Jesus moved between Him and the mob," and "the murderous throng . . . staggered back. Priests, elders, soldiers, and even Judas, fell as dead men to the ground."[1] But then Jesus allowed Himself to be arrested. That's when Peter decided it was time for action and whipped out his sword to defend his Master. But Jesus did the strangest thing. He ordered His disciple to put his sword back in its sheath. How totally incomprehensible that must have seemed to Peter!

The disciples followed Jesus to the home of the high priest, then to the Sanhedrin, then to Pilate's judgment hall, then to Herod, and back to Pilate. All the while they waited with bated breath for Him to assert His power. "Just flash Your divinity, Jesus! Show Your power! Take over the armies of Israel and lead them to victory over the Romans!"

But He never did.

Instead, Jesus allowed Himself to be led away to Golgotha, where Roman soldiers nailed Him to a cross, and He died. *He really, truly died!* Nicodemus and Joseph of Arimathea took His body down and buried it in Joseph's tomb.

Do you understand a bit better now the anguished cry of the two disciples on the road to Emmaus: " 'We had hoped that he was the one who was going to redeem Israel' " (Luke 24:21)? Talk about the great disappointment!

But then Jesus came back to life.

What a miracle! He had raised Lazarus from the dead, and now He had even raised Himself from the dead. What a military leader Jesus would make! The enemy couldn't possibly destroy Him or His army. So this was the plan! The disciples spent the next forty days waiting for Him to outline the steps in the establishment of His kingdom. But on that subject Jesus was strangely and to-tally silent. Finally, on what seemed to them a particularly auspicious occasion, they broached the subject again: " 'Lord, are you at this time going to restore the kingdom to Israel?' " (Acts 1:6).

Old ideas do die hard.

Please notice that *it was wrong thinking about the end time* that caused the disciples so much confusion and grief. Do you begin to understand why it's so important that *we* understand how to think about the end time?

Join me some 1,800 years later. October 22, 1844. It's the end time again. Jesus is coming! He's coming today! The people gather in little groups, looking into the sky. Waiting for the flaming cloud. The trumpet call. The graves breaking open. The saints ascending to heaven. But mid-night comes, and there's no flaming cloud, no trumpet call, no Jesus. In-stead, to quote the anguished words of one who passed through that time, "Our fondest hopes and expectations were blasted, and such a spirit of weeping came over us as I have never experienced before. . . . We wept, and wept, till the day dawn."[2]

It was the second Great Disappointment.

And why? Because, again, God's people misunderstood the prophecies. I realize that there's a great difference between the first disappointment and the second one. Jesus warned His disciples repeatedly about His approach-ing trial and death, but they refused to listen. Thus, they brought their great disappointment on themselves. The situation was different during the Mil-lerite movement of the 1830s and early 1840s. In the words of Ellen White, God's hand "was over and hid a mistake in some of the figures, so that none could see it, until His hand was removed." He "covered a mistake in the reckoning of the prophetic periods."[3] The point is that *a misunderstanding of prophecy always leads to erroneous expectations, regardless of the cause.*

Seventh-day Adventists today, together with many other Christians, believe that we truly do live in the end time. I share that conviction. The question that confronts us is this:

Will there be a third great disappointment?

I'd like to answer that question with the words of Jesus Himself:

"Not everyone who says to me, 'Lord, Lord,' will enter the kingdom of heaven, but only he who does the will of my Father who is in heaven. Many will say to me on that day, 'Lord, Lord, did we not prophesy in your name, and in your name drive out demons and perform many miracles?' Then I will tell them plainly, 'I never knew you. Away from me, you evildoers!' " (Matthew 7:21-23).

Our ideas about the end of the world and the establishment God's eternal kingdom are based on Bible prophecy, and for Seventh-day Adventists, the prophetic writings of Ellen White. It can't be any other way, unless we're prepared to accept the babblings of the psychics or the questionable predictions of the so-called apparitions of the Virgin Mary. Therefore, it's imperative that we have a correct understanding of the prophecies. Because if we don't, *we will misunderstand the fulfillment of those prophecies even as we live through the events that fulfill them.*

Satan was extremely successful at deceiving the Jews about Christ's first coming. He got them to believe that the Messiah's primary mission would be to deliver them from the Romans. He twisted their calling to be God's *special* people into the perversion that they were His *exclusive* people. He caused them to be so zealous for the law that they twisted it into an impossible burden. And because of these false beliefs and expectations, they rejected their own Messiah when He came.

I can assure you that Satan is also doing everything he can to introduce false beliefs and false expectations into our minds about the second coming of Jesus. And with many of us he will succeed, for Jesus warned that Satan will be so successful that even God's own elect will be in danger of succumbing to his deceptions, if that were possible (see Matthew 24:24). Those who are truly the elect won't be deceived. But many who *think* they are among the elect *will* be deceived. For Jesus also warned that " 'many will say to me on that day, "Lord, Lord, did we not prophesy in your name, and in your name drive out demons and perform many miracles?" Then I will tell them plainly, "I never knew you" ' " (Matthew 7:22, 23).

False ideas and expectations about the end time will be among Satan's major deceptions in our day. That's why it's so important that we *think correctly* about the end time. For if our thinking is confused on that issue, at best the final crisis will be much more difficult for us as we're passing through it, and at the worst we will end up on the wrong side when it's over. That's why I invite you to consider with me in the remainder of this book:

How to Think About the End Time.

---

1. *The Desire of Ages*, 694.
2. From a fragment of a letter written by Adventist pioneer Hiram Edson.
3. *Early Writings*, 74; *The Story of Redemption*, 362, 363.

the
Final Crisis

I'm sure you've read the book of Daniel and you know that Daniel's angel interpreter told him the full meaning of his prophecy was "closed up and sealed until the time of the end" (Daniel 12:9). Seventh-day Adventists believe this "time of the end" began in 1844. We divide the time of the end into at least two periods—a longer one from 1844 to the "time of trouble," with the time of trouble itself being the shorter one.

Differences exist as to exactly when this time of trouble will start. Some believe it will begin *with* the close of probation. However, I prefer to start it with the judgments of God that will begin falling on the earth shortly *before* the close of probation. I call the period from the beginning of these judgments of God until the second coming of Christ "the final crisis."[1] Here is a simple diagram of that crisis as I understand it:

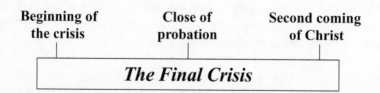

Beginning of the crisis	Close of probation	Second coming of Christ

The Final Crisis

The purpose of this chapter is to provide a very brief overview of the final crisis for readers who may not be familiar with it. If you have read my books, *The Crisis of the End Time* and *The Coming Great Calamity,* you already have a good idea of what I mean by "the final crisis," and you may wish to go on to the next chapter.

Revelation's picture of the final crisis

According to Revelation 13, a global conflict between the forces of good and evil will erupt shortly before the second coming of Christ. A one-world, religio-political government will be set up, and it will launch a fierce attack against God's people:

> [The first beast of Revelation 13] was given power to make war against the saints and to conquer them. And he was given authority over every tribe, people, language and nation (Revelation 13:7).

> [The second beast] was given power to give breath to the image of the first beast, so that it could speak and cause all who refused to worship the image to be killed (verse 15).

It's hard for us to imagine a global religio-political government with that kind of authority even existing in today's world, much less that such a government would launch an attack of that magnitude on religious dissenters. We might conceive of this happening in certain Muslim societies—but in the secular, freedom-loving West? Hardly! Nevertheless, Bible prophecy predicts it, and if the world is now in its final countdown as Seventh-day Adventists have taught for 150 years, then a global government such as this is not too far distant. The question is, How could such a dramatic turn of events happen anytime in the foreseeable future?

That's what the final crisis will be about.

Global calamities

Revelation 7:1 pictures four angels "holding back the four winds of the earth to prevent any wind from blowing on the land or on the sea or on any tree." However, according to the next three verses, at a certain point these angels will be commanded to release those winds, and when that happens the land, sea, and trees will be harmed. I understand this to mean that terrible natural disasters will fall upon our planet, causing severe ecological devastation.[2] This crisis will launch the world into the " 'time of distress such as has not happened from the beginning of nations until then' " that was spoken of by the prophet Daniel

(Daniel 12:1). Jesus paraphrased Daniel's prediction and added some words of His own that give us additional insight into the magnitude of the crisis. He said:

> "For then there will be great distress, unequaled from the beginning of the world until now—and never to be equaled again. If those days had not been cut short, no one would survive, but for the sake of the elect those days will be shortened" (Matthew 24:21, 22).

These words say more than we might realize at first glance. Notice: The coming time of distress will be so severe that if God didn't cut it short "*no one would survive.*" In other words, without God's intervention to halt the distress, the human race would become the next extinct species! If this sounds extreme to you, pay careful attention to the following words by Ellen White:

> Calamities will come—*calamities most awful, most unexpected;* and these destructions will follow one after another.[3]

> Something great and decisive is soon to take place, *else no flesh would be saved.* The character of God will not be compromised. Under the wrath of God, *universal desolation* will soon reach all parts of the known world.[4]

> O that God's people had a sense of the impending *destruction of thousands of cities,* now almost given to idolatry.[5]

Calamities most awful, most unexpected; no flesh would be saved; universal desolation; thousands of cities destroyed! I propose that as a result of the chaos arising out of these global natural disasters the world will recognize that "God is trying to tell us something," and religious laws will be enacted that would be unthinkable today. All this will happen very swiftly. We do not know when these events will occur, but they have been foretold by both the Bible and Ellen White, and believing these sources to be inspired by God, I have no doubt that the crisis they predict will become very real at some point in the future.

Two end-time groups

Out of this chaos two groups will emerge, both of which are forming today. The larger group, consisting of the vast majority of the world's population, will enforce a global form of worship. Revelation describes this group with three symbols: A sea beast, a land beast, and an image to the sea beast that the land beast will set up. While these beast powers are described in very symbolic language, it's obvious that they will be in rebellion against God.

The other group will be God's remnant—a small minority who will resist the false worship of the two beast powers. God's people will be given a special endowment of His Spirit that will enable them to stand up to these global forces of evil with a power that is far superior to their small numbers. Their stand will be similar to that of Shadrach, Meshach, and Abednego, who challenged the laws of Babylon and allowed themselves to be cast into a burning fiery furnace rather than yield their allegiance to the true God.

These two groups will actually be the human representatives of God and Satan—the two powers outside our world that are contending for control of the universe. Each group will proclaim its message with great power, and every human being will become sufficiently aware of the issues on both sides to make a personal, irrevocable decision. When each person on earth has made his or her final decision, God will close probation, and from that time forth no one will be able to change his or her loyalty from God to Satan or from Satan to God.

The close of probation will mark the end of Christ's mediatorial ministry in the heavenly sanctuary. Immediately after that, the seven last plagues will begin to fall—the final outpouring of God's wrath on the wicked. During this time God's people will have to "live in the sight of a holy God without an intercessor."[6] Many Adventists believe that God's people must be sinlessly perfect in order to live without a Mediator after the close of probation—an idea that we will examine in some detail later in this book.

From our study of the prophecies of Daniel and Revelation, Adventists understand that the forces of evil during the final crisis will be under the leadership of the Roman Catholic Church, while God's people will accept the message that we have been proclaiming since the mid-1800s.

Seventh-day Adventists also understand, for reasons that will become more clear in succeeding chapters, that the primary spiritual issue in the conflict between the forces of good and evil at that time will be the law of God, particularly the Sabbath commandment. Laws will be enacted, enforcing Sunday as the exclusive day for worship, and those who refuse to obey these laws will be prosecuted and eventually condemned to death.

Spiritualism

Jesus, Paul, and John all warned of false christs and false prophets in the last days who will bring the whole world under the power of spiritualism.[7] Protestants and Catholics will join hands with each other and with spiritualism to create a false religious system. Demons masquerading as angels of light will unite the entire world into this false religious system. They will claim to have come to save the human race from the terrible calamities that are falling on the world. Eventually, Satan himself will appear on the earth in the guise of Christ. He will be a glorious being of intense light, and the entire world will bow down and worship him.

God's remnant are the only ones who will resist these spiritualistic forces. They will point out that these false christs are actually demons. Because God's people refuse to submit to the religious dogmas of the majority, they will become "objects of universal execration."[8] Eventually, they will be condemned to die for their faith, and a decree will go forth "giving the people liberty, after a certain time, to put them to death."[9] Two forces will drive the world to this extreme. The first will be the natural disasters that devastate our planet to the point that human life will be threatened. The other force will be demons.

Before the end comes, it will appear from a human point of view that God's people have lost in their conflict with earth's forces of evil. But at the very last moment Jesus will return as a Warrior from heaven (see Revelation 19:11-21). He will defeat the world's evil powers and rescue His people from what had appeared to be certain doom. " 'The God of heaven . . . will crush all those kingdoms and bring them to an end' " (Daniel 2:44).

The final crisis, as I have described it, seems impossible at the present time. However, if the Bible and Ellen White are correct, then these events will indeed transpire in the not too distant future. We live prior to that time, though how much before we don't know. However, this book is only indirectly about the final crisis. It deals more with how we *think* about the final crisis.

Because God wants us to be prepared to go through the crisis on His side, He has given us a great deal of information about it in both the Bible and the writings of Ellen White. Unfortunately, it's very easy to misinterpret these inspired sources and thus to arrive at unwarranted conclusions. It's easy for our emotions and our preconceptions to cast a meaning on these sources that they don't actually support. I have studied the end time for many years. I have also written a great deal on end-time events. Because of this, and because I am the editor of Signs of the Times®, I have received many letters and other inquiries about the end time. These letters and inquiries have helped me to realize that there is a good bit of misunderstanding about the end time among us.

Following are some of the topics I will consider with you in the rest of this book:

- What constitutes a valid sign that the final crisis and the second coming of Jesus really are near? How can we know what is—and what isn't—a sign?
- If Sunday laws are to be a key issue in the final conflict, then why don't we see them being more widely enacted and enforced today?
- How can we really be sure the final crisis and Christ's second coming are near today when it's been 2,000 years since the disciples said His coming was near and 150 years since the pioneers began proclaiming His soon return?
- If the Catholic Church is supposed to be one of the chief antagonists against God's people in the end time, what should be our attitude toward Catholics today? And in light of the Catholic Church's current attitude of religious toleration, wouldn't it be a good idea for us to modify our view of its role during the final crisis?
- What does it mean to be perfect in order to live without a Mediator after the close of probation? How can I know whether I'm good enough?
- Does our teaching about the time of trouble really have to be so scary? How can I ever be ready to live through that time?
- Are Adventists God's "remnant" that will withstand the forces of evil during the final crisis, and what does it mean if we are?

These are some of the questions I will discuss with you in this book. I don't claim that my conclusions are the last word on each topic or that they are all correct. I do hope that what I say will stimulate you to further study and reflection on your own so that all of us can think as correctly as possible about the end time.

---

1. I didn't invent the term the final crisis. There is clear evidence for it in the writings of Ellen White. Sometimes she called it "the final crisis." At other times she spoke of it as "the great crisis," "the crisis of the ages," or simply "the crisis." (See for example *Testimonies,* 6:404; 9:11; *Christ's Object Lessons,* 178; *Prophets and Kings,* 278.) A careful examination of her understanding of this crisis also makes it clear that she understood it would begin some time before the close of probation.

2. I say this because it's the land, the sea, and the trees that will be harmed when the angels release the four winds.

3. *Evangelism*, 27, italics added.

4. *Review and Herald*, November 27, 1900, italics added; see also *Special Testimonies A*, 1-b, page 38; *The Ellen G. White 1888 Materials*, 447, 448.

5. *Evangelism*, 29, italics added.

6. *The Great Controversy*, 614.

7. See Matthew 24:23, 24; 2 Thessalonians 2:9, 10; Revelation 13:11-14; 16:12-14.

8. *The Great Controversy*, 615.

9. Ibid., 615, 616.

HOW TO THINK ABOUT

Signs
of the
Times

Signs
of the
End

I get asked a lot of interesting questions as editor of *Signs of the Times*®. Often, people send me newspaper clippings and magazine articles, and occasionally they will ask what I think of them in light of the end time. Please read the following newspaper story someone sent me, which is the first of three "end-time scenarios" that I will share with you in the next couple of pages:

Scenario number 1

EL CENIZO, Texas—As ceiling fans puffed at the big American flag on the community center wall, the dozen residents at the City Council meeting Thursday [August 12, 1999] poised hands over hearts for the Pledge of Allegiance.

Then they commenced their town's modestly historic council meeting, possibly the first in the United States to be conducted by city ordinance in Spanish.

Far-flung, sun-battered and mostly poor, this former *colonia* of trailers and frail bungalows found itself in the middle of a political vortex two weeks after enacting a pair of surprising laws.

Under one ordinance, all city government business must take place in Spanish. And under the second, city employees—all six of them—are forbidden to help the U.S. Border Patrol catch undocumented immigrants, at risk of being fired.

That innocuous bit of news was allotted five whole inches on the front page of the *Los Angeles Times* for August 13, 1999, continuing with a quarter of a page on the inside. When I first read that story in my home-town newspaper, *The Idaho Statesman*, I took it as a commentary on the fascinating variety of life just north of the Mexican border and promptly forgot about it. Until a reader of *Signs of the Times®* sent me the version from the Los Angeles newspaper with an interesting question: Wasn't the part about conducting all city business in Spanish an ominous portent of Sunday laws and Christ's return?

She was sure the answer was Yes.

My answer was No.

Scenario number 2

Another *Signs* reader called me during the war in Kosovo early in 1999 asking whether I thought that conflict didn't portend imminent Sunday laws. He went on to explain his reasoning: Prophecy suggests that the United States will become a superpower during the end time, and in that role it will institute Sunday laws. The war in Kosovo is evidence that America is now a superpower. Therefore Sunday laws must be just around the corner. Didn't I agree?

I said No.

Scenario number 3

I'm sure everyone reading these words remembers the acronym Y2K—shorthand for the year 2000 and the much-anticipated and much-feared global millennium computer meltdown associated with it. Some people predicted that fearful chaos would erupt beginning January 1, 2000: Empty shelves in the grocery stores, all major utilities shut down, and the national guard called out to quell the rioting in the streets. Fearing the worst, some people bought houses in the wilderness complete with water wells, generators, a year's supply of food and fuel, and guns and ammunition to protect their hoard from the starving masses.

I'm glad to tell you that most Adventists kept their wits about them through all of this. Nevertheless, there was some speculation that Y2K just might lead the world into the final crisis and usher in the second coming of Jesus. I remember seeing an article in a respectable Adventist publication titled "Is Y2K 666?" I wrote an article by the same title in my *Signswatch®* newsletter, and again, my answer was No, Y2K won't be 666.

None of these scenarios impressed me as a significant sign that either Sunday laws or the second coming of Christ were imminent. However, these stories do convey a very important lesson to all of us who are anticipating the soon return of Jesus: We need to think carefully about what constitutes a valid sign of the end. I'd like to analyze the emotions and motivations behind these stories and many others like them.

What's our mindset?

Nearly all readers of this book have waited their turn in line at grocery store check-stands, and most of us have probably spent at least some of those moments looking at the tabloids that decorate the racks along the side. Think back on the headlines you've read on these scandal sheets. A significant number of them focus on predictions about the future—psychics telling us what the movie stars are going to do next year or some obscure theologian forecasting the imminent end of the world. Most of us dismiss these prognostications with a shrug and a smile.

But I propose an interesting experiment. Go to the nearest public library, browse through a copy of *Business Week* or *Investors Business Weekly*, and see how much space these magazines devote to divining the future of the stock market or the next year's sales potential for cars and soybeans. I suspect the percentage of space the business journals devote to forecasting the future is fairly close to that of the tabloids. At the most basic level, the prognostications of the tabloids and those of the business magazines are identical. Both exemplify the fundamental human desire to know the future. *We want to know what will happen tomorrow.*

And that, I suggest, is what lies behind the Adventist (and Christian) fascination with signs of the end. *We want to know what the future holds.*

Most of us would probably agree, however, that there is quite a difference between the prognostications of the tabloids and those of the business magazines. I, for one, assume that the predictions of the tabloids are based on some astrologer's hocus pocus (more respectfully called a "hunch"), while the predictions in the business magazines have a rational basis. Few of us would make a life-changing decision based on the predictions of a tabloid. We consider their primary value to be entertainment. Businessmen, on the other hand, are continually making life-changing decisions based on the predictions of their business magazines.

Jesus also made some extremely significant predictions about the future. He promised us a world free of fear, pain, and death. Naturally, we long to see that prediction fulfilled. Unfortunately, often, mixed in with this very normal desire is a tabloid mentality that's willing to accept anything as a sign of the end as long as it's sensational. *And all too often our motivation is more the need for an emotional charge than it is a genuine desire for Jesus to come.*

I know from experience that what I just said is true. Most of those reading this book shortly after its publication in 2001 were probably old enough at the time Communism fell in Eastern Europe to remember the excitement Adventists felt over those events. We said "Wow! Ellen White told us the final events would be rapid ones, and they sure are!" I don't know about you, but I got quite an adrenaline rush out of those six or eight months. Desert Storm hit the world a year or so later, and that was good for another adrenaline rush. Next it was Gorbachev out and Yeltsin in—the end of the Soviet Union—and another adrenaline rush. Alongside these events was the growing political power of the Christian Coalition, which seemed to fulfill Ellen White's predictions about the end-time union of church and state, the ultimate result of which will be Sunday laws. And with this, of course, came another adrenaline rush.

I can still remember reflecting on my emotions as they related to end-time events and signs of Christ's coming. I'd had enough exposure to addiction theory by then that I was able to recognize my adrenaline rush for what it was—a surge of emotion. I also knew that chemistry, and the pleasure induced by the chemistry, is the basis of all addictions, whether the chemical is introduced *into* the body or produced *by* the body. And it occurred to me that the adrenaline rush of end-time events has the potential to become quite addictive. I can tell you from experience that the surge of emotion over an event that seems to be a sign of the end *feels good,* and I would like to get it again. And again. And again.

Now I happen to believe, given Ellen White's description of end-time events and our Adventist understanding of Daniel and Revelation, that the Christian Coalition's growing political power back in the early 1990s was one piece of a trend that suggests the coming of Jesus is near. So was the Roman Catholic Church's role in the demise of Communism in Eastern Europe. Realistically, events that hold this much end-time significance don't come along every day, *but the addict's need for the adrenaline rush that such events provide is ongoing.* The unfortunate result is that, when the daily news doesn't provide us with enough events having end-time significance, we'll impose an end-time significance on *ordinary* events in order to keep the adrenaline rush going.

This is one of the most important reasons why it's so critically important that we learn how to *think* clearly about the end time and not just *react emotionally* to signs of the end, including those that are genuine. We need to evaluate our motives in this area very carefully. For when our response to end-time events is purely emotional—when it's just another way to pump adrenaline into our blood stream—the motive is dysfunctional and ultimately destructive. Worse yet, we're likely to "see" signs of the end where they don't exist.

How to evaluate signs of the end

So how *should* we evaluate events to determine whether they are signs of the end? Following are three of the guidelines that I follow.

Trends rather than events. In my opinion, very few individual *events* qualify as signs of the end in the sense that they fulfill a specific end-time prediction in either the Bible or the writings of Ellen White. I would probably consider a Sunday law passed by the United States Congress to be a sign of the end, and the appearance of Satan as Christ surely will be a sign of the end when it occurs. Beyond these two and maybe a few others, I can't think of any *single event* that would constitute for me a sign of the end. However, I do believe that, in combination with similar events, individual events can have *end-time significance*. And the combination of similar events with end-time significance can form a *trend* that I *am* willing to interpret as a sign of the end.

For example, by itself—if there were no other events of an ecumenical nature—I would not consider the recent Catholic-Lutheran accord on justification to be a sign of the end. However, this joint statement does have *end-time significance*, and in combination with many similar events it forms an ecumenical trend. And that trend I do consider to be a sign of the end. So my recommendation for the vast majority of events is to look for that *end-time significance* and its relationship to similar events that may form a *trend*.

What is the inspired evidence? In order for either an event or a trend to have end-time significance, it must relate to an end-time issue that is defined in either the Bible or the writings of Ellen White. The relationship may be indirect, such as modern witchcraft, which is not spiritualism per se but contributes to the present trend toward the spiritualism that both the Bible and Ellen White tell us will be rampant during the final crisis.

The challenge is to be sure the event or trend truly does have support in the inspired evidence. It's easy to read into the Bible what we want it to say, and it's easy to read into events a meaning we want them to have, but when we do either of these we are very likely to come up with incorrect conclusions about what constitutes a "sign of the end." We will be examining examples of this kind of distorted thinking in future chapters.

Did it really happen? In their anxiety for signs of the end, some Christians see signs in "events" that have not happened. Such "events" get the attention of Christians who need another shot of adrenaline, but because they never happened they can't possibly be signs of the end. They're mere distractions that get our attention off of the real issues having to do with the end time. Since I've devoted the next chapter in its entirety to this topic, I won't discuss it further here. The point is that we need to verify that what might be an event in the future, or what we're told is an event in the past, actually happened before we ask whether it has end-time significance.

Let's apply these guidelines to the three examples of "signs of the end" that I shared with you at the beginning of this chapter. Why did I say that the newspaper clipping about the Spanish-language city council meeting in El Cenizo, Texas, is not a sign of Sunday laws or of the end? Well, you tell me, How does that event relate to *anything* the Bible or the writings of Ellen White tell us about the end time?

Regarding the war in Kosovo, both the Bible and Ellen White make it quite clear that the United States will be a superpower in the end time,[1] and perhaps the world's only superpower. If the individual who called me about that war had asked if I thought it was significant in relation to the Bible's prediction about the status of the United States in the end time, I might have given a guarded Yes (keeping in mind that it was NATO that conducted that war, not the United States, though we probably contributed 90 percent of the firepower). But there's simply no evidence that the war in Kosovo has *any* relationship to Sunday legislation.

How about Y2K, which many Christians and some Adventists were sure would precipitate the final crisis and the end of the world. Why did I say No? For two reasons. First, it was a nonevent until the worst-case scenario some people predicted actually happened. And second, I knew of absolutely *nothing* in either the Bible or the writings of Ellen White to suggest that the turmoil of the end time will be brought on by some human technological screw-up. To the contrary, the evidence suggests that the final crisis will be under God's control, and it will happen when He's ready for it to.

Other possible "signs"

Before closing this chapter, I'd like to examine two other areas where Adventists tend to see "signs" of the end. The first is Roman Catholicism. Because we believe that Catholicism will be the leading force in end-time apostasy, we tend to pay careful attention to what's going on in the Vatican. Unfortunately, some Adventists see an event with end-time significance in just about every news story that comes out of Rome. But is John Paul's canonization of a saint or two an event with end-time significance? No. Why? Because nothing in the inspired evidence relates canonization of saints to the end time. On the other hand, John Paul's ecumenical outreach to the Anglican and Orthodox churches does have end-time significance, for two reasons. First, Ellen White predicts an end-time union of churches,[2] and second, John Paul's ecumenical outreach is one of many similar events in today's world that create a definite ecumenical trend.

The second area where Christians in general, Adventists included, tend to see signs of the end is in wars. At the time of both World War I and World War II, Adventist evangelists got large audiences to attend their meetings with handbills that proclaimed Armageddon to be just around the corner. But Armageddon never developed, because wars, in and of themselves, are not signs of the end. Christians tend to see wars as signs of the end because Jesus spoke of "wars and rumors of wars" in response to His disciples' questions about signs of the end (see Matthew 24:6-8). But speaking of these wars Jesus specifically said that " 'the end is still to come' " (verse 6) and " '*that* is not yet the end' " (verse 6, NASB).

Let's take a moment to summarize the key points to keep in mind in evaluating whether an event has end-time significance:

- *Trends*. While very few events, by themselves, constitute a sign of the end that fulfills a specific prediction in either the Bible or Ellen White's writings, many events do have end-time significance. And a cluster of such events can form a trend that can be considered a sign of the end.
- *Inspired evidence*. To have end-time significance, an event must have a basis in the inspired evidence. It's not a sign of the end just because it's sensational or because it's about Catholics. And we need to read the inspired evidence carefully to be sure it says what we think it says.
- *Factuality*. When we hear of something that seems to have end-

time significance we must verify that it actually occurred before we conclude that it has end-time significance.

• *Watch our emotions.* While Christ's second coming will be a time of great joy, we should evaluate evidence for the nearness of His return as rationally as possible, lest our emotions prevent us from a realistic assessment.

I hope these suggestions have been helpful to you. We now need to turn to the question of the factuality of an event. *Did it really happen?*

---

1. Based on our traditional interpretation of the second beast of Revelation 13.
2. See for example *The Great Controversy*, 445.

Conspiracy Theories
and
Urban Legends

Back in the early 1960s when I was a ministerial intern in Pomona, California, the pastor under whom I worked suggested that I go door-to-door looking for people to whom I could give Bible studies. I will always remember one family that I became acquainted with as a result of this assignment. I don't recall ever giving a Bible study to *them,* but they sure tried to impress their political ideas on *me.*

Their great burden was the Illuminati, a super-secret cabal that they said had been running the world politically and economically for centuries and that was scheming to set up a one-world government under their control in the immediate future. They loaded me down with their literature, which I took home and devoured.

Wow! This was *The Great Controversy* in twentieth-century language! The prophecies of the Bible and Ellen White were being fulfilled before my very eyes! For several weeks I kept going back for more.

However, after the initial "shock," I began reflecting on what I was reading, and I noticed something extremely significant: Their books and magazines were all put out by obscure publishers, and they provided absolutely no documentation by which I could verify whether these astounding claims were really true. I was just supposed to *believe it* because the books and magazines *said it.*

I asked my friends if they could provide me with reliable sources. How

31

about articles from established magazines and major newspapers? How about books put out by well-known publishers?

"Oh, you can't trust these sources," my friends said. "They're all controlled by *them*."

I also noticed that the literature these people gave me focused strictly on political and economic issues. There was a lot of talk about the global crisis this one-world government would create, especially for dissenters such as my friends, but there wasn't a word about spiritual preparation for that crisis.

There was also a lot of paranoia about the coming one-world government. I recall sitting in the home of one woman who wept because she felt so unsure what she and her husband should do when the armies of the coming one-world government started mopping up the country. She asked if I thought they should buy a house out in the desert and stock it with food, guns, and ammunition! I said No, I didn't think they should do that.

Conspiracy theories and urban legends

What I have just described to you is a conspiracy theory. There are also "urban legends"—stories that circulate widely and are believed to be true by a large number of people. Certain conspiracy theories and urban legends find a ready acceptance among some Adventists because they appear to be signs of the approaching end. But as I pointed out in the previous chapter, we need to be sure that what *looks* like a sign really *is* a sign, or perhaps more correctly, that what looks like an event with end-time significance really has end-time significance. In this chapter I'll discuss how to evaluate conspiracy theories and urban legends that have—or appear to have—end-time implications. We'll start with conspiracy theories.

PART 1
CONSPIRACY THEORIES

First things first: What is a conspiracy theory? *Webster's New World Dictionary* defines *conspiracy* as "a planning and acting together secretly, esp. for an unlawful or harmful purpose, such as murder or treason"; and it defines *theory* as "a speculative idea or plan as to how something might be done." So a conspiracy theory is *a speculation about a secret plan of action by an individual or group of individuals whose plan, if carried out, would harm those whom it will affect.*

Given this definition, it's not surprising that Adventists and others who believe we are living in the end time tend to find conspiracy theories meaningful. After all, the primary objective of Revelation's end-time beast powers will be to harm God's people. Thus, any entity we hear about that appears to threaten our freedom, especially our religious freedom, is a candidate for being one of these beast powers or one of its coconspirators. And since Adventists tend to view Catholicism as the primary end-time persecutor of God's people, we especially tend to pay attention to anything that appears to implicate Catholics as conspirators.

So how do we separate the genuine from the false? Following are three guidelines that I have found helpful in evaluating conspiracy theories. The same guidelines will be useful in evaluating urban legends when we come to them later in the chapter:

- *Doubt it*. I have found that the majority of conspiracy theories and urban legends are false. So my first response on hearing a new story is to ask, "Is it really true?"
- *Check it*. And obviously, the only way to answer that question is to check it out. I try to go to the source: Who gave me the information, and what credentials does this person have for being an authority on the topic? If the person passing the story along to me is not personally an authority, I ask who gave the information to him or her. I trace it back as far as possible, and I refuse to believe anything I can't verify as coming from a reliable source.
- *Determine its relevance*. Even if I determine that the source is reliable and the story credible, is it relevant to the end time as described by the Bible and Ellen White? For example, a story about a group of conspirators trying to undermine the New York Stock Exchange might be credible but quite irrelevant to end-time events.

Let's examine some conspiracy theories and apply these guidelines to them. We'll start with the Illuminati, since I already brought that one up.

The Illuminati

Illuminati is a Latin word that means "enlightened." The English word *illuminate* comes from the same Latin original. The idea of an organization called the Illuminati is not totally false. Any good encyclopedia will tell you that an organization by that name was founded in Germany in 1776 or shortly thereafter by Adam Weishaupt, a professor of canon law at the University of Ingolstadt in Bavaria. The two encyclopedias I consulted[1] affirmed that Weishaupt's Illuminati was a secret society, its aim being to replace Christianity with a religion of reason. The society had a close relationship with the Masons, but it was short-lived. The Bavarian government shut it down in 1785.

The word *Illuminati* was also used of a group in the 1600s that claimed direct communion with the Holy Spirit, and because of this they said that the outward forms of religious life were unnecessary. The Rosicrucians and the followers of the mystics Jakob Boehme and Emmanuel Swedenborg also adopted the name Illuminati. However, all of these groups were (or are)[2] primarily religious, and it's highly unlikely that anything of political significance ever came from them.

The real question for us today is whether the Illuminati still exists as an international political and economic organization, and if it does, whether it's a super-secret society of individuals who are powerful enough to control the world from behind the scenes without themselves ever being discovered. That in a nutshell is what my friends back in the early 1960s claimed, and it's what believers in the Illuminati still claim. And let me assure you, those who believe this *believe it with a passion*. They are not easily dissuaded.

So let's apply the guidelines I suggested above to the Illuminati.

Doubt. I did not doubt the story when I first heard it back in the early 1960s. As I told you at the beginning of the chapter, my first reaction was very positive—enthusiastic would not be too strong a word. Fortunately, by then I'd been through four years of college and a year of graduate school, where I'd learned to look for demonstrable evidence before accepting something as true. My doubts about the Illuminati arose when I began doing that.

Evidence. Forty years have passed since then (I'm writing this book in the year 2000), and I haven't found any evidence from a credible source that would validate the existence of an Illuminati of the sort described by my friends in the early 1960s. So I'm compelled to conclude that, as a secret organization in today's world, the Illuminati is a fiction. Those who believe in it are for the most part sincere, well-meaning people, but I believe they are wrong.

Relevance. What about the third guideline I suggested above—the relevance of a theory to end-time events? If a theory truly is false, then it obviously has no relevance to the end time. Those who believe in the Illuminati will no doubt dispute my conclusion that it's a fiction, and I must admit that I cannot prove that the Illuminati does *not* exist. I am only saying that I have not seen the kind of evidence I need in order to believe it *does* exist. Therefore, the Illuminati has no relevance to the end time for me, and I believe this conclusion to be correct.

Other "conspiracy" organizations

The people who talk about the Illuminati will also tell you about two other organizations called the Council on Foreign Relations and the Trilateral Commission, which, along with the United Nations, are intent on establishing a one-world government. These are conspiracy theories, because the critics of these organizations believe there's something bad about a one-world government—a conclusion I tend to agree with.

So let's apply the guidelines.

There is probably not a soul on planet Earth—with the possible exception of an aborigine from the hinterlands of New Guinea—who would question the existence of the United Nations. And while doubt about whether the Council on Foreign Relations and the Trilateral Commission exist is appropriate for anyone who's never heard about them, I've learned enough about them over the years to assure you that they *do* exist and that the establishment of a one-world government is probably one of their more significant objectives. Having assured myself of their reality, the next question is whether their existence is relevant to our Adventist understanding of the end time.

The Bible does make it clear that a one-world, religio-political government *will* come into power for a very short time just before Jesus returns. This is very evident from a couple of statements in Revelation:[3]

[The first beast of Revelation 13] was given authority over every tribe, people, language and nation (Revelation 13:7).

"The ten horns you saw are ten kings who have not yet received a kingdom, but who for one hour will receive authority as kings along with the beast. They have one purpose and will give their power and authority to the beast" (Revelation 17:12, 13).

Numerous forces exist in our world that are moving us toward a one-world *political* and *economic* system. However, the one-world government predicted in Revelation will also be a *religious* system, and at this point I'm not aware of any evidence that the United Nations, the Council on Foreign Relations, or the Trilateral Commission are trying to establish any kind of theocracy.[4] The end-time significance of these organizations lies in the possibility that the one-world *political* system they establish might be taken over by the coming apostate *religious* system when the time is ripe. That *is* worth keeping an eye on.

Jesuits in the Adventist Church

An interesting conspiracy theory that I hear about occasionally from very conservative Adventist sources is the idea that the General Conference and our colleges and universities have been infiltrated by Jesuits. Once or twice I've even heard mention of the name of some prominent Adventist who is supposedly a closet Jesuit. And once or twice I've even been accused of it myself, though I think more in jest.

Let me give you a very simple method by which you can verify for yourself, usually very quickly, whether a particular person is a Jesuit infiltrator in the Adventist Church. Start with this simple question: Is he (Jesuits are all males) married? If so, your search just stopped, because Jesuits are Catholic *priests,* and Catholic priests don't marry!

If by chance your suspect is single, then your verification process is a bit more difficult, but fairly straightforward. Keep in mind that a Jesuit is at least as well trained as a medical doctor or a Ph.D., which means four years of college and at least that many years of graduate school. So follow your suspect through his educational career: High school, college, and university. If all his training was exclusively in some combination of Adventist schools, other Protestant schools, or public schools, you can rule out that part of his life as a time when he might have become a Jesuit priest, because Jesuits have to attend *Catholic* schools, at least at the college and graduate level.

Next, follow your suspect through his career as a denominational employee. In what conference or institution did he begin his service for the Church? How long was he there? Where did he go after that, and after that, and after that? Did he ever work near a Catholic university, and if so, did he take course work there? If you can verify that your suspect attended a Catholic school during his service for the Church, find out whether that school has a seminary that trains Jesuits. If it does, did your suspect obtain a degree from the university, and if so, was it from the seminary? If it was, and if your suspect was unmarried at the time he graduated from this training, then maybe you really have discovered a Jesuit priest operating within the Adventist system!

My point is that the training of a Jesuit priest is an arduous process that takes years to complete, and it's impossible for anyone to hide that fact from inquiring minds. It would be next to impossible for a genuine Jesuit to infiltrate any Adventist institution without being recognized.

Even if you could verify that a certain individual had attended a Jesuit seminary, there's one more question you need to ask: How loyal has this person been to the Adventist faith during the time of his denominational service? The best way to determine that is to read what he's written and listen to tapes of sermons he's preached and seminars he may have conducted. If he's a Jesuit trying to undermine the Adventist Church, you'll find evidence of it in his writing and in his speeches. If no such evidence shows up, and if in fact everything he says proves him to be a loyal Adventist, then he certainly is.

Frankly, I know of only one individual who has worked in the Adventist system who has also attended a school that trains Jesuits, and that's Samuele Bacchiocchi. Sam obtained his Ph.D. from the Gregorian University of Rome, which does indeed train Jesuits. But I'm well enough acquainted with Sam to know that the notion that he's a Jesuit priest is laughable. If Sam is a Jesuit intent on destroying the Adventist Church from within, he's doing a very miserable job of it. He's a prodigious speaker and writer, as just about every Adventist knows, and everything he preaches and everything he writes is on the very conservative side of Adventism.

I said a moment ago that even I have been accused of being a Jesuit priest, though never seriously, so far as I know. Actually, in jest, I sometimes tell people myself that I'm a Jesuit infiltrator in the Adventist Church, because I do qualify on one count: I spent one year in the early 1970s studying at the University of Dallas in Texas, which happens to be a Catholic institution. And UD, along with being a liberal arts institution, has a seminary that trains Franciscans (not Jesuits). However, never mind that I studied in the liberal arts part of the university, not the seminary. Never mind that I spent one year there, not four, five, or six. And never mind that my degree was in writing, not theology. I offer myself as "evidence" for anyone looking for Jesuit infiltrators in the Adventist Church. And for anyone who's foolish enough to believe that I really am a Jesuit, I offer the same rebuttal that I gave for Sam Bacchiocchi: Read what I've written, listen to the sermons and seminars I give in churches and at camp meetings all across the United States and Canada each year, and I think you'll have your answer.

A variation on this Adventist conspiracy theory is the claim by Jack Chick of Chick Publications in Chino, California back in the early 1980s that a converted Jesuit priest by the name of Alberto Rivera had infiltrated and destroyed Protestant churches; that he converted to Christ in the mid-1960s; and that from that time on he made it his mission to expose the villainy of the Catholic Church.

Let's put the Alberto Rivera story to the test of our guidelines: Doubt, evidence, and relevance. I was suspicious of the story from the time I first heard it. It just didn't *seem* right. But, of course, doubt alone isn't sufficient reason to reject something as false.

What about the evidence? Several years ago I saw a video tape of an interview with "Alberto" that gave him a very positive rating, but the tape was put out by an Adventist independent ministry that I consider to have a reputation for being sensational and highly unreliable.

Roman Catholics adamantly deny the Alberto story. The weekly Catholic newspaper *Our Sunday Visitor* offered $10,000 to anyone who could prove that the allegations made by Jack Chick were true. *Christianity Today* published an investigation that exposed Rivera as a liar and a fraud, as did the Adventist *Liberty* magazine. [5] When the only people supporting the Alberto Rivera story have a very poor reputation for accuracy, and when sources, which I know provide their readers with accurate reporting, expose him as a fraud, I am compelled to conclude that his story is a hoax.

What about relevance? Unfortunately, some Adventists were taken in by this story simply because it involved a Catholic and sounded sinister. *But nothing is true just because it's sinister and about Catholics!* Truth is about facts from reliable sources. And if it can't be determined to be true, then it has absolutely no end-time significance. This is what I had in mind in the previous chapter when I said that we must be sure an event has actually happened before we attach end-time significance to it. And what's true of conspiracy theories is also true of urban legends.

PART 2
URBAN LEGENDS

I'm not sure where the term *urban legend* originated, but I know what it means. It's a story that is circulated widely and believed by a large number of people to be true. While some urban legends are true, most are either of dubious origin or false. One of the most common in Christian circles, including Adventism, is the disappearing hitchhiker story. I think I first heard this one back in the 1950s, and I've run across several versions of it since. You may have heard it. It goes like this: A couple picks up a hitchhiker who, after the introductions, announces from the back seat that "the coming of Jesus is sooner than you think." But when the startled couple turn around to look at the hitchhiker, he's disappeared.

That's an urban legend.

I respond to stories like this with the same guidelines I use for checking out conspiracy theories: Doubt it, check it, and ask about its relevance to the end time.

The disappearing hitchhiker story obviously has end-time relevance—if its true! Unfortunately, I am compelled to conclude that it's a pious hoax. Why? Because I have yet to meet a single person who will tell me that it happened to him or her. Neither have I ever met anyone who told me that they had met anyone who claimed to have given this hitchhiker his ride. The story is always several layers removed from the alleged couple who had this astounding encounter.

The Internet has proved to be a marvelous medium for the spread of urban legends and conspiracy theories. Please be advised, though, that *the Internet is one of the most unreliable of all sources for these stories*. People get them, read them, ooh and ah over them, and without verifying a thing (if it sounds good, it must be true), they zap them through to a dozen friends, each of whom reads, oohs and ahs, and zaps them through to a dozen of their friends, again without bothering to check. And thus within twenty-four hours the legend has spread all over the world. Literally!

The Janet Reno legend

Let's look at an example. Several times during the past couple of years individuals have sent me an email warning that back in 1994 U. S. Attorney General Janet Reno stated in an interview on *60 Minutes* that

> a cultist is one who has a strong belief in the Bible and the second coming of Christ; who frequently attends Bible studies; who has a high level of financial giving to a Christian cause; who home schools their children; who has accumulated survival foods and has a strong belief in the second amendment; and who distrusts big government. Any of these may qualify but certainly more than one would cause us to look at this person as a threat, and his family as being in a risk situation that qualified for government interference.

This urban legend also qualifies as a conspiracy theory because it suggests that the United States government is "out to get" Bible believing, end-time-loving, patriotic Americans. So let's apply our three guidelines. We begin by doubting. Why? Because we don't accept anything like this as valid just because someone hands it to us or sends it to us over the Internet. Doubt was my immediate reaction when I first heard this story. It had the "feel" of being a hoax.

However, doubt is not a valid reason for rejecting an urban legend or conspiracy theory. It has to be checked out first. But how does one go about checking an urban legend like the Janet Reno story? Fortunately, there's a very easy way to do that. Barbara and David Mikkelson and the San Fernando Folklore Society check out every one of these urban legends that is brought to their attention, and they have set up a public Web site for anyone interested in verifying the authenticity of a particular story. The URL address is www.snopes.com.

Snopes[6] has developed a rating system for reporting the determination of the authenticity of each story. Beside the title of each item is a colored ball. A green ball means the story is true or probably true; a red ball means it's false or probably false; a yellow ball identifies items for which the available evidence is too contradictory or insufficient to determine whether they are true or false; and a white ball is for stories that *could* have happened to someone, somewhere, at some time, but for which there is no evidence to make a determination. Clicking on a key word in each item will take you to a link that explains in detail the reason for the Society's conclusion. I trust snopes.com as a source to check out urban legends for several reasons:

- Its Web site identifies who are the sponsors of this organization.
- It provides a detailed explanation of its rating system. (You can read it by going to www.snopes.com/info/ratings.htm.)
- It gives detailed and sensible reasons for its conclusions, and it lists its sources. People can go to the books and magazine articles on which it bases its conclusions and evaluate the evidence for themselves.
- In order to ensure its accuracy, it asks readers to send in any verifiable information that either agrees or disagrees with its conclusions.[7]

I'm not going to tell you that every conclusion of the people who operate the Snopes web site is correct. I still have to exercise my own judgment after reading their evaluation, and I do occasionally question one of their conclusions. The reason I trust them is that they give all the signs of *trying* to be accurate. I consider them to be a reliable way to check out urban legends because of their forthrightness and apparent honesty.[8] Thus, when I heard the story about Janet Reno on *60 Minutes*, I checked with Snopes and found that their investigation shows the story to be totally false. Here is the first paragraph of Snopes' detailed refutation of this urban legend:

> The date of the putative interview varies depending upon the source, but 26 June 1994 seems to be the most commonly men-

tioned one. It doesn't matter, because Janet Reno was not interviewed by "60 Minutes" on that date or at any other time during 1994, nor did she ever make such a statement.

Given the fact that the Snopes sponsors investigate carefully the stories they report on, I assume that they are correct when they say that Janet Reno was never interviewed by *60 Minutes* during 1994 and that she never made such a statement. Going back, now, to our three guidelines: I doubted the Janet Reno legend the moment I heard it, and since a quick check with Snopes gave me good reason to consider it to be false, relating it to the end time was unnecessary.

An Adventist urban legend
What could be called an Adventist urban legend made the rounds a couple of years ago. It was a sheet of paper that purported to be a "Special Document From the Vatican" outlining a "Catholic Plan to Evangelize Seventh-day Adventists." Among the objectives stated in the document were:

- To infiltrate, among the Adventists, ideas and projects that could aid in bringing about a Catholic-Adventist closeness.
- To demonstrate to the Seventh-day Adventist Church that its origin as a church has no biblical basis.
- To demonstrate to the Seventh-day Adventists the falsehood of the writings of Ellen White.
- To make sure that Seventh-day Adventists understand that a failure to unite with Catholics and Protestants in a common search for world peace would cause them to be blamed for all the evils and/or disasters that might befall the world.

When I first saw this "document," my immediate reaction was skepticism. That wasn't too hard, because the document had the appearance and the tone that goes along with the work of an amateur. It didn't *look* credible and it didn't *sound* credible.

My next approach was to ask the individual who gave me the document where he got it. He said a Spanish pastor in California gave it to him. I asked him the name of the Spanish pastor, and when he told me who it was, I called the pastor on the phone. The pastor said, Yes, he had indeed given the document to my "friend." So I asked the pastor where he got it. "Oh," he said, "some of us from my church went on a week-long mission trip to Honduras, and one of the laymen down there gave it to me." Now I was *sure* the document was a fraud, not because I think our laymen in Honduras are deceptive, but because the source was simply not credible.

Several other people asked me about the document after that, so I knew it was making the rounds in the Adventist Church. And sure enough, two or three months later the General Conference published a statement in the *Adventist Review* that it had checked out the document, and it was a fraud.[9]

PART 3
HOW IMPORTANT IS TRUTH?

In the previous chapter I pointed out that for an event to have end-time significance it must actually have happened. Another way to state that is to ask: Is it true?

Pilate asked Jesus one of the most important questions of all time: What is truth? Equally important is the question: How important is it that we be sure what we *think* is truth really *is*? Paul answered that question in 2 Thessalonians 2:9, 10:

> The coming of the lawless one will be in accordance with the work of Satan displayed in all kinds of counterfeit miracles, signs and wonders, and in every sort of evil that deceives those who are perishing. *They perish because they refused to love the truth and so be saved.* (Italics supplied.)

We must love the *truth*, because if we don't love the *truth*, we are in great danger of perishing. And loving the *truth* means far more than having a love for the doctrinal teachings of the Seventh-day Adventist Church. It means loving *all* truth. It means getting to the bottom of everything, including even nonreligious issues, to be sure they're *true*—that they really happened. And it means refusing to believe anything until we can confirm to the best of our ability that it did happen.

This chapter is about something far more important than conspiracy theories and urban legends. It's about how to *think* about these issues in such a way that we penetrate beyond what titillates our emotions to discover the *truth* and believe only the *truth*. I propose that the deceptions of the end time will be so subtle that those who have failed to train their minds to believe only that which can be verified as truth will be deceived while thinking they have the truth.

I hope that what you've read in this chapter will inspire you to pursue the *truth* and *only* the truth on all issues of importance until you're sure you've found it.

1. I looked up "Illuminati" in the *Encyclopedia Britannica* and the *Columbia Encyclopedia*.

2. The Rosicrucians are still around.

3. This is not a contradiction of our traditional interpretation of Daniel 2 and 7, which say that Rome was the last empire to dominate Europe and the Middle East. The global government just before the second coming of Christ will exist for only a very short time. Daniel's prophecies did not provide that kind of detail, but Revelation does.

4. The United Nations held summits of both religious leaders and political leaders in late August and early September 2000, but there was no suggestion at any of them that the UN intended to transform itself into a *religio*-political system.

5. *Christianity Today*, March 31, 1981, 50-53; *Liberty*, September/October 1981, 5-7.

6. Snopes is the name of a family of characters who appear throughout the works of American writer William Faulkner.

7. In a link "Send comments" at the bottom of their main Web page they say: "Feel free to challenge the truth value of any of the entries on our site. As always, the more specific information you can provide, the better. If you know of any sources that support our conclusions but aren't mentioned here, we'd like to hear about them, too."

8. You can verify all kinds of urban legends with Snopes. At the time I'm writing this chapter, its religion section lists a dozen or so stories, including the following: NASA scientists discovered a day lost in time: *False*; scientists drilling in Siberia punched through to hell (You knew that one would be false, didn't you?); you must sign a petition to stop Jesus from being portrayed as a homosexual in an upcoming film: *False*; by proclamation of Governor George W. Bush, 10 June 2000 was "Jesus day" in Texas: *True*.

9. The General Conference acknowledged that some Catholic cleric or lay person may have planted this document in an effort to embarrass Seventh-day Adventists, but it did not originate with the Vatican, and none of the objectives stated in the document are legitimate Catholic objectives toward Adventists.

Sunday Laws

Sunday, September 17, 2000, an article appeared in my newspaper, *The Idaho Statesman*, titled "Pursuit of Greenbacks Erases Blue Laws." That title tells a significant story about America in the first year of the new millennium: Materialism is gaining over spirituality. In cities across the South, as the article in the *Statesman* put it, "the last bastions of blue laws are succumbing to the pressures of the almighty dollar."

That's a significant change from even twenty or thirty years ago, when you couldn't buy groceries or hardware on Sunday throughout much of the South. But as retail giants such as Wal-Mart and Home Depot move into Southern communities, the pressure is growing for laws that allow businesses to remain open all day every day. In addition, a lucrative tourist trade has sprung up throughout the region, and, as everyone knows, tourists bring along spending money. Thus, according to Jim Hatchell, the director of the South Carolina Merchants Association, "Retail commerce has developed to the point where blue laws don't work any more."

History of blue laws

Blue laws originated in Connecticut, and at first they referred to rigid enactments covering all manner of vices. These statutes were published in 1650 on blue paper—hence the name "blue laws." However, the term soon came to be used exclusively of laws that regulated activities on Sunday. With the passing of the colonial era, blue laws passed into disfavor. They remained on the books in most states, but they were largely ignored. However, a resurgence occurred during the late 1800s, when temperance groups such as the Women's Christian Temperance Union pushed for both Sunday blue laws and laws regulating the sale of alcoholic beverages.

In the late 1880s and early 1890s, several Southern states began strict enforcement of these laws, and a number of Seventh-day Adventists were prosecuted as a result. The first, Samuel Mitchel of Quitman, Georgia, spent thirty days in a county jail on a charge of violating a Sunday law. It was in Tennessee, however, where enforcement was the most harsh. In 1885 three Adventists—William Dortch, W. H. Parker, and James Stem—were fined and imprisoned and spent several weeks working on a chain gang. In 1889, and again in 1890, R. M. King was arrested for plowing corn and hoeing in his potato patch on Sunday. Three years later, five Adventists were brought to trial for violating Tennesee's Sunday ordinance, and they also spent time on a chain gang.

During this same period, the advocates of Sunday legislation succeeded in having several bills introduced in the Congress of the United States. One of their chief allies was Senator H. W. Blair, who introduced a bill in 1888, the purpose of which was "To Secure to the People the Enjoyment of the First Day of the Week, Commonly Known as the Lord's Day, as a Day of Rest, and to Promote Its Observance as a Day of Religious Worship." This bill was defeated, in large part because of the vigorous opposition of the Seventh-day Adventist Church under the fiery leadership of Alonzo T. Jones.

It was also during this period that Ellen White wrote *The Great Controversy*—her own most extensive statement about end-time events—in which she described the Sabbath-Sunday conflict during the final crisis in great detail.

It's understandable that Seventh-day Adventist end-time emotions were aroused to a fever pitch during the late 1880s and early 1890s. Ellen White had just published *The Great Controversy*, and events transpiring in Congress and the Southern United States seemed to conform her scenario. The end was in sight! Just a few more years, and Jesus would come!

The demise of Sunday laws

However, the enforcement of Sunday laws died down after about 1895, and ever since, these laws have been disappearing from the Ameri-

can scene. This has been very puzzling to Seventh-day Adventists, because for 150 years we have viewed Sunday observance as the key apostasy of the Christian world during the end time, and we have seen Sunday laws as the preeminent sign of the approaching end of the world.
We have responded to the demise of Sunday laws in three ways. By far
the majority of us have simply trusted that the final crisis, including
Sunday laws, *will come* in God's good time. However, there have been
two more extreme responses.

A significant number of Adventists, in their anxiety to see evidence of
the final crisis, have tended to interpret every suggestion of a Sunday law
in some obscure American village as a sign of the end. Usually, the language in the literature published by this segment of Adventism is shrill and
alarmist. We are warned that the agitation for a city Sunday ordinance in,
say, "Podunk, Arkansas" is sure evidence that the final crisis can't be much
more than six months away. Perhaps I'm exaggerating a bit, but you get the
point. The conspiracy buffs that I described in the previous chapter tend to
be a part of this group.

This attitude is very unrealistic. It overlooks the fact that the final
crisis will be global, not local. It forgets that the attitude of religious
conservatives who may happen to dominate politics in a local situation
is a far cry from the national and international emergency that will
bring on the final crisis. It fails to take into account that Ellen White
predicted a change in the Constitution of the United States as a sign of
the end, not a change in the status of church-state separation in a local
community.

This latching on to every local Sunday ordinance as a sign of the
impending end of the world springs from the addictive attitude toward
end-time events that I spoke about a couple of chapters back. Its agita-
tors profess to be very concerned about our "preparation for the end
time," but their attitude is so unrealistic that it will cause us to be *less*
prepared for the real end time, not *better* prepared. *I do not hesitate to
say that we all need to avoid this alarmist way of thinking about Sunday laws.*

However, the opposite response to waning Sunday laws has also begun
to surface among some Adventists. Ellen White's prediction of end-time
Sunday laws arose out of events transpiring around her at the time she
wrote *The Great Controversy*, they say, and that's how the final conflict
would have developed had it transpired in her day. A hundred years later, it
will likely revolve around other issues.

I disagree with this conclusion for a number of reasons. First, the

Adventist understanding of Sunday laws as the mark of the beast had its origin, not with Ellen White in the 1888 *The Great Controversy*, but with Joseph Bates in an 1847 pamphlet titled *The Seventh-day Sabbath a Perpetual Sign*.[1] In this pamphlet Bates developed, for the first time, the view that the mark of the beast will be the observance of Sunday when it is enforced by law. The following year James and Ellen White endorsed Bates's views in a pamphlet of their own titled *A Word to the Little Flock*, which they co-published. Thus, when Ellen White wrote out her end-time views in the 1888 edition of *The Great Controversy*, she was merely expanding on an interpretation of the mark of the beast that Adventists had held for more than forty years.

Having said this, I do not doubt that events occurring in the late 1880s influenced the way Ellen White described end-time Sunday legislation in *The Great Controversy*. However, rather than dismissing her words as mere Adventist hysteria, it seems more reasonable to me to conclude that God caused her to write her book at that very time *because* those events would influence the intensity with which she described the final conflict.

I might be more willing to concede that the final conflict will revolve around issues other than the Sabbath-Sunday controversy had Ellen White made only one or two passing references to it during her seventy-year prophetic ministry. However, she reiterated the point over and over and over again. The legal enforcement of the false Sunday-Sabbath lies at the very heart of the final conflict, as she understood it. Take that away, and for her there would be no final conflict. Thus, if she was indeed a prophet of God, as we have maintained for the past 150 years, we have to conclude that what she said about end-time Sunday legislation is correct.

The final conflict in Scripture

Scripture is the third and most important reason why I believe the final conflict *will* revolve around the Sabbath-Sunday issue in our day.

Daniel predicted that a "little horn" power would emerge in world history after the fall of the Roman Empire that would "try to change the set times and the laws" (Daniel 7:25). We have always understood this little horn to be the papacy of the Middle Ages, and we have said that the prediction that it would change times and laws was fulfilled by the papal change of the Sabbath from the seventh day of the week to the first. It's extremely significant that John included several of the characteristics of Daniel's little horn power in his description of the first beast of Revelation 13. Thus, it's clear that the end-time antichrist will be a modern form of the medieval papacy.

From Revelation we also learn that the final conflict will revolve around God's law. This point is both *explicit* and *implicit* in Revelation 12–14. It's *explicit* in the fact that twice God's end-time people are described as commandment keepers:

> Then the dragon was enraged at the woman and went off to make war against the rest of her offspring—*those who obey God's commandments* and hold to the testimony of Jesus (Revelation 12:17, italics added).

> This calls for patient endurance on the part of the saints *who obey God's commandments* and remain faithful to Jesus (Revelation 14:12, italics added).

Obedience to God's law as a key issue in the final conflict is *implicit* in the image to the beast that is described in Revelation 13:14, 15. The second beast of Revelation 13 sets up this image and demands that every human being on planet Earth worship it, on pain of death. This symbol is drawn directly out of the account in the third chapter of Daniel of the conflict between King Nebuchadnezzar and Shadrach, Meshach, and Abednego over the worship of his golden image. Just as it would have been a violation of one of the Ten Commandments for these three Hebrews to worship Nebuchadnezzar's image, so it will in some way be a violation of the Ten Commandments for God's end-time people to worship the image that is set up by the second beast of Revelation 13.

But which commandment?

The first angel's message of Revelation 14:6, 7 contrasts the false worship of the two beast powers with worship of the true God: " 'Worship him who made the heavens, the earth, the sea and the springs of water.' " Notice that the reason for worshiping God is His creatorship. That is the very same reason given in the fourth commandment for keeping the Sabbath. In fact, these words in Revelation 14:7 are almost a direct quote from the fourth commandment:

> "Worship him *who made the heavens, the earth, the sea and the springs of water*" (Revelation 14:7, italics added).

"For in six days *the Lord made the heavens and the earth, the sea, and all that is in them,* but he rested on the seventh day. Therefore the Lord blessed the Sabbath day and made it holy" (Exodus 20:11, italics added).

Bringing all of this evidence together, it's obvious that the final conflict will involve the legal enforcement of a form of false worship by the world's civil governments, and there is a clear suggestion that this false worship will be in contrast to true worship according to the fourth commandment. Thus, Ellen White's conclusion in *The Great Controversy* that the final conflict will revolve around enforced Sunday observance in opposition to the fourth commandment is fully in harmony with the description of the final conflict that we find in Revelation 13 and 14. That's the most important reason why I reject the idea that Sunday laws might have been the way the end-time crisis would have developed in Ellen White's day, but not in ours.

Developments that are significant

From what I have said up to this point, you might easily conclude that I see nothing happening today that might have prophetic significance with respect to our Adventist expectation of a Sabbath-Sunday conflict during the final crisis. However, that is not the case. Certain factors will have to be present in American society in order for Sunday laws to be enacted, and I do see some of these factors beginning to develop. I will mention two.

John Paul's apostolic letter Dies Domini. As Ellen White describes it, a popular demand for Sunday laws will lead to their enactment. She said, for example, that "even in free America, rulers and legislators, in order to secure public favor, will yield to *the poplar demand for a law enforcing Sunday observance.*"[2]

Now, popular demands have a history. They don't just pop up one morning and take everyone by surprise. And I consider John Paul's apostolic letter *Dies Domini,*[3] which urges upon all Catholics the importance of keeping Sunday holy, to be significant in this regard. Much of the pope's letter is in harmony with the Adventist understanding of the Sabbath.[4] However, two considerations are meaningful to the present discussion. First is the mere fact that John Paul published a letter[5] urging the faithful to keep Sunday holy. Papal pronouncements have far more impact on a culture than do those of lesser ecclesiastical figures. While John Paul's letter will hardly turn the tide of American popular opinion toward Sunday laws (it hasn't so far), it sets a precedent that will surely influence people's thinking when the events of the end time begin to unfold.

Second, John Paul's apostolic letter supports civil legislation of Sunday as a day of rest and worship. He said, for example, that "my predecessor Pope Leo XIII in his Encyclical *Rerum Novarum* spoke of Sunday rest as a worker's right which the state must guarantee" and "in the particular circumstances of our own time, Christians will naturally strive to ensure that civil legislation respects their duty to keep the Sabbath holy."[6]

That's the significance I see in John Paul's letter *Dies Domini*. However, it's also important to keep in mind that the Catholic Church has spoken out in favor of Sunday laws several times in the past two hundred years, and the pope's recent letter is no more strident than some of these other statements. John Paul's letter is simply an ecclesiastical pronouncement. His call for the protection of Sunday cannot have the force of law until it is acted upon by a government legislative body.

Church-state union. Another factor that must be present in the American culture in order for a national Sunday law to become a reality is antagonism toward church-state separation. End-time Sunday legislation, of the sort described by Ellen White in *The Great Controversy* and similar sources, would be in clear violation of this requirement of the U. S. Constitution. Thus, there will have to be a change in the Constitution, or at least in the way it is interpreted by the Supreme Court, before the kind of Sunday legislation envisioned by Ellen White can be enacted. She herself was very aware of this. That's why she said that only under the influence of the three-fold union of Protestantism, Catholicism, and spiritualism, will "our country . . . repudiate every principle of its Constitution as a Protestant and republican government." When that happens, she said, we can know "that the time has come for the marvelous working of Satan and that the end is near."[7]

Furthermore, before there can be a change in the U.S. Constitution that would permit Ellen White's type of national Sunday law, a change will have to take place in the attitude of the American people, their legislators, and their judges toward church-state separation. And that change has already begun.

I can still remember hearing Pat Robertson express a very negative attitude toward church-state separation back in the early 1980s. And this attitude has hardened significantly in the years since. It's not at all uncommon today to hear Religious Right Protestants in America say things such as "The words 'church-state separation' appeared in the constitution of the

Soviet Union, not the American Constitution." Perhaps most significant is a statement several years ago by William Rehnquist, the Chief Justice of the United States Supreme Court, that "the 'wall of separation between church and state' is a metaphor based on bad history, a metaphor which has proved useless as a guide to judging. It should be frankly and explicitly abandoned."[8] And in the late 1990s, Representative Earnest Istook (R, Okla.) sponsored a "religious freedom" amendment to the U.S. Constitution in the House of Representatives that would have seriously weakened the principle of church-state separation had it been enacted. Fortunately, the proposed amendment was defeated, but it had the zealous support of the Christian Coalition and other Religious Right forces.

Two issues having to do with church-state separation have come to national prominence in the United States in recent years. One is the posting of the Ten Commandments in government buildings. This controversy was sparked by Alabama Judge Roy Moore, who refused to remove the Ten Commandments from his courtroom. But now the Ten Commandments are popping up in public schools and courthouses all over the United States, especially in the South. The more the courts forbid posting the Ten Commandments in public places, the more the people put them up!

A similar development is the conservative Protestant opposition in this country to Supreme Court rulings of the past forty years that forbid public schools from initiating or leading out in classroom prayers. As I write these words, the Supreme Court's most recent ruling, which struck down school-sponsored prayers at football games,[9] has aroused the holy wrath of conservative Christians to the point that the crowds attending these games are responding with spontaneous prayers from the bleachers. Emotional issues such as this are causing Religious Right activists to rebel against the constitutional principle of church-state separation. And that *is* a significant development in laying the groundwork for an eventual national Sunday law.

In view of the fact that church-state separation will have to be dismantled in the United States before a national Sunday law could be enacted, any trend in that direction is a significant end-time development. And the major development along that line at the present time is the strong, almost vicious, opposition to church-state separation on the part of many Religious Right Protestants in America since about 1980.

Ellen White's prediction of end-time Sunday laws has increasingly been a puzzle for Seventh-day Adventists since about 1900. Indeed, I think it's safe to say that this has been one of the major challenges to our thinking about the end time in recent years. It's easy for us, on the one hand, to see evidence of Sunday laws where it doesn't exist and, on the other, to conclude that we (and thus Ellen White) have been wrong all along. I consider both conclusions to be out of harmony with the evidence in the world at the beginning of the twenty-first century.

This issue surely will continue to challenge our thinking as time goes on!

---

1. The full title of Bates's pamphlet is *The Seventh-day Sabbath a Perpetual Sign From the Beginning to the Entering Into the Gates of the Holy City According to the Commandment.*

2. *The Great Controversy*, 592, italics added.

3. Published May 31, 1998.

4. *Dies Domini* traces the origin of Sabbath to Creation, contrary to some Protestants and former Adventists, who claim that the Sabbath did not begin until Sinai.

5. The letter was almost certainly written for John Paul by his aides, with him giving approval to the final draft.

6. *Dies Domini*, Chapter 4:66, 67.

7. *Testimonies*, 5:451; see also *The Great Controversy*, 588.

8. *Church and State*, October 1991, 24.

9. *Santa Fe Independent School Dist. V. DOE* (99-62). The courts have consistently held that students have the right to pray on their own in public schools. Thus, Religious Right advocates felt they had a strong case when the public school district in Santa Fe, Texas allowed students to elect one of their own number to lead out in prayer before high school football games. However, the court ruled against them on the grounds that while the students provided the individual to say the prayers, the school provided the forum and the public address system over which the prayers were said.

HOW TO THINK ABOUT

the
Time
of
Christ's Return

the
Delay
in
Christ's Return

Back when I was a kid, my mother, who grew up in Wyoming, used to enjoy telling me of an incident in her life when she was about ten years old. She said to her mother one day, "I wonder who I'll marry when I grow up. Maybe he's way down in Texas!"

Her mother, my grandmother, said, "Oh, Honey, you won't ever grow up. Jesus is going to come before you're old enough to get married."

That probably happened around 1915. Some sixty years later, in the mid-1970s, my grandmother died at the ripe old age of ninety-six. My mother—who did marry a Texan, by the way—died in 1996, when she was ninety. By the time you read these words I'll be in my mid-sixties, and my children—Grandma's great grandchildren, no less—will be well on their way to their forties!

When I was a student at Southwestern Junior College (now Southwestern Adventist University), a fellow student and I were discussing end-time events, and I remarked that I thought Christ might return within twenty-five years. My friend was horrified. He declared with absolute certainty that Jesus' coming couldn't possibly be more than five years distant. However, since that time my friend has devoted nearly an entire career to ministry in the Adventist Church, and, like me, is approaching retirement.

Shortly after Pacific Press appointed me the editor of *Signs of the Times*®, an Adventist reader wrote and said, "I hope you'll be the magazine's last editor"—and he didn't mean he hoped I'd fail so miserably that I'd cause the magazine to fold!

A mistaken emphasis?

All these statements reflect our deep Adventist conviction that Jesus is coming soon. Yet they also raise an extremely significant question: One hundred and fifty years after our first Great Disappointment, are we about to confront a second one? Can we still believe that Jesus is coming *soon?* Since about 1975, and probably even earlier, Adventists have increasingly been wondering out loud whether our emphasis these past 150 years may not have been a mistake.

For example, several years ago, a friend who knows that I speak and write a great deal on end-time events wrote me a letter that included the following paragraph:

I don't mean to suggest I'm skeptical of *your* particular perspective on the topic of last-day events. I'm skeptical of all of them. I remain open and interested in the possibility of Christ's soon return. I'm willing to suspend disbelief, but I'm frankly skeptical. I do understand, in terms of our traditional story, that last-day events is our primary *reason to be,* but I wonder how long that idea can suffice as the decades rumble along—and nothing happens. Here we are 152 years beyond the Great Disappointment, still waiting, still wondering.

Those who decide that our emphasis on Jesus' soon coming has been wrong often go on to conclude that no one will ever know when His coming is near. This was reinforced for me back in the late 1980s when I had lunch one day with an Adventist professional. The conversation drifted to Christ's second coming, and my friend thought a moment, then said, "I know only one thing for sure. He *is* coming again someday. It could be tomorrow, but it could also be a thousand years from now."

Some Adventists, concluding that our emphasis on the soon coming of Jesus is wrong-headed, have proclaimed our entire movement to be nothing more than an interesting blip in the 2,000-year history of Christianity that will eventually be relegated to the history books.

There's no question about it, thoughtful Adventists are beginning to ask serious questions about our traditional emphasis on the nearness of Christ's coming.

Is this bad? Of course not! These questions are very sensible and perfectly normal. We *have* to ask them. There would be something wrong if we *didn't* ask them. At the very least, we'd be hiding our heads in the sand. We *need* to talk about the delay, because that's the only way we're going to reach a correct understanding of it. And we all need to listen to everyone's ideas—liberal, conservative, and all those in between. I've found helpful suggestions at both extremes as well as in the middle.

In recent years a number of books have been written on the topic of the delay, so obviously we aren't going to answer all the questions that can be raised in the short space of one chapter. However, I would like to discuss three issues that are relevant to the problem of the delay in Christ's return. First, we will look at the delay from a biblical perspective. Next, we will examine three explanations that Adventists have given for the delay. In the third section I will share with you some factors to consider in relating to the delay.

PART 1
THE DELAY FROM A BIBLICAL PERSPECTIVE

In His famous sermon on signs of His coming in Matthew 24 and 25, Jesus told His disciples that " 'no one knows about that day or hour, not even the angels in heaven, nor the Son, but only the Father' " (Matthew 24:36). It's reasonable to assume that today Jesus does know the day and hour of His return, and that perhaps even the angels have that information by now. But Jesus Himself did not know the date at the time He spoke these words to His disciples. When the disciples came to Him shortly before His ascension and asked if the time had come for the establishment of His eternal kingdom, He said in essence, "That's not for you to know" (see Acts 1:7).

We can say without hesitation, then, that it has never been God's intention that believers know when He will come. Rather, He advised His disciples over and over—and through them He advises us—to maintain a constant watchfulness for His return:

- " 'Therefore keep watch, because you do not know on what day your Lord will come' " (Matthew 24:42).
- " 'So you also must be ready, because the Son of Man will come at an hour when you do not expect him' " (verse 44).
- " 'Therefore keep watch, because you do not know the day or the hour' " (25:13).

Parables of the delay

In addition to these cryptic statements, two of Jesus' parables in Matthew 24 and 25 give specific advice on relating to the delay.

The two servants. In the first parable, Jesus tells of a servant who was placed in charge of his master's household " 'to give them their food at the proper time.' " He said, " 'It will be good for that servant whose master finds him doing so when he returns' " (Matthew 24:45, 46). But Jesus warned that matters would not go so well for the servant who said to himself, " ' "My master is staying away a long time" ' " and then began to " 'beat his fellow servants and to eat and drink with drunkards.' " He said that " 'the master of that servant will come on a day when he does not expect him and at an hour he is not aware of. He will cut him to pieces and assign him a place with the hypocrites, where there will be weeping and gnashing of teeth' " (verses 48-51).

The whole point of this parable is the delay and how to relate to it. And please notice that the faithful servant didn't spend time pondering when the master might return, nor did it trouble him that the master was staying away much longer than he had expected. He simply kept on carrying out the duties the master had assigned him. The unfaithful servant, on the other hand, was very conscious of the delay. When the master didn't return as soon as he expected, the unfaithful servant decided that the master would continue to stay away for a long time, and he neglected the responsibilities the master had assigned to him in favor of having his own good time.

How could Jesus have said it more plainly? *He doesn't want us to be overly concerned about the delay.* In fact, the servant who was most conscious of the delay is the one whose attitude got him in trouble! Until He returns, Jesus wants us to keep on with the work He gave us to do—feeding the world with spiritual food, which means fulfilling His Great Commission.

The wise and foolish virgins. Jesus' second parable about the delay—the parable of the ten virgins—is actually a prophecy that gives us a peek at what the end time will be like. And, according to the parable, one of the chief characteristics of the final years of world history is that *there will be a delay in the coming of the Bridegroom.* Jesus actually *predicted* the delay! That means we should *expect* a delay, and we should be neither surprised nor disappointed when it happens. Jesus' prediction would fail if there *were no* delay.

The parable of the ten virgins is Jesus' commentary on our personal preparation for His second coming. You know, of course, that the oil in the girls' lamps represents the Holy Spirit. The wise girls carried extra oil with them, which is a symbolic way of saying that genuine Christians maintain their relationship with Jesus even though He doesn't come as soon as they expect Him to. The wise girls didn't like the delay, but they were prepared for it. The foolish girls, on the other hand, failed to bring extra oil with them. They neglected the all-important spiritual preparation for Jesus' return. They made it safely enough through the delay, but they were unprepared for the arrival of the bridegroom.

A parable of His soon coming
The delay would be much easier for us to deal with if Jesus had stopped with the advice to wait patiently till He comes. However, His parable of the fig tree stimulates us to look for signs of His return, and our enthusiasm over these signs all too easily overshadows our patience in waiting. I'm sure the parable of the fig tree is familiar to everyone reading this book. Nevertheless, for the record, here it is:

> "Now learn this lesson from the fig tree: As soon as its twigs get tender and its leaves come out, you know that summer is near. Even so, *when you see all these things, you know that it is near*, right at the door. I tell you the truth, this generation will certainly not pass away until all these things have happened" (Matthew 24:32-34, italics added).

So, while we'll never know the exact *date* of Jesus' return, the signs He gave will alert us when it's *near*. That sounds simple enough, but there's a huge problem. In nearly every age of the Christian era, some believers have been convinced that world events in their day fulfilled Jesus' signs, and they have concluded that Jesus' return would surely occur during their lifetime. The reality is, though, that 2,000 years have passed, and Jesus still hasn't come.

What the apostles believed
It's fairly common knowledge that the New Testament writers believed Jesus would come in their day. Paul revealed his thinking rather subtly in 1 Thessalonians 4:16, 17:

> For the Lord himself will come down from heaven, with a loud command, with the voice of the archangel and with the trumpet call of God, and the dead in Christ will rise first. After that, we who are still alive and are left will be caught up together with them in the clouds to meet the Lord in the air.

Notice who Paul expected to be "still alive" when Christ returned: "We"—that is, he and the Christians in Thessalonica. And in Romans he came right out and said it:

> And do this, understanding the present time. The hour has come for you to wake from your slumber, because our salvation is nearer now than when we first believed (Romans 13:11).

By "our salvation," Paul meant the second coming of Christ.[1] When Paul wrote his letter to the church in Rome—probably sometime between A.D. 55 and 58—he had been a Christian for a little over twenty years, and the members of the church in Rome had probably been Christians for ten or fifteen years. So when Paul said, "our salvation is nearer now than when we first believed,"[2] he indicated that he expected Jesus to return in the very near future.

And Paul wasn't the only apostle who believed this. James wrote that "the Lord's coming is near" (James 5:8). Peter said, "The end of all things is near" (1 Peter 4:7). John said, "This is the last hour" (1 John 2:18). And three times in the last chapter of the Bible Jesus Himself said, " 'I am coming soon' " (Revelation 22:7, 12, 20).

How are we to understand these positive declarations from Bible writers? Can inspired prophets be wrong? More to the point of our discussion, if the apostles believed 2,000 years ago that Jesus was coming in their day and He still hasn't come, how can we be so sure He's coming in our day? Is it possible that the world might last another 2,000 years? Adventists have always responded No in answer to that question. Even the 150-year delay since the founding of our movement has not caused the majority of us to give up our belief that His coming is near. Nevertheless, increasingly we are asking ourselves, Why the delay? And traditionally, we have given three answers.

PART 2
ADVENTIST EXPLANATIONS OF THE DELAY

The three Adventist responses to the delay have been the "finishing the work" explanation, the "perfection of character" explanation, and the "saving more souls" explanation. Let's take a look at each one.

Finishing the work

In Matthew 24:14 Jesus said, " 'This gospel of the kingdom will be preached in all the world as a witness to all the nations, and then the end will come.' " Again, shortly before He left this Earth, Jesus said to His disciples " 'Go and make disciples of all nations,' " and " 'surely I am with you always, to the very end of the age' " (Matthew 28:19, 20). From these verses the idea has developed that Jesus' second coming depends on our rolling up our sleeves and "getting the job done." Ellen White reinforced this idea by her suggestion that Jesus would have returned "ere this" if the church had carried out God's purpose "in giving to the world the message of mercy."[3]

Church leaders, who have been charged by their constituents with directing the Church in the fulfillment of its mission, are probably the most likely to point to an unfinished work to explain the delay. They also tend to use this explanation as a motivation for members to join with them in fulfilling the Church's mission. Several General Conference initiatives in the last twenty-five years of the twentieth century had precisely this focus, including the "Finishing the Work" document that was approved by the 1976 annual council,[4] the "Thousand Days of Reaping" strategy that came out of the annual council of 1987, and Global Mission, which was established at the 1990 General Conference session. These initiatives have been extremely successful. The explosive growth of the Seventh-day Adventist Church since in the late 1980s is a direct result of the strategies of the "Thousand Days of Reaping" and "Global Mission."

It's important to understand that faithfully carrying forward God's work in the earth is the emphasis in one of Jesus' parables about the delay that I mentioned earlier. The unfaithful servant, who was interested only in his own pleasure, neglected the responsibility that his master had given him. The faithful servant, who saw to it that the members of his master's household received their food " 'at the proper time,' " is the one whom the master commended and promoted (Matthew 24:45).

However, does the fact that Christ has not returned mean that we have not been doing God's work? Conversely, if we were to carry out God's work more persistently and somehow more effectively, would that hasten Christ's return? Is the Adventist Church's explosive growth beginning in the late 1980s an indication that we *are* getting the job done, and that we can therefore expect Jesus to come sooner than He would have had we not carried out initiatives such as "Global Mission" and the "Thousand Days of Reaping"? I'll respond to these questions later in this chapter.

Perfection of character

The second reason for the delay that Adventists have traditionally given is that God's people are not spiritually prepared. One sentence, on page 69 of Ellen White's book *Christ's Object Lessons*, summarizes the idea succinctly: "When the character of Christ shall be perfectly reproduced in His people, then He will come to claim them as His own."

Biblically, this view is probably most often defended from the description of the 144,000 in Revelation 7:1-4 and 14:1-5. In chapter 7, the 144,000 are sealed before the four winds blow—that is, before the time of trouble comes upon the earth (verse 3). The seal of God is the spiritual preparation that God's people will need in order to pass through that time without losing their faith in the face of the tyranny of the oppressive beast powers of Revelation 13. Chapter 14 says of the 144,000 "No lie was found in their mouths; they are blameless" (verse 5). The word *blameless* suggests perfection, what some would term a sinless character.

Some Adventists have focused on the 1888 message of righteousness by faith, and particularly the Adventist failure to adopt that message, as the reason for the delay in Christ's return. Thus, Denis Priebe, writing in the January 2000 issue of the magazine *Our Firm Foundation*, said:

> What is the [1888] message that could have produced the latter rain and the loud cry then, and will produce it today if we accept it? The message can be summed up in one Bible verse—Christ *in you*, the hope of glory. Colossians 1:27. The 1888 message was focused on preparing God's people for translation; thus it had much to say about how to be perfect in Christ and thus be ready for the close of probation. . . .
>
> Right here is the difference between justification as taught by Evangelicals and justification in the 1888 message. Only in the 1888 message do we hear about power to keep from sinning.[5]

Elsewhere in his article Priebe applied this conclusion to hastening the return of Jesus:

> If you want to see Christ return to this earth very soon, then I plead with you to reorder your lives if necessary. Make the study of the 1888 message your top priority, and spend more time in study and prayer than ever before in your lives.[6]

For at least a hundred years, some Seventh-day Adventists have explained the delay in Christ's return by the failure of Adventist members to adopt the 1888 message of righteousness by faith and develop perfect characters. So to what extent is it reasonable to conclude that the delay in Christ's return is the result of our lack of spiritual preparation? I'll respond to that question shortly.

Saving "a few more souls"

A less frequently mentioned reason for the delay is that Jesus is waiting for a few more people to accept His offer of salvation. This reasoning probably gives comfort to those who are hoping their friends and/or loved ones will accept Jesus before it's too late. However, it's nonsense as far as a reason for the delay, because there will always be "a few more souls" to save. If Jesus waits a year in order to save a few more souls, there will still be a few more souls left to save, and a year later there will be a few more, and the year after that there will be a few more. There is no end to it! At what point is God going to say, "OK, I've saved enough souls. The rest will have to just be lost"?

The "saving a few more souls" reason does make some sense in the context of the close of probation. However, the issues there are considerably more complex than God waiting to save a few more souls, so I'll reserve that discussion for the chapter "How to Think About the Close of Probation."

PART 3
FACTORS TO CONSIDER

We need to consider several other factors before we rush to the conclusion that the delay is the result of our failure either to "finish the work" or to "reflect the image of Jesus." In this section, I will discuss two things with you. First, we'll take another look at these two Adventist reasons for the delay and then we'll examine a couple of other explanations.

Adventist reasons for the delay

One of the first things that jumps out at us when we look at Jesus' parables is the similarity between the two Adventist reasons for the delay and what Jesus said. In the parable of the two servants, the master commended the first servant because he carried on faithfully with the master's work in spite of the delay. On the other hand, the master condemned the unfaithful servant because he allowed the delay to interfere with his responsibility to do the master's work. It's extremely important that we not allow the delay either to discourage us from doing God's work or to conclude that since His coming appears to be a long way off we can neglect His work. Notice, however, that *there is no hint in the parable that the faithful servant's consistent discharge of his duties hastened the master's return or that the unfaithful servant's failure to fulfill his duties hindered the master's return.*

The spiritual preparation of God's people for Christ's second coming—the second reason Adventists have given for the delay—is clearly reflected in the parable of the ten virgins. The five wise girls were spiritually ready for the bridegroom's appearing and the five foolish girls were spiritually unprepared. However, again, *there is no indication in the parable that the girls' preparation or lack of preparation had anything to do with the time of the bridegroom's arrival.* In both parables—the two servants and the ten virgins—the master and the bridegroom arrived when *they* were ready, not when the servants or the virgins were ready. In fact, in both parables exactly half of the people were *not* ready, but the master and the bridegroom came anyway!

Other reasons for the delay

I do not wish to minimize the importance of our Church doing its work or of our members being diligent in making a spiritual preparation for Christ's return. However, I would like to suggest a couple of other reasons for the delay.

The cup of iniquity. Seventh-day Adventists have long stressed that God commanded the Israelites to destroy the Canaanite tribes upon entering the Promised Land because the people living there had passed the boundary of their probation. However, God specifically commanded them not to destroy several of these tribes, because they had not yet "filled their cup of iniquity." Only when evil had reached a certain point in the history of these tribes were the Israelites permitted to destroy them. For example, speaking of the Amorites, Ellen White said:

> Although this nation was conspicuous because of its idolatry and corruption, it had not yet filled up the cup of its iniquity, and God would not give command for its utter destruction.[7]

With the "cup of iniquity" principle in mind, notice what Ellen White said about the wickedness in the world in our day as a condition for God to initiate end-time events:

> Everything is preparing for the great day of God. Time will last a little longer *until the inhabitants of the earth have filled up the cup of their iniquity,* and then the wrath of God, which has so long slumbered, will awake, and this land of light will drink the cup of His unmingled wrath.[8]

The Lord has appointed a time when He will visit transgressors in wrath for persistent disregard of His law.[9]

The emphasis in these statements is on God's punishment of the wicked during the time of trouble (the day of His wrath) rather than on the second coming of Christ. However, since the time of trouble immediately precedes Christ's return, by implication we can say that Jesus cannot come until the world has reached a level of iniquity that God has predetermined.

So, if God is waiting for evil to increase to a certain level in the world before He initiates the final events leading to Christ's second coming, then regardless of how much work we do or how much character perfection we develop, if God's predetermined level of global evil has not been reached, Jesus won't come. We can keep on berating ourselves for our failure to finish the work or develop a character like Christ's, "till the cows come home," as the colloquial expression says, but what if, instead, God is waiting for evil in the world to reach a certain level?

God's perspective. The second alternate reason I will give for the delay is God's broad view of world events as they relate to the cosmic conflict between good and evil.

Allow me to illustrate. Imagine that you and I are tiny ants running around in the grass in a pasture. Imagine, also, that our ant culture has an ancient prophecy that the world will end someday and that the sign for the end of the world will be a shadow crossing the sky. One day we all see a dark shadow cross the sky, and we get excited, thinking the world is surely about to end. But life continues as usual. Some time later another shadow crosses the sky, and we get excited again. But again, life continues as usual. This keeps on happening until the "wise ones" among us proclaim the whole prediction a myth at best and a hoax at the worst. But then one day a huge shadow crosses the sky, and in a short while our home is flooded and many of our comrades die.

Now suppose that one of the ants happens to climb onto the claw of a bird that's pecking at some seeds in the pasture and gets a ride through the air. This ant now has a much different perspective on the pasture from it's fellow ants crawling around in the grass, and it realizes that the temporary shadows were simply cows walking through the pasture, some of them perhaps pausing right over the ant hill to munch on some grass. But then one day a thunderstorm pours water down on the pasture, and the ant hill is flooded.

I propose that, like the "flying ant," God's view of events in our world, and the relationship of these events to the universal conflict between good and evil, is much broader than ours. Thus, events that seem to us to be signs of the end may not be so to Him at all, or if they are, the timeline He's working on is much longer than ours.

Yet, because He understood our point of view—because He knew that we would tend to misinterpret world events as signs of Jesus' return "within five years"—He warned us of a delay. The delay is from our perspective, not His. In this regard, I like the advice of Dr. Fritz Guy, a professor of theology at La Sierra University:

> The advent hope is appropriately modest in the presence of transcendence [that is, in the presence of God]. It remembers that in the biblical revelation God insists that "my thoughts are not your thoughts, neither are your ways my ways" (Isaiah 55:8). That is to say, from God's perspective on reality there may well be a quite different evaluation of what is and what ought to be. . . . The idea of delay may be more a matter of human perception or misperception than of ultimate reality. . . .
>
> The fact that the planet on which humanity resides is part of a larger universe, and that our struggle with personal and collective sin is part of a cosmic controversy between good and evil means that there may be other transcendent factors for the delay of Christ that will remain entirely unknown to us until the coming of Christ. As in the biblical drama of Job, there may be reasons for the absence of God that remain unknown to humans until after the new beginning of human existence when we enter the immediate presence of God.[10]

> Guy goes on to say:

> even if we could demonstrate that the reason Jesus has not come is that the church has failed to proclaim the gospel to all the world, or that its people have not reached a sufficient level of spiritual growth, we would still be lacking essential information. For it would be God alone who would define the necessary extent and persuasiveness of the proclamation and the necessary level of maturity.[11]

Please do not think I am minimizing the importance of diligent effort on the part of God's church either to finish the proclamation of the gospel or to develop a character like Christ's. The two parables we have considered in this study make it clear that we *must* be seriously and energetically involved in both. Furthermore, Ellen White said we *could* hasten Christ's second coming through cooperation with Him. Here are two of several statements that could be cited:

> By giving the gospel to the world it is in our power to hasten our Lord's return. We are not only to look for but to hasten the coming of the day of God (2 Pet. 3:12, margin).[12]

> He has put it in our power, through cooperation with Him, to bring this scene of misery to an end. "This gospel of the kingdom shall be preached in all the world for a witness unto all nations; and then shall the end come." Matt. 24:14.[13]

In both of the statements above, Ellen White gave "finishing the work" as the way in which God's people might hasten Christ's return, and I'm not particularly in disagreement. However, I'm not sure it's spiritually beneficial to castigate ourselves for the delay. There are better motivations for these activities than guilt over a perceived failure on our part to hasten the return of Jesus. The best motive I know for diligent effort to proclaim the gospel is love for lost humanity, and the best motive for diligent effort in character development is love for Christ and a desire to be like Him. And I also propose that we will come the closest to actually hastening the coming of Jesus when we carry out our missionary activities and our personal character development for these better reasons.

When the disciples asked Jesus whether He was " 'at this time going to restore the kingdom to Israel,' " Jesus replied, " 'It is not for you to know the times or dates the Father has set by his own authority' " (Acts 1:6, 7). Jesus said, in essence, "You are not in control of the time of My return. God is." I do not doubt the sincerity of those of us who wish to finish the work or to perfect our characters so that Jesus can come. But I fear that in doing so, and especially in berating ourselves for not having done so, we are trying to take control of that which God has reserved for His control.

PART 4
HOW SHOULD WE RELATE TO THE DELAY?

I will conclude this chapter with one bit of advice about our relationship to the delay. Jesus said "Occupy till I come" (Luke 19:13, KJV). Every now and then some sincere Adventist couple asks me whether, in light of Christ's imminent return and the time of trouble that must take place between now and then, I think it would be wise for them to have children. My reply has always been Yes. I remember people asking me that question when I first entered the ministry. Their children are now approaching forty.

"Occupy till I come."

Young people sometimes wonder whether they should finish college. "Why should we waste time getting an education?" they ask. "Since Jesus is coming so soon, wouldn't it be better for us to get out there and help 'finish the work'?" Young people have been asking that question for the better part of 150 years. Those who first asked the question went on to college, put in their forty years, retired, and have long since died! So to all the young people who wonder whether they should waste time getting an education, my advice is to *get the education*. It's not wasted time!

"Occupy till I come."

Many years ago the United States Social Security Administration offered pastors the opportunity to "opt out" of paying into the social security system by signing a waver. Some young pastors, assuming that Jesus surely would come before they'd see a dime of that Social Security money, signed the waver. Many of them are now having second thoughts! Another concern of some young people just getting started on a career is whether to invest money in mutual funds as part of a retirement plan. "Jesus is going to come before we have a chance to retire," they say. My answer to all these questions is, Plan for the future. Plan for your retirement.

"Occupy till I come."

Events in the world suggest that the coming of Jesus is indeed near. However, we still do not know how near that is. We have no idea how much longer the delay will continue. From our human perspective, and given our great desire to see Jesus return, it's natural for us to think that surely He'll be here "in the next few years." That's what our parents thought, and our grandparents, and our great grandparents. But basing major long-range plans on this expectation is a mistake. Even if Jesus *should* come before we finish college, before our babies have a chance to grow up, or before we reach retirement age, the advice is still the same.

"Occupy till I come."

---

1. Commenting on the word *salvation* in this verse, *The SDA Bible Commentary* says, "By 'salvation' Paul evidently means the coming of Christ in power and glory" (6:629).

2. Writing in the Greek, Paul said "when we believed." The word *first* is implied. *The SDA Bible Commentary* says, "The tense of this verb in the Greek points back to the first acceptance of the Christian faith" (Ibid.).

3. *Testimonies*, 6:450. Ellen White also said that "had Adventists, after the great disappointment in 1844, . . . proclaim[ed the third angel's message] to the world, . . . Christ would have come ere this to receive His people to their reward" (*Early Writings*, 299; *Selected Messages*, 1:68).

4. The "Finishing the Work" document stated that " 'finishing the work' means one thing: communicating God's message through the power of the Holy Spirit to all of earth's population so that God can proclaim His work finished. *When this happens, Jesus will come*" (page 12, italics added).

5. Dennis Priebe, "Is Jesus Really Coming Soon?" *Our Firm Foundation*, January 2000, 16.

6. Ibid.

7. *Christian Experience and Teachings of Ellen G. White*, 186.

8. *Testimonies*, 1:363, italics added.

9. Ibid., 9:93.

10. Fritz Guy, "Dynamics of the Advent Hope" in *Pilgrimage of Hope*, Roy Branson, ed. (Takoma Park, Maryland: Association of Adventist Forums: 1986), 118.

11. Ibid.

12. *The Desire of Ages,* 633.

13. *Education*, 264.

the Nearness of Christ's Return

After reading the previous chapter, you may be tempted to think that I don't believe in the nearness of Christ's second coming at all. Fortunately, I can assure you that nothing could be further from the truth. I could write an entire book on this topic, so in this short chapter we can touch on just a few of the highlights. I will share with you *two reasons* why I believe the coming of Jesus to be near and *three signs* that persuade me His return is indeed near.

PART 1
TWO REASONS WHY I BELIEVE JESUS' COMING IS NEAR

There's no incontrovertible proof that the coming of Jesus is near. However, neither are we left with blind faith. Half way between these two extremes is evidence that can provide us with reasonable certainty. It's this evidence that I would like to discuss with you on the next few pages. The two reasons confirming my faith that the coming of Jesus is near are (1) Daniel's outline prophecies and (2) his time prophecies. We will begin by examining two of his outline prophecies.

The two great outline prophecies of Daniel
I'm sure you're familiar with Nebuchadnezzar's dream of the great image that is recorded in Daniel 2. You'll recall that Daniel told the king

that he (Nebuchadnezzar) was the head of gold—meaning that Babylon was the first in a line of four ancient empires. Medo-Persia followed next, represented by the arms and chest of silver. Greece was represented by the waist of brass, and Rome by the legs of iron. Then came the feet of iron and clay, the ten toes of which symbolized the nations of Europe, the Middle East, and North Africa that arose from Rome's ashes. In the final part of Nebuchadnezzar's dream, a stone struck the image on the feet and shattered it, and the stone became a great mountain that filled the whole earth.

Daniel explained to the king that the stone meant that " 'the God of heaven will set up a kingdom that will never be destroyed, nor will it be left to another people. It will crush all those kingdoms and bring them to an end, but it will itself endure forever' " (Daniel 2:44). It must have taken a lot of courage for a wiseman in training—a young hostage from a defeated nation—to stand before the most powerful monarch in the world and tell him that his kingdom was doomed! But Daniel fearlessly proclaimed the truth.

Daniel's basic message was this: No earthly kingdom will ever be eternal. Only the God of heaven can establish an eternal kingdom, and when He does, He will destroy every other nation. Premillennialist Christians have fairly consistently identified the establishment of God's eternal kingdom with the second coming of Christ. That has certainly been the Seventh-day Adventist understanding for more than 150 years. Thus, we have the following order of events in Nebuchadnezzar's dream of the great image:

Babylon
Medo-Persia
Greece
Rome
Divided Europe
Second coming of Christ

Years later Daniel received a similar vision, though the symbols were quite different. In this vision, recorded in chapter 7, Daniel saw four great beasts arise out of the sea: A lion, a bear, a leopard, and a nondescript beast that I'll call a dragon. These represented the same four ancient kingdoms—Babylon, Medo-Persia, Greece, and Rome. On the dragon's head were ten horns, representing the division of Europe, the Middle East, and North Africa into the nations we know today. However, two new elements were added to Daniel's vision that did not appear in Nebuchadnezzar's dream. The first was a "little horn" that uprooted three other horns and defied the God of heaven. Adventists have historically identified this horn with the medieval papacy. Immediately following the description of this little horn, Daniel saw a judgment scene in heaven: God seated on His throne with millions of angels standing around Him. This, we have always said, represents an "investigative judgment" that began in heaven in 1844.

The purpose of this court session is to judge between the little horn and God's people, whom it had been attacking. When the verdict is pronounced, God's people are vindicated and the little horn is condemned. Immediately following the rendition of the verdict, " ' "the sovereignty, power and greatness of the kingdoms under the whole heaven will be handed over to the saints, the people of the Most High. His kingdom will be an everlasting kingdom, and all rulers will worship and obey him" ' " (Daniel 7:27). Again, the vision culminates with the second coming of Christ. Now we have this order of events:

Babylon
Medo-Persia
Greece
Rome
Divided Europe
The medieval papacy
The investigative judgment
The second coming of Christ

Both of these prophecies came to Daniel while he was still living under the dominion of the Babylonian Empire. He received the second one very near the end of his life, when Babylon was about to fall to the Medes and Persians, so he was fully aware of the identity of the first two kingdoms. In a subsequent vision, God identified the third kingdom as Greece (see Daniel 8:20). But Daniel could not have known about Rome, which followed Greece, and there is absolutely no way he could have known that Rome would break into the nations of Europe we know today. Human wisdom could as well have suggested that Rome would be followed by a fifth empire. And Daniel's prediction of a religio-political power that would persecute God's people during the period of divided Europe is even more astounding. From a human point of view, there is no way that Daniel, on his own, writing in the fifth century B.C., could have predicted this outline of world history so accurately.

My point in bringing these two outline prophecies in Daniel to your attention is this: The supernatural nature of these visions assures us that they had their source in God, and if everything in both visions has been fulfilled save for the second coming of Christ, then we can know that the second coming of Christ is near.

The two great time prophecies of Daniel

God also gave Daniel two time prophecies—the 1,260 days/years of Daniel 7:25 and the 2,300 days/years of Daniel 8:14. The 1,260 years began in A.D. 538 and ended in 1798, while the 2,300 years began in 457 B.C. and ended in A.D. 1844. Please notice that these two visions began more than 1,000 years apart, but they ended less than fifty years apart. Only the God of heaven could start two time prophecies rolling a thousand years apart in ancient history and end them less than fifty years apart in our day!

Furthermore, after giving Daniel the prophecy about the 2,300 days, twice the angel told him that the vision concerned the "time of the end" (Daniel 8:17, 19). Thus, we know that *ever since 1844 we've been living in the time of the end*. Our pioneers were aware of this too, and they expected Jesus to come in their day. He didn't, as we all know. It's now been more than 150 years since the time of the end began rolling, and the obvious question is How much longer does it have to go? We don't know, of course. But several signs tell me clearly that the time of the end is rapidly winding down.

PART 2
THREE SIGNS THAT TELL ME JESUS' COMING IS NEAR

In the chapter "How to Think About Signs of the End" I said that clusters of events that make up a trend are much more likely to be signs of the end than are individual events. And a number of trends in today's world do appear to me to be leading toward the final crisis and the second coming of Christ. I will share three with you.

The gospel to all the world

Toward the end of Jesus' life on this earth, His disciples asked Him what would be the sign of His coming and of the end of the world (see Matthew 24:4). He gave them several signs, the most specific of which is found in Matthew 24:14:

And this gospel of the kingdom shall be preached in all the world
for a witness unto all nations; and then shall the end come (KJV).

This verse does not say that the entire world will be converted. It doesn't
even say that every human being will *hear* the proclamation of the gospel.
It says the end will come *when the gospel has been preached in all the
world*. However, although the preaching of the gospel to the entire world is
the most specific sign of the end that Jesus gave, it will be impossible for
us to know when it has been fulfilled. Only God will know that. So what
difference does this sign make to us? Why did Jesus even bother to give it?
Because, although we cannot know exactly when the gospel has been
preached to all the world, we have a pretty clear indication that the time
has almost come for that to happen.

Allow me to give you a bit of background before we go further. Go
back with me a little more than 500 years to Mainz, a city in Germany.
A man in that city by the name of Johann Gutenburg invented movable
type and thus introduced the world to printing.[1] The first major work to
be printed was the Bible, sometime in the 1450s, and by the end of the
century, small printing presses had been established throughout
Europe.

Next we will go to Wittenburg, also in Germany. An Augustinian monk
by the name of Martin Luther became convicted of the biblical truth of
justification by faith. In October 1517, he nailed ninety-five propositions
to the church door in Wittenburg challenging the Catholic practice of indulgences. The document was an instant success. Within a few months it
had been translated into the various languages of Europe, and printing
presses all over the continent had spread it far and wide. By the time the
church caught on to what was happening, it was too late to stop its dis-
semination.

I propose that the printing press, in addition to the guidance of the
Spirit, was one of the primary reasons Luther's effort to reform Christianity succeeded whereas other attempts in the previous two or three centuries had failed. *God brought printing technology at just the right time for
the Reformation to succeed.*

I believe we can see the same thing happening in our day. In addition to printing, we have television, radio, a global telephone system,
global air travel, FAX machines, and just in the 1990s, the Internet.
Most important of all, we now have satellite technology that makes it
possible for one person standing in one spot on earth to preach *live* to
the entire globe! And I propose that *God has brought all of this tech-*

nology at just the right time for the proclamation of His final warning message to the world.

Thus, while we cannot know when the gospel has been preached to the entire world, we do know that the technology is in place to accomplish the task practically overnight!

> **That's why I suggest that the recent development of technology that makes it possible to quickly preach the gospel to all the world is a significant indication that the time of the end is drawing near.**

And please notice that much of the technology to accomplish this has been in place only since about 1975.

The rise of modern spiritualism

The Bible gives several descriptions of what the world will be like during the months and perhaps years just before Jesus comes, and these can be signs of the end even though the Bible doesn't call them that. When we see trends leading us toward that kind of a world, we can have reasonable assurance that the coming of Jesus is near. That is the case with the next two signs I will share with you, the first of which is the rise of modern spiritualism. Notice the description of this by Jesus, Paul, and John:

Jesus

"If anyone says to you, 'Look, here is the Christ!' or, 'There he is!' do not believe it. For false Christs and false prophets will appear and perform great signs and miracles to deceive even the elect—if that were possible" (Matthew 24:23, 24).

Paul

The coming of the lawless one will be in accordance with the work of Satan displayed in all kinds of counterfeit miracles, signs and wonders, and in every sort of evil that deceives those who are perishing (2 Thessalonians 2:9, 10).

John

He [the second beast of Revelation 13] performed great and miraculous signs, even causing fire to come down from heaven to earth in full view of men. Because of the signs he was given power to do on behalf of the first beast, he deceived the inhabitants of the earth (Revelation 13:13, 14).

The sixth angel poured out his bowl on the great river Euphrates, and its water was dried up to prepare the way for the kings from the East. Then I saw three evil spirits that looked like frogs; they came out of the mouth of the dragon, out of the mouth of the beast and out of the mouth of the false prophet. They are spirits of demons performing miraculous signs, and they go out to the kings of the whole world, to gather them for the battle on the great day of God Almighty (Revelation 16:12-14).

The seven last plagues are the final series of events to happen in the world before Jesus comes. In fact, the seventh plague *is* the coming of Jesus, and the sixth plague occurs just *before* His return. The last passage cited above describes the sixth plague. It says that demons will go forth to government leaders all over the world to organize the battle of Armageddon. That's how widespread spiritualism will be just before the second coming of Jesus!

Spiritualism obviously does not have that kind of influence in the world today, but it's clearly on the way. In recent years, spiritualism has gone mainstream. Millions of people play with Ouiji boards and consult astrology charts. Angels have been the rage since about 1990, which isn't too bad if we're "raging" about the right kind of angels. Unfortunately, most of the talk about angels that you'll read about in the popular press is about the wrong kind.

Fifty years ago, paganism was something that happened in the undeveloped part of the world. Today, it's mainstream in America and other Western countries. Wicca is growing so fast (it's the fastest growing religion in America today) that the U.S. military has appointed at least one Wicca chaplain.

Some of the occult messages in our society are beamed directly at children. There are TV programs such as *Sabrina, the Teenage Witch*, which a Sabrina Web site says "consistently demonstrates what happens when a normally curious teenager has the powers of witchcraft." According to the Web site, *Sabrina*'s 2000-2001 season will include "a precocious witch from the Other Realm." And in the TV series *Charmed*, three sisters discover that they are witches and regularly consult their dead mother.

There are also books about witchcraft for kids. *U.S. News and World Report* said that *Teen Witch: Wicca for a New Generation* was "flying off the shelves" of bookstore giants like Borders and Barnes and Noble. Then, of course, there's the Harry Potter books, which are loaded with occult themes. The amazing thing is their popularity. Amazon.com sold nearly 400,000 copies of the fourth Harry Potter book (in a seven-book series) before it had even come off the press, and Barnes and Noble had 360,000 pre-publication orders! Author J. K. Rowling has announced plans for other kids' projects when she's completed the Harry Potter series.

Go to the World Wide Web, type "New Age" into several search engines, and see what you come up with. Alta Vista listed 364,746 pages for me, and Lycos gave me the option of choosing any one of 5,565,118 Web sites! Think of just about any word having to do with the occult: Witches, witchcraft, reincarnation, karma, chakra, ascended masters, etc. Type them in, and you'll come up with a world of occult, spiritualist, New-Age sites and information.

There are also issues that are less directly occult, but that have major implications for spiritualism and the popular view of life after death. I'm thinking, for example, about UFOs and extraterrestrials (which are popularized in motion picture and TV shows such as *Star Wars* and *Star Trek*). And, of course, there's the ever-popular near death experiences and out of body experiences that even many Christians are convinced provide proof that the spirit survives the body in a conscious form.

All these evidences for an emerging spiritualism in our culture prompt me to suggest that the rise of modern spiritualism is a significant indication that the time of the end is drawing to a close.

And the significant point to keep in mind is that all of this fascination with the occult has exploded in our Western culture since about 1975.

Religion involved in politics

The third sign telling me the coming of Jesus is near is the recent upsurge in religious politics, both in the United States and around the world. I base this conclusion on Revelation 17, which describes events in the world during the seven last plagues:

> One of the seven angels who had the seven bowls came and said to me, "Come, I will show you the punishment of the great prostitute, who sits on many waters" (verse 1).

As most Seventh-day Adventists are aware, a woman in Bible prophecy represents the Christian church. A virtuous woman represents the church in its apostolic purity, while an evil woman represents the church in deep apostasy. The prostitute in Revelation 17 is obviously an evil woman. Thus, the Bible is telling us that immediately before Jesus comes the Christian church will be in deep apostasy. What will be the nature of that apostasy? The next verse tells us:

> "With her the kings of the earth committed adultery and the inhabitants of the earth were intoxicated with the wine of her adulteries" (verse 2).

Adultery is a relationship between a man and a woman that God forbids. So Revelation is telling us that at the end of time the Christian church will be in an adulterous relationship with "the kings of the earth." Very few monarchies are left in the world. Most of today's governments are led by presidents and prime ministers. However, when Revelation speaks of the "kings of the earth" committing adultery with the "woman," the point is not the form of government that will exist at the end of time but simply that the church will be involved in a relationship with the governments of the world that God forbids. There will be an unholy union of the church with the state. So what will be the nature of that union? Verse 3 answers the question:

> Then the angel carried me away in the Spirit into a desert. There I saw a woman sitting on a scarlet beast that was covered with blasphemous names and had seven heads and ten horns.

There is an apparent contradiction here that we need to deal with before I comment on this verse. The woman is riding a *beast*, and Adventist students of prophecy know that a beast represents a major world power. Notice that the beast the woman is riding is *singular*, whereas in verse 2 she was committing adultery with "kings," *plural*. I understand this to mean that the nations that exist at the time of Christ's return will be pretty much the ones we know today, with one "super government" over all. This super government will very likely be the United Nations or some derivative thereof. This, I believe, is the "beast" in Revelation 17.

Now please notice that *the woman is riding the beast*. Conventional wisdom says that any time a human being rides an animal, the human being is supposed to be in control. (The only exception I've ever seen is in a rodeo.) Thus, this symbolic word-picture in Revelation suggests something very important about the world just before Jesus comes—that *the church will be in control of politics, at least at the global level.* The question is: Do we see this beginning to happen? And the answer is Yes—on the national level with American Protestantism, and on a global level with Catholicism.

American Protestantism. I hardly think I need to tell you that the Religious Right had a powerful influence on American politics during most of the 1990s. The Christian Coalition and similar Religious Right organizations played a major role in the switch from Democratic to Republican control of both houses of the United States Congress in 1994. For several years after that, conventional political wisdom dictated that any Republican who aspired to national political office had to show up at the Christian Coalition's annual Road to Victory Conference. George W. Bush did not personally attend the 2000 Road to Victory Conference, nor did his running mate Dick Cheney. They sent, instead, Jim Nicholson, the chairman of the Republican National Committee. Pat Robertson fumed, but couldn't do much about it.

The influence of the Religious Right over American politics appears to have waned during the last few years of the 1990s. However, the point is not so much the influence of the Religious Right at any one moment. The point is that conservative American Protestants have shown that they can exercise their political muscle when issues that concern them are at stake. Seventh-day Adventists understand, from both the Bible and Ellen White, that a day is coming when a conservative Protestant and Catholic political ideology will dominate American politics, and significant evidence exists that this development has begun.

Global Catholicism. The Vatican is gaining increasing influence over politics on a global scale. Practically everyone on our planet is aware of John Paul's feverish travel schedule since he assumed the papal office in 1978. What many people may not be so aware of is the fact that John Paul and Ronald Reagan joined hands back in the 1980s for the express purpose of bringing down Communism in Eastern Europe. *And it worked!* The first nation to break away from Communism, in June 1989, was John Paul's own homeland of Poland. When the other nations of Eastern Europe saw what Poland got away with, they tried it too. Czechoslovakia and Hungary were next, and we all watched with bated breath as the Berlin Wall came crashing down on November 9, 1989. By the end of the year, the only two Communist countries that had not broken away from the Soviet orbit were

Romania and Albania. And by the end of 1990 both of those nations were free of Communist domination. Then, in late December 1991 it was Gorbachev out, Yeltsin in, and the Soviet Union ceased to exist. *Communism was out in Europe.*

The Vatican's role in these dramatic events is underscored by this paragraph in *Time* magazine dated December 4, 1989:

> John Paul helped inflame the fervor for freedom in his Polish homeland that has swept like brush fire across Eastern Europe. While Gorbachev's hands-off policy was the immediate cause of the chain reaction of liberation, . . . John Paul deserves much of the longer-range credit.[2]

It's political power when a church can bring down the government of an entire nation.

And, if we can believe Malachi Martin, John Paul has much higher ambitions for his church than vanquishing Communism in Poland and Eastern Europe. Martin, a former Jesuit and at one time a professor at the Vatican's Gregorian University in Rome, wrote a book with the rather lengthy title *The Keys of This Blood: The Struggle for World Dominion Between Pope John Paul II, Michael Gorbachev, and the Capitalist West.* Martin begins the book with a wordy statement that a one-world government is inevitable in the near future:

> Willing or not, ready or not, we are all involved in an all-out, no-holds barred, three-way global competition. Most of us are not competitors, however, We are the stakes. For the competition is about who will establish the first one-world system of government that has ever existed in the society of nations. It is about who will hold and wield the dual power of authority and control over each of us as individuals and over all of us together as a community; over the entire six billion people expected by demographers to inhabit the earth by early in the third millennium. The competition is all-out because, now that it has started, there is no way it can be reversed or called off.[3]

Martin went on to say that "those of us under forty will surely live under [the new world order's] legislative, executive and judiciary authority and control."[4] Then he made the following remarkable statement:

It is not too much to say, in fact, that the chosen purpose of John Paul's pontificate—the engine that drives his papal grand policy and that determines his day-to-day, year-by-year strategies—is to be the victor in that competition, now well under way.[5]

In other words, John Paul wants his church to rule the coming one-world government! Seventh-day Adventists have predicted for 150 years that the Vatican would dominate the world politically someday. That sounded like political nonsense when we first said it back in the 1850s. The Vatican had just lost political authority over Europe only about fifty years earlier. But we said it because we believed the Bible predicted it. And now it's not just Adventists who are saying it. Malachi Martin assures us that global political domination is John Paul's own highest ambition!

That's why I suggest that the growing trend toward religion in politics—on a national scale with American Protestants and on a global scale with the Vatican—is a significant sign that the time of the end is drawing to a close.

And please notice that this trend has been going on only since about 1980.

Summarizing the evidence
I have offered two reasons and three signs why I believe that the coming of Jesus truly is near in our day. The two reasons are:

- *The two outline prophecies of Daniel.* These prophecies give a snapshot of world history down to the end of time, and the only thing left to be fulfilled is the second coming of Christ.
- *The two great time prophecies of Daniel,* including the 2,300-day prophecy, which tells us that ever since 1844 we have been living in the time of the end.

So the only question is how much longer the time of the end has to run, and I shared with you three trends in today's world that tell me it's drawing to a close:

- *The gospel to all the world.* The gospel must be preached to all the world before the end can come, and the technology is in place to accomplish that task almost overnight, including satellite broadcasting, which has been with us since about 1975, and the Internet, which began to have a global impact during the 1990s.

•*Spiritualism*. The Bible predicts that spiritualism will be rampant throughout the world just before the second coming of Jesus, and we have seen that trend developing rapidly since about 1975.

•*Religion in politics*. Based on the prophecies in Revelation, Adventists have historically said that near the end of time Christianity will be deeply involved in politics on both a national scale with American Protestantism and on a global scale with Catholicism. And a trend in that direction began about 1980.

I could discuss a number of other trends indicating that we are nearing the second coming of Christ, including the ecumenical movement, the increase in natural disasters around the world during the 1990s, crime and violence, and the breakdown of earth's ecology. *And all of these increased in their intensity during the last quarter of the twentieth century.*

It's these major trends, and especially their acceleration in recent years, that persuades me the world is approaching its end. Numerous events have end-time significance in the context of these trends, and keeping each event in the context of trends helps me to avoid giving any one event more significance than it deserves.

As a Christian who is anxious to see Jesus return and put an end to sin and suffering, I would like nothing better than to assure you that Jesus will come within the next five to ten years. *I wish I could do that.* However, I *cannot*, and I *will not*, because *I don't know*. And neither does anyone else. God has His timetable, and when the fullness of time has come, Jesus will return to claim us as His own.

PART 3
WILL WE EVER KNOW FOR SURE?

The most you and I can say about the nearness of Christ's coming at the present time is that we have been living in the end time for a little over 150 years and that certain trends suggest it is drawing to a close. Beyond that—even to speculate that He might be here in five, fifteen, or twenty-five years—is unwise. So the question naturally arises, will we *ever* know that the coming of Jesus truly *is* near? Some people answer that question with a definite No. However, I disagree. I believe there will come a time when we can know that it is significantly nearer than it is today. And the closer we come to His return, the more certain we can be of that conclusion. There are several reasons why I say this.

The final crisis. I shared a snapshot of the final crisis with you in chapter 2, so a summary is adequate here. The final crisis will have the following characteristics, among others:

- Global natural disasters that threaten the survival of the human race.
- A worldwide proclamation of the gospel by God's people under the powerful influence of the Holy Spirit.
- Spiritualism uniting with Protestantism and Catholicism to create a global religious system in opposition to the gospel.
- A union of this false religious system with the governments of the world, including the one-world government, to suppress the proclamation of the truth with persecution and threats of death.

When this condition develops in the world, God's people will surely know it, and this will give them reasonable certainty that the coming of Jesus is likely to occur within their lifetime.

A statement by Ellen White. Ellen White made a statement that suggests we can know when the second coming of Jesus is near. She said:

> By the decree enforcing the institution of the papacy in violation of the law of God, our nation will disconnect herself fully from righteousness. When Protestantism shall stretch her hand across the gulf to grasp the hand of the Roman power, when she shall reach over the abyss to clasp hands with spiritualism, when under the influence of this three-fold union, our country shall repudiate every principle of its Constitution as a Protestant and republican government, and shall make provision for the propagation of papal falsehoods and delusions, then we may know that the time has come for the marvelous working of Satan and that *the end is near.*[6]

Please note: W*e can know that the end is near* when the conditions stated in the paragraph have been met. Of course, we will need to be sure that all the conditions have been met. One of the great temptations, for those of us who are anxious to see Jesus come, is to conclude that a prediction has been fulfilled when only some of the conditions have been met. We also tend to see certain events as the "fulfillment" of a prediction when a careful examination of the inspired evidence compared to what happened would show that no fulfillment had occurred. The events didn't really match the requirements of the prophecy.

The close of probation. No one will know when probation has closed. However, assuming that the seven last plagues are literal, as we have always taught, we should be able to recognize them when they begin to fall. This will be evidence that probation has closed and that the return of Jesus is near.

The death decree. Ellen White made three statements that suggest we will have a fairly accurate knowledge of the time of Christ's return shortly before it happens. She said:

> I saw the leading men of the earth consulting together, and Satan and his angels busy around them. I saw a writing, copies of which were scattered in different parts of the land, giving orders that unless the saints should yield their peculiar faith, give up the Sabbath, and observe the first day of the week, the people were at liberty *after a certain time* to put them to death.[7]

> A decree will finally be issued against those who hallow the Sabbath of the fourth commandment, denouncing them as deserving of the severest punishment and giving the people liberty, *after a certain time*, to put them to death.[8]

> A general decree has *fixed the time* when commandment keepers may be put to death.[9]

This "certain time" and "fixed time" could be a condition that must be met. However, if it is a specific date, then God's people who are alive at that time can know that Jesus will come to deliver them *before* that date.

How to think about the nearness of Christ's return

There's an inevitable tension between Christ's warning that no one knows the day or the hour of His return and His assurance that we can know when it is near. And there will always be those who want to take a position at one of those extremes. Some will always be sure that His coming will occur within five years, while others will say it might be a thousand years in the future. Finding the middle ground isn't easy, but in the end I believe it's the only way to be both realistic and sane about the time for Christ's return. We need to recognize that we've been living in the time of the end since 1844 and that the quickening of signs since about 1980 indicates that the end is near. Yet we must refuse to speculate about how soon that might be. Like the disciples, I'm human enough to want to know whether this is the time when Jesus is going to "restore the kingdom to Israel" (Acts 1:6). But I recognize that, while the signs and trends suggest that it is near, we do not know how near that is.

---

1. Gutenburg was born in Mainz. There is some evidence that his actual inventing of printing may have occurred in Strasbourg.

2. *Time*, December 4, 1989, 74.

3. Malachi Martin, *The Keys of This Blood* (New York: Simon and Schuster, 1990), 15.

4. Ibid., 16.

5. Ibid., 17.

6. *Testimonies*, 5:541, italics added.

7. *Early Writings*, 282, italics added

8. *The Great Controversy*, 615, 616, italics added.

9. Ibid., 631, italics added.

Dates
and
Time Setting

The Great Disappointment of October 22, 1844 should have cured Adventists of all efforts to set dates for Christ's second coming. Ellen White stated categorically that ever since the passing of the time in 1844, she had warned against setting dates for Christ's return.[1] And in 1892 she wrote in the *Review and Herald* that "we are not to be engrossed with speculations in regard to the times and the seasons which God has not revealed, . . . for 'of that day and hour knoweth no man.' "[2]

You'd think that would be enough to stop us from setting dates for Christ's return. Unfortunately, it hasn't been so in the past, and it almost certainly won't be in the future.

Following the Great Disappointment, some Millerite Adventists speculated that Jesus would return on October 22, 1845. James White himself was one of these. He said "That Christ would then come we firmly believed." In fact, a few days before this date he was at the point of preaching about it when Ellen White, in a vision at Carver, Massachusetts, saw "that we should be disappointed." James and others who believed in her revelations dropped the prediction and were not disappointed.[3] When the 1845 date passed, those who refused to follow her counsel predicted that Christ would return in 1846. Then they set a date in 1849, followed by other dates in 1850, 1851, 1854, 1866, and 1877![4]

For 150 years, some Seventh-day Adventists have been very creative in their time setting.

Various dating schemes

Joseph Bates came up with a theory that sounds amusing to us, but which he and others at the time took quite seriously. He interpreted the seven *times* that the priest in the earthly sanctuary was to sprinkle blood upon the altar on the Day of Atonement[5] to mean seven *years*, which would be the length of time it would take Christ to cleanse the heavenly sanctuary. Thus, in 1850, he published a tract suggesting that Christ would return in the fall of 1851—seven years following October 22, 1844. Some Sabbath-keeping Adventists took his suggestion quite seriously, until Ellen White published instruction from the Lord that Bates was wrong. To his credit, Bates dropped his theory, and the infant church was spared his fanatical time-setting scheme.[6]

However, this didn't keep Adventists from setting more dates for Christ's return. Some Adventists suggested 1884 as a date for Christ's return, based on the speculation that as the Israelites wandered forty years in the wilderness, so Christ would come forty years after 1844.[7] I haven't heard whether any Adventists promoted 1914 as the year for Christ's return,[8] but it would have made a good speculation, based on the seventy years that the Jews were captive in Babylon. Certainly there were Adventists in the early 1900s who, based on Jesus' statement that " 'this generation will certainly not pass away until all these things have happened' " (Matthew 24:34), expected Jesus to return by about 1930. The stars fell in 1833, and the 1930s, they said, would be about the latest one could expect a few people from that generation to still be alive.

I began my ministerial internship in 1961 in Pomona, California, and I can still remember the pastor of the church preaching a fiery sermon that Christ would come in 1964. He based this on the 120 years that it took Noah to build the ark. The math is quite simple: 1844 plus 120 equals 1964. Presumably, if Christ hasn't returned by about 2250, some Adventists will speculate that He will return in 2274, based on the 430 years that the Israelites spent in Egypt before their return to Canaan. For obvious reasons, that date doesn't attract a lot of attention today.

Hal Lindsey proposed 1988 as the year for Christ's return. He based this on the view held by dispensationalist Protestants that the restoration of the Jews to their homeland in 1948 had prophetic significance.[9] Jesus said that " 'this generation will certainly not pass away until all these things have happened' " (Matthew 24:34). Lindsey assumed a biblical generation to be forty years, hence his date 1988. And because dispensationalists believe that the tribulation that immediately precedes Christ's return will last exactly seven years, he also speculated that the tribulation might begin in 1981.

Harold Camping, the founder of the *Family Radio* program, published a book in 1992 in which he predicted that Christ's coming would be "on the Day of Atonement, September 15, 1994," or at the very latest September 27 of that year.[10] In the introduction to his book, Camping wrote: "I would be very surprised if the world reaches the year 2000."[11] I trust that Camping celebrated his surprise on January 1, 2000!

However, Camping was not the only one who speculated that Christ might return in 1994. So did a number of Adventists, though their argument is not as complex as Camping's, which took him 550 pages to write! The Adventist 1994 date is based on the jubilee theory. A jubilee equals forty-nine years.[12] Assuming that A.D. 34 (when the seventy weeks of Daniel 9:24, 25 ended) was a jubilee year, forty jubilee cycles from that date would indeed end in 1994. The math works.[13] The rest of the theory obviously doesn't, since Christ didn't return in 1994. Some people speculated that if Christ didn't return in that year, perhaps the time of trouble would begin then, but that didn't happen either.

I could wish that, with the passing of 2000, Adventists and all other Christians would be cured of setting dates for Christ's return. Unfortunately, that is not to be. As long as humans are numbered among the Christians on planet Earth, some among us are bound to figure out more schemes for dating the end of the world. I've already heard one proposal for a date in the new millennium: the year 2027. Jesus was baptized in A.D. 27, so that theory goes, and two millenniums after that will be 2027—the new date for Christ's return!

The 6,000-year theory

There's also the famous 6,000-year theory, which I've left for last because I want to comment on it in some detail. You've probably heard it, but for the record, it's based on the assumption that the millennium that God's people spend in heaven will be a *sabbatical* millennium. According to James Ussher's chronology of the Bible,[14] Creation occurred in 4004 B.C. If that calculation is correct, the date for the end of the sixth millennium was A.D. 1996. And, based on the 6,000-year theory, some people speculated that Christ might return at that time. When He didn't, and when the time of trouble didn't begin in 1996, the next logical date was 2000. And a *lot* of speculation surrounded that year, as you no doubt know. Nor was it just

Adventists or even Christians who were doing the speculating. Psychics of all shades and colors predicted everything from the appearance of the antichrist to the beginning of World War III to a global earthquake in that year. However, as you now know, nothing out of the ordinary happened in 2000.

The 6,000-year theory has been the most persistent scheme for dating Christ's return. Some Christians were proposing it as far back as the third century A.D., and Ellen White made a number of statements that appear to support it. I have reproduced several of these statements below. In each one, I have placed the words "six thousand years" in italics—although they are not emphasized in the original statement. I will not comment on each quotation. Rather, I will invite you to notice that all of them are in the context of the close of the great controversy, the second coming of Christ, and the millennium that follows His return:

> The great controversy between Christ and Satan, that has been carried on for almost *six thousand years,* is soon to close.[15]

> For *six thousand years,* Satan has struggled to maintain possession of the earth. Now God's original purpose in its creation is accomplished. "The saints of the most High shall take the kingdom, and possess the kingdom for ever, even for ever and ever." Daniel 7:18.[16]

> As the church approaches her final deliverance, Satan is to work with greater power. . . . For *six thousand years* that mastermind that once was highest among the angels of God, has been wholly bent to the work of deception and ruin.[17]

> For *six thousand years* the great controversy has been in progress; . . . Now all have made their decision; the wicked have fully united with Satan in his warfare against God. The time has come for God to vindicate the authority of his downtrodden law.[18]

> For *six thousand years,* Satan's work of rebellion has "made the earth to tremble." . . . For a thousand years, Satan will wander to and fro in the desolate earth, to behold the results of his rebellion against the law of God.[19]

Some people have used these statements to impress on Adventists that the end is near. However, there are several problems associated with the 6,000-year theory that make that conclusion less than satisfactory. I will mention three.

Ellen White's statements. Ellen White never did say that Christ would return exactly 6,000 years after the creation of the world. On numerous occasions she said "about six thousand years" or "nearly six thousand years." Thus, we should understand her comments about 6,000 years of earth's history to be generalizations rather than exact chronological statements. I pointed out earlier in this chapter that Ellen White consistently opposed efforts to fix a date for Christ's return. She would certainly be horrified to know that some people today have used her 6,000-year statements to speculate about Christ's return in 1996 or 2000.

Furthermore, Ellen White's 6,000-year statements were nearly all in the context of the history of sin, but we have only a vague idea of how much time passed from the creation of the world till Adam and Eve rebelled and were cast out of the Garden of Eden. What we do know is that Seth was born when Adam was 130 years old.[20] Cain and Abel were born after the fall but prior to the birth of Seth, and both of them were old enough to be offering sacrifices on their own prior to Seth's birth. Thus, while the brevity of the biblical record makes it seem unlikely, it's possible that as much as a hundred years might have transpired between the Creation and the Fall.

The imprecise nature of biblical chronology is the second problem associated with arriving at even an approximate date for the creation of the world, which of course affects our calculation for the end of the 6,000 years. The problem is that the biblical data are not as exact as they would have been had we written the Bible. There are two problems. The first has to do with the ages of pre-and post-Flood patriarchs.

Ages of the patriarchs.[21] The Bible lists ten patriarchs before the Flood and ten after—twenty in all. The wives of nine of these gave birth to their first son when the father's age was a multiple of ten—that is, his age ended in at least one zero and in some cases two, which would be a multiple of a hundred.[22] However, the statistical probability of a son being born when the father's age ended in a zero is one out of ten. Thus, we could statistically expect that two out of the twenty patriarchs would have his first son when his age was a multiple of ten—not nine out of twenty as the record has it.

One might argue that these patriarchs *planned* the births of their sons that way. However, it's not likely that they planned their own deaths that way. Nevertheless, eight of the twenty patriarchs lived an additional number of years that also ended in a multiple of ten,[23] and five of them lived an additional number of years ending in a multiple of one hundred. Statistically, the odds of that actually happening are close to impossible!

Biblical scholars thus reasonably ask whether, in giving the ages of these patriarchs, the author of Genesis may not have had some stylistic objective in mind rather than the strict chronological considerations that would be of primary concern to people living in the twenty-first century A.D. This conclusion is strengthened when we note that the genealogical chart in the first chapter of Matthew differs significantly from a similar chart in the first chapter of Luke. Modern scholars are not sure why these differences exist, but they speculate that they have to do with the differing purposes of the two authors.

Differences among ancient sources.[24] A second reason to question Ussher's interpretation of biblical chronology is that it was based exclusively on the Masoretic text of the Old Testament. Just as we have many versions of the English Bible today, so the Masoretic text is a "version" of the Hebrew Old Testament. All modern translations of the Bible are based on this Masoretic version of the Hebrew Bible.[25] However, two other versions of the chronological data for the pre- and post-Flood patriarchs are available. One is the Septuagint—a Greek translation of the Old Testament—which differs in significant ways from the Masoretic text, including the ages of the pre- and post-Flood patriarchs. The other version is the Samaritan Pentatuch. The Samaritans, descendants of the Jews that were left in Palestine after the Babylonian captivity, were still around in Christ's time, and because of the hostility that existed between them and the Jews, these Samaritans accepted only the five books of Moses (the Pentatuch) as genuine Scripture. And the Samaritans had their own version of the Pentatuch. The ages of the patriarchs in this Samaritan Pentatuch differ significantly from the ages given in both the Masoretic text and the Septuagint. According to the Masoretic text, the total number of years from Creation to the birth of Abraham was 1,946. The total for the same period in the Septuagint is 3,412 years, and in the Samaritan Pentatuch it's 2,247 years.

Given these two problems associated with the ages of the patriarchs—(1) the apparently stylistic nature of their ages as given in the

Bible and (2) the differences among the various ancient sources—it's extremely unlikely that Ussher's simple addition of these ages, as they are listed in the King James Version and other versions based on the Masoretic text, can provide us with an accurate date for Creation. Thus, it's virtually certain that neither 1996 nor 2000 are valid dates for the conclusion of 6,000 years since Creation. The difference could go several hundred years either way! However, I don't know of anyone who is prepared to get excited about the fact that, if we had the chronology absolutely straight, the 6,000 years might actually end in 2300 or 2400!

Within "the next five years"

I can't remember when I first heard an Adventist say, "Surely the coming of Jesus will be within the next five years," but it's been a long time. And I've heard it every now and then since. Occasionally it comes out more subtly, such as when someone mentions an event he or she anticipates happening in five or ten years—graduation from college, retirement, long-range job goals, etc.—and the person he or she is talking to will remark, "I hope we're in heaven by then."

I wish we could all bring ourselves to stop saying things like that, because *it's actually a mild form of time setting,* and like all time-setting schemes, it has the potential to create major spiritual problems. This is tragically illustrated in the following story, which Ken Wade tells in his book *Jesus for a New Millennium:*

> Years ago when I was in college, my wife told me about a visit she'd had with an elderly gentleman who had lost his hope. "When I was a young boy," he told her, "I expected Jesus to come any day. I've been hoping He'd come for the past eighty years. But now I don't believe it anymore. I just can't believe it. It's been too long."[27]

I think I'm safe in assuming that this man didn't invent the notion of Christ's return "within five years" himself. So who put it in his head? *It was the well-meaning parents, Sabbath School teachers, church school teachers, and preachers in his life.* When you and I talk about Jesus surely coming "in the next five years," we plant the same seeds in the minds of our children and even in the thoughts of spiritually immature adults. And one day those seeds are likely to sprout into the same doubts that the old man had in Ken Wade's story. Ellen White's advice is still good today:

You will not be able to say that He will come in one, two, or five years, neither are you to put off His coming by stating that it may not be for ten or twenty years. . . . We are not to know the definite time either for the outpouring of the Holy Spirit or for the coming of Christ.[28]

So how should we think about setting a date for Christ's return? I have just one word of advice for myself and anyone else who is tempted to do it:

Don't!

1. *Testimonies*, 1:72.

2. *Review and Herald*, March 22, 1892; cited in *Evangelism*, 221.

3. See Arthur W. Spaulding, *Origin and History of Seventh-day Adventists* (Washington, D.C.: Review and Herald, 1961), 1:145, 146.

4. Spaulding, *op. cit.*, 1:136.

5. See Leviticus 16:17, 18.

6. Spaulding, *op. cit.* 1:146, 147.

7. I cannot cite a source for this, but I have read it, and I have talked with others who said they had read it.

8. The Jehovah's Witnesses still teach that He did return *spiritually* in that year.

9. Seventh-day Adventists reject this interpretation of prophecy.

10. Harold Camping, *1994?* (New York: Vantage Press, 1992), 521, 525.

11. Ibid., xv.

12. See Leviticus 11:8-13.

13. 40 x 49 = 1960 + 34 = 1994.

14. James Ussher (1581-1656), an Irish clergyman, worked out the system for dating biblical events, including the Creation in 4004, that for several centuries was used in many editions of the King James Bible.

15. *The Great Controversy*, 518.

16. *Amazing Grace*, 370.

17. *The Great Controversy*, 88.

18. Ibid., 656.

19. Ibid., 658, 659.

20. See Genesis 5:3.

21. For a complete discussion of this topic see James L. Hayward and Donald E. Casebolt, "The Genealogies of Genesis 5 and 11: A Statistical Study," *Origins*, 9:75-81.

22. These chronological statistics are recorded in Genesis 5:3-32 (pre-Flood patriarchs) and Genesis 10:10-26 (post-Flood patriarchs). (1) Adam was 130 when Seth was born; (2) Enosh was 90 when Kenan was born; (3) Kenan was 70 when Mahalalel was born; (4) Noah was 500 years old when Shem was born; (5) Shem was 100 years old when Arphaxad was born; (6) Shelah was 30 years old when Eber was born; (7) Peleg was 30 years old when Reu was born; (8) Serug was 30 years old when Nahor was born; and (9) Terah was 70 years old when Abraham was born.

23. These chronological statistics are recorded in Genesis 5:3-32 (pre-Flood patriarchs) and Genesis 10:10-26 (post-Flood patriarchs). (1) Adam lived 800 years after the birth of Seth; (2) Kenan lived 840 years after the birth of Mahalalel; (3) Mahalalel lived 830 years after the birth of Jared; (4) Jared lived 800 years after the birth of Enoch; (5) Enoch lived 300 years after the birth of Methuselah; (6) Shem lived 500 years after the birth of Arphaxad; (7) Eber lived 430 years after the birth of Peleg; and (8) Serug lived 200 years after the birth of Nahor.

24. For a complete discussion of this topic see Lawrence T. Geraty, "The Genesis Genealogies as an Index of Time," *Spectrum*, 1974, volumes 1, 2, pages 5-18.

25. Translators take into consideration the Septuagint and other sources that differ from the Masoretic text, but the modern translations as a whole are based on the Masoretic text.

26. Ken Wade, *Jesus for a New Millennium* (Nampa, Idaho: Pacific Press®, 1999), 12.

27. *Evangelism*, 221.

HOW TO THINK ABOUT

Catholics

Catholics
and the
Antichrist

On February 2, 2000, George W. Bush spoke at Bob Jones University in Greenville, South Carolina. This was a smart enough move. Bush was campaigning for the Republican nomination for president of the United States. South Carolina is a conservative Christian state that leans heavily toward the Religious Right. And BJU is a staunchly conservative university.

In many ways, BJU would make any conservative Adventist proud. It has a strict campus code for student dress and behavior—even to the kind of music students can listen to. And it maintains the historic Protestant view of the papacy as the antichrist, the beast of Revelation 13, the whore of Revelation 17.

Which is what got George W. in trouble.

Never mind that every Republican candidate for president beginning with Ronald Reagan had spoken at BJU during his campaign. So why not Bush? But this time it backfired. Senator John McCain, the Republican senator from Arizona with whom Bush was in a dead heat for the Republican primary at the time, used Bush's BJU speech to garner Catholic votes in Michigan. Michigan is a strongly Catholic state, so the week before the Michigan primary, McCain issued a "Catholic Voter Alert" informing the state's Catholics that BJU is anti-Catholic and that Bush had failed to distance himself from that anti-Catholicism.

And, of course, the media—which is no lover of religion to start with—

picked up on the flap and turned it into a national debate. *Time* magazine called the university's views Catholic bashing. "BJU's acrid exclusivism," *Time* said, "raise[s] troubling questions about how close beneath the surface some old intolerances run."[1] The media pressure got so heavy that on February 27 Bush wrote a contrite letter to Cardinal John O'Conner, the Catholic Archbishop of New York, apologizing to all Catholics for failing to make clear that he did not support BJU's anti-Catholicism.

And, as a final drum roll, Mr. Robert Torricelli, Democratic senator from New Jersey, introduced a resolution in the United States senate "condemning the discriminatory practices prevalent at Bob Jones University." Among other things, the resolution castigated Bob Jones University for branding Catholicism "a satanic system and the religion of the anti-Christ."

BJU's president Bob Jones III responded that the religious convictions of Bob Jones University are none of the Senate's business. "What other religious belief will find itself in the gunsight of the U. S. senate next?" Mr. Jones asked. What about Islam's doctrine that men are superior to women or the Jewish doctrine that a marriage between a Jew and a non-Jew is not recognized? "Would you desire to see them persecuted by the senate, by Presidential candidates, or by the media because their beliefs are not yours and may even offend you? We wouldn't!"[2]

I agree with Mr. Jones.

The real issue

However, important as is the point that he makes, it's not what I want to discuss with you in this chapter. Our question here is not how Bob Jones University should think about Catholics, how Senator McCain or Governor Bush[3] should think about Catholics, or how the U. S. Senate should think about Catholics. Our question is how *Adventists* should think about Catholics—and how we should talk about them.

I will introduce this discussion by calling your attention to an article I wrote in the June 1999 issue of *Signs of the Times*® titled "Who Is the Antichrist?" The article reviewed the New Testament evidence for the antichrist and concluded that "one individual—possibly Satan himself—will be the ultimate antichrist just before Jesus comes."[4] My conservative Adventist readers were disappointed that I did not identify the pope as the ultimate antichrist. Here are several of the responses that came to *Signs*:

> I was enticed by your June '99 cover, which read in bold print "Who Is the Antichrist?" I was about half way through when I

realized that what I had been hungering for would go unfulfilled. I can't believe that you did not identify the antichrist for your readers after luring them in with your cover. Once you baited the hook and threw your line in the water, you should be prepared to deliver what you promised to all the fish that come along to take your bait. It reminded me of a politician anxious to be reelected yet trying to sidestep the media questions when cornered and asked how he stands on a certain issue.

I was curious to find out how you would address this controversial topic. To my disappointment, you failed to adequately identify who is "the ultimate antichrist just before Jesus comes."

I looked forward to reading the article "Who is the Antichrist?" I was disappointed, however, that the answer to the question was left so incomplete.

One particularly distressed reader wrote: "Mr. Moore, you owe the church an apology for this article!"[5]

Public discussion of the antichrist

I agree with the traditional Adventist view that the first beast of Revelation 13 is the papacy. I agree that at the very least the papacy was *the* antichrist during the Middle Ages and will be an important antichrist during the final conflict.[6] The question is: *How should we present that view to the public?* The more traditionally-minded Adventist readers of *Signs* obviously thought I should have named the pope as the antichrist in my article.

In addition to the letters I received, a number of people approached me either by phone or in person with their objection that I did not identify the pope as the antichrist. And I always began my response with a question: Would you want an evangelist to identify the pope as the antichrist on the opening night of a series of meetings in your church? The immediate response was always No! I don't recall a single individual, no matter how conservative, who would have thought it appropriate for an evangelist to identify the papacy as the antichrist on the opening night of a crusade.

I then pointed out to these individuals that *Signs of the Times*® is published for non-Adventists. We know from our records that of our current 200,000[7] circulation, only 8 to 10 percent are Adventists. The rest are non-Adventist readers. If we assume that each copy of each issue is read by at least two people, then close to 400,000 non-Adventists read *Signs of the*

Times® each month, and I believe it's safe to also assume that each month thousands of these are first- or second-time readers. In other words, *Signs of the Times*® *is like the opening night of an evangelistic crusade.*

It's not a denial of our faith to avoid putting our more controversial beliefs front and center on the opening night of a series of public meetings—whether it's our belief in the Sabbath, the state of the dead, or the papacy as the antichrist. And for the same reason, neither is it a denial of our faith to avoid putting that detail in *Signs of the Times*®.

The principle to follow

One of the basic principles to follow is this: Always treat other people's religious faith with courtesy and respect, and *insofar as possible it's important to be perceived by the public as showing that respect.* I'm not talking about mere window dressing for public consumption. I'm talking about one of the graces of the Christian spirit, which takes into consideration other people's feelings before we speak or act. How will Catholics feel about our statement that the pope is the antichrist? How will the general public perceive it?

And I propose that in today's religious climate it's virtually impossible to show the kind of respect I'm talking about and at the same time openly identify the papacy as the antichrist *unless people have had a significant introduction to the background of our belief on this point.* And by *background* I mean that people need to understand that we aren't just spouting bigotry, that our views are solidly based on a particular interpretation of prophecy. And the facts are that (1) it's impossible to give this background in a 1,250-word article, and (2) without that background people will almost inevitably conclude that we are simply being bigoted.

One of the correspondents who responded to my article in *Signs* said that the article reminded her of "a politician anxious to be reelected yet trying to sidestep the media questions when cornered and asked how he stands on a certain issue." The flap over George Bush's speech at Bob Jones University puts this issue in sharp focus. Bush *is* a politician; he *was* embarrassed by the media's questions; and it could be argued that his apology to Cardinal O'Conner was mere window dressing. But does this mean that I was simply playing good politics in refusing to identify the pope as the antichrist in my article in *Signs*? Am I suggesting that Adventists sidestep questions about our beliefs if the answers would be embarrassing?

Absolutely not! But it's extremely important that we be careful about how we introduce our understanding of the antichrist lest we be *perceived* as something we are not. I honestly don't believe that Seventh-day

Adventists, as a whole, are bigoted toward Catholics. But we will be *perceived* as bigots if we aren't careful.

Our choice of words

Another very important consideration when discussing the antichrist and similar controversial issues is our choice of words. To introduce this aspect of the topic, I will state an important principle to keep in mind as we choose those words: *We cannot use the same language to talk about Catholics today that our pioneers used a hundred years ago.*

Allow me to explain.

Ellen White's magnum opus on the end time—*The Great Controversy*—was written in the late 1800s when anti-Catholic feelings were running strong in American Protestantism. This sentiment was still strong during most of the first half of the twentieth century. As *Time* magazine put it, back in the 1920s "anti-Catholicism was a staple of conservative American Protestantism. Americans, alarmed at the influx of Irish and Italian immigrants, took solace in Reformation descriptions of the Pope as the Whore of Babylon."

Time went on to point out, however, that "eventually most American Protestants left anti-Catholicism behind, and from the 1950s on, Billy Graham led many Evangelicals toward a greater tolerance."[8]

Greater tolerance indeed! We live in a time when this so-called tolerance is running so strong that some Lutherans are beginning to anticipate the day when they will return to the "mother church"! Obviously, today's relationship between Protestants and Catholics in America is the polar opposite of what it was a hundred years ago.

I should hasten to point out that I do not consider this to be all bad. Much of the attitude a hundred years ago was blind prejudice, which resulted in a number of instances of severe persecution of Catholics. In some cases Catholic property was destroyed, and in a few instances Catholic people lost their lives. I don't think anyone but the most rabid member of the Ku Klux Klan would want America to return to that religious climate.

On the other hand, we must not suppose that all the differences between Catholics and Protestants have been resolved or should be papered over. Adventists are not the only Protestants who disagree with Roman Catholics over such doctrines and practices as purgatory, indulgences, images, the veneration of saints, the Mass, and Mary's role in salvation—to name a few. And disagreement with Catholics over these doctrines and practices does not in itself constitute anti-Catholic bigotry.

But *we must always keep in mind the religious climate of the times in which we live when we state these differences. Time* magazine is absolutely right in saying that the religious climate in America, and indeed throughout the world, is much different today than it was a hundred years ago. As I read Ellen White's assessment of Catholicism in *The Great Controversy*, I agree with every basic point she makes. *But I would not in every case use the same language to express those ideas that she used back then.* We don't need to apologize for the way she wrote, but we do need to recognize—and clarify for those who may misunderstand—that her choice of words is a reflection of the time in which she lived.[9]

The difference between her time and ours in the way we say things is evident in something as simple as the title to chapter 35 of *The Great Controversy*. This chapter was originally called "Aims of the Papacy." Today, in editions that are sold by our literature evangelists, it's titled "Liberty of Conscience Threatened."[10] Ellen White used terms such as "Romish" and "popery" that were acceptable in her day but sound prejudiced today. Where she said that the Catholic Church "possesses the same pride and arrogant assumption that lorded it over kings and priests,"[11] I might say "Catholics still adhere to the political theory that the church is superior to the state." The meaning is the same, but her language was better suited to her day, mine to our day.

I believe it's possible to express Ellen White's ideas in public in a way that is both honest and truthful and that will, at the same time, be perceived as respectful by all but perhaps the most harsh critic. And I believe we have an obligation to both our Catholic friends and the general public to state our views in this manner. But as I said earlier, it's virtually impossible to do that and call the pope the antichrist in a 1,250-word article in *Signs of the Times*®!

Ellen White's counsel

Some conservative Adventists may yet feel that I'm suggesting compromise in order to—as one of my correspondents put it—"sidestep the media questions [like a politician] when cornered and asked how he stands on a certain issue." My response is that sensitivity to our public image doesn't necessarily have anything to do with political compromise. Ellen White certainly didn't think so, and in defense of that statement I will call your attention to something she said in *The Great Controversy*:

> The followers of Christ, as they approach the time of trouble, [should] make every exertion to place themselves in a proper light before the people, to disarm prejudice, and to avert the danger which threatens liberty of conscience.[12]

I propose that we can't follow this counsel and continue using the same *language* our pioneers used, including in some instances the language that Ellen White herself used, which was not considered offensive in her time but is today.

I realize that some conservative Adventists may disagree with what I just said, so I will repeat a point I made earlier: I am in basic agreement with every one of the *ideas* about Catholics that Ellen White expressed in *The Great Controversy* and in other parts of her massive written output over a period of seventy years. But in some cases I would use different words to state those ideas because the words she used a hundred years ago, which were not perceived as offensive back then, would definitely be perceived so today and therefore would be misunderstood by the average non-Adventist reader.

So what did Ellen White mean when she said that God's people should "make every exertion to place themselves in a proper light before the people"? She herself suggested two answers: (1) to disarm prejudice, and (2) to avert the danger, which threatens liberty of conscience.

What does it mean to place ourselves in a proper light before the people *in order to disarm prejudice?* At the very least, it means to be sure that people have a correct understanding of what we believe. An Adventist friend once said to me, "I don't mind people disagreeing with me over something I truly believe. What I don't like is when they disagree with me over something I *don't* believe." Many Christians, for example, claim that because Adventists observe the Sabbath on Saturday, we are trying to be saved by works. This simply is not true, and we need to do our very best to make that clear. That's putting ourselves "in a proper light before the people."

We do not compromise a single principle of our faith by clarifying the misunderstandings people have about us. This is simply common sense. It has nothing to do with politics or sidestepping embarrassing questions.

Second, Ellen White said we should try to put ourselves in this proper light in order to "avert the danger which threatens liberty of conscience." Could the public's misunderstanding of our teaching about the antichrist be a threat to liberty of conscience? I call your attention to the action of the United States Senate condemning "the discriminatory practices prevalent at Bob Jones University" in the wake of George Bush's speech. The religious convictions of Bob Jones University, its students and staff, are absolutely none of the Senate's business! Nevertheless, the Senate jumped into the fray when BJU's beliefs became a matter of public controversy.

That is a threat to liberty of conscience.

What about *The Great Controversy*?

The foregoing discussion raises a significant question: Should we continue circulating *The Great Controversy*? And the answer is Yes, of course. But I believe we must pay attention to how we do it. I am personally opposed to taking armloads of the books down the street and dropping one on every door step or handing a copy to every person we meet. I realize that some Adventists have made quite a mission for themselves of doing that very thing, but I'm reminded of the Adventist pastor who found a pile of the books on the doorstep of his church the day after a well-meaning (but, in my opinion, unwise) group of Adventists had covered his town with them.

Someone may point out that Ellen White said we should circulate her books "like the leaves of autumn." I did a search on the Ellen G. White CD ROM for all the occurrences of the words "leaves of autumn" in her published works. There are fifty-one. Of these, eight are not related to Adventist publications at all, and most of the rest are about our publications in general rather than about Ellen White's own books. Time after time she speaks of scattering tracts, pamphlets, and leaflets—in other words, very inexpensive literature—"like the leaves of autumn." In only one instance do two of her own books—*Christ's Object Lessons* and *Ministry of Healing*—appear in the context of these words. I think it's safe to say that Ellen White's statements about scattering Adventist publications "like the leaves of autumn" refer to literature that would be most appropriate to those least acquainted with our teachings.

Ellen White did suggest that *The Great Controversy* be "widely circulated,"[13] but that's quite different than saying it should be "scattered like the leaves of autumn." In harmony with the words "widely circulated," it's perfectly appropriate to give *The Great Controversy* to people who show an interest in our church, particularly after they've had a bit of instruction about our beliefs, including our understanding of prophecy.

The advice of Jesus

I will close this chapter with a statement Jesus made to His disciples that gives us some good insight on how we should relate to our non-Adventist friends regarding sensitive topics such as the papacy and the antichrist. Following the meal in which He instituted the ordinances of foot washing and the Lord's Supper, He said, " 'I have much more to say to you, more than you can now bear. But when he, the Spirit of truth, comes, he will guide you into all truth' " (John 16:12, 13).

Two thoughts are especially relevant to our discussion. First, Jesus was sensitive to the fact that His disciples were unprepared to understand, or deal with, certain issues, and He refused to confront them with those issues prematurely. Rather—and this is my second point—He said that when the time was right, the Holy Spirit would help them to understand.

Even after the momentous events of Christ's death and resurrection, the disciples were still consumed with the idea that the Jews would conquer the Romans, gain their freedom, and even rule the world someday. Hence their question to Jesus shortly before His ascension: " 'Are you at this time going to restore the kingdom to Israel?' " (Acts 1:6). Jesus could have said, "That's not how it will happen. From now on My work on earth will be carried out by the church." Instead He said, " 'You will be my witnesses in Jerusalem, and in all Judea and Samaria, and to the ends of the earth' " (verse 8). Notice that He told them what *they would* do, not what Israel *would not* do.

And when we read the story of the spread of the gospel in the New Testament, that's exactly how it spread. The first six chapters of Acts deal with the spread of the gospel in Jerusalem. While the writer of Acts does not say so, we can assume that this included Judea. That would have been familiar territory, and acceptable to them. Following the death of Stephen, the Christians in Jerusalem fled to other regions, and the gospel spread to Samaria and Antioch. God gave Peter the vision of the sheet filled with unclean animals and commanded him to preach to the Roman centurion, Cornelius. Then followed Paul's ministry to the Gentiles throughout Asia Minor (now Turkey) and Greece.

The question is: When the disciples came to Jesus with their question, "Are you at this time going to restore the kingdom to Israel," why didn't Jesus just tell them? And the answer is very simple: They would not have understood; indeed, they would probably have rejected the idea, the same way they rejected His repeated statements prior to His death that He would be killed by the Jews in Jerusalem. Jesus didn't have much choice but to allow the disciples to be traumatized by His death. But He commissioned the Spirit to lead them gently into the new understanding about His abandonment of Judaism and the role of His church. *Jesus led them slowly out of their life-long commitment to Judaism.*

The issue for us is almost identical. We also are trying to lead people from a life-long commitment to one religious tradition into another. And we need to be just as understanding of their biases as Jesus was of the preconceptions of His disciples. We need to lead them as gently as He and His Spirit did the disciples. *We are always safe in following Jesus' method of helping people to learn new truth.*

1. "Catholic Bashing?" *Time*, March 6, 2000, 52.

2. From the Bob Jones University Web site, <www.bju.edu>.

3. I wrote this chapter in the spring of 2000, while Mr. McCain was still a United States senator from Arizona and Mr. Bush was still governor of Texas.

4. "Who Is the Antichrist?" *Signs of the Times*, June 1999, 10.

5. I shared with you only the relevant parts of these letters, and in none of the selections I quoted is it evident that those who wrote them were chastising me for failing to identify the pope as the antichrist. However, I can assure you, that's exactly what they meant.

6. The ultimate antichrist at that time will be Satan. Ellen White called his personation of Christ during the final conflict "the crowning act in the drama of deception" and "the strong, almost overmastering delusion" (*The Great Controversy*, 624).

7. I wrote this chapter in April 2000.

8. *Time*, March 6, 2000, 52.

9. One Adventist scholar has pointed out that "Sabbatarian Adventists of this period (1860s) were certainly no more anti-Catholic than members of most other Protestant denominations. In fact, they often showed greater restraint in expressing anti-Catholic sentiments . . . than in many sectors of nineteenth-century American Protestantism. Ellen G. White," he says, "was certainly no more anti-Catholic than most Protestants and fellow Adventist leaders of her day." He also points out that "Protestant misgivings about Catholic(s) . . . became increasingly strong during the 1870s and 1880s," and "a considerable amount of anti-Catholic propaganda circulated during the 1800s and 1890s." Ellen White's *The Great Controversy*, was published in 1888. (Quotations are from Reinder Bruinsma, "Adventists and Catholics: Prophetic Preview or Prejudice?" *Spectrum*, 27:3, Summer 1999, 47, 50, 48.)

10. The Conflict of the Ages series, which is published for Adventist use only, also gives the chapter the new title, but it includes the original title beside the new one in italics and in parentheses.

11. *The Great Controversy*, 571.

12. Ibid., 616.

13. *Review and Herald*, February 16, 1905; cited in *Colporteur Ministry*, 123.

the
Antichrist
and
Adventist Evangelism

The February 1997 issue of *Signs of the Times*® carried an article on John Paul II by Samuele Bacchiocchi, and we put a photograph of the pope on the cover. Because *Signs* is an Adventist magazine, the question naturally arises: Why did I, as editor, put a Catholic pope on the cover? Why did I include an article about him on the inside? I actually had a very good reason for doing that.

The mission of *Signs* is to communicate the Adventist message to those who are not of our faith, and we need to keep in mind several factors in our efforts to fulfill that mission. First and most important is the need for doctrinal articles that set forth our teachings in clear, simple language. I obviously did not put John Paul on the cover of *Signs* because he is an advocate for Adventist teachings. I did it because of a second important consideration—getting people to open the magazine and read it. Even if the articles we publish are the clearest and most readable in the world, until people open the magazine and read those articles, it's as though we hadn't published them. I put John Paul on the cover of *Signs* because I knew that his picture would attract some people to the magazine who otherwise might not be interested in it, prompting them to open it and hopefully to read it.

The article discussed in a very respectful way the positive contribution that John Paul had made up to that point in his pontificate, but it also acknowledged that significant differences exist between Adventists and Catholics. It did not spell out those differences in any great detail. It simply acknowledged them.

Dr. Bacchiocchi is nobody's flaming liberal, as anyone who is even casually acquainted with him surely must be aware. And that's one of the reasons I published the article. I felt that if anyone could write about John Paul in a way that would be appropriate for an Adventist magazine, surely it would be Dr. Bacchiocchi, who in addition to being quite conservative also knows Catholics well, since he obtained his doctoral degree from the Gregorian University of Rome. This was an editorial judgment that I felt at the time was appropriate, and I still believe it was.

Nevertheless, I received at least fifty letters from Adventists who were very upset that I had put John Paul II on the cover and that the article on the inside was not sufficiently critical of him. One of these letters was particularly intense, though I did not receive it in the mail, as you will see in a moment.

A week or so after the article appeared, I had the opportunity one morning of spending several hours visiting the campus of an independent ministry that is quite critical of the Adventist Church and its leadership. I spent most of the time dialoguing with the leaders of the group about theological and doctrinal issues. I'm glad to say that, while there were frank differences of opinion, the discussion was cordial. At the conclusion of our meeting, one of the members of the group invited me to his home for lunch, and this was a pleasant social occasion.

However, when I returned to my car, I found several hand-written sheets of yellow legal paper on the windshield. Removing them, I read an unsigned "letter to the editor" that was an utterly scathing rebuke. Never before or since have I've received a letter that condemned me as harshly as did the writer of those pages. He castigated me both for the article about John Paul and the photograph of him on the cover. I did not keep the letter, so I can't share with you exactly what it said—which is probably just as well.

That letter reflected what I find to be an unfortunate attitude toward Catholics among some people in the Adventist Church. You can call it animosity, hatred, bigotry, or prejudice. Take your pick. The point is that some of us have an intense dislike for anything Catholic, and this dislike goes beyond doctrinal disagreement. To say anything positive about Catholicism, in these people's minds, is to play the devil's advocate.

Anti-Catholic evangelism

Unfortunately, this attitude is reflected in the "evangelistic methods" that some of these Adventists use. Several years ago, an independent group in Florida put up billboards around Orlando condemning the pope and advertising a special edition of *The Great Controversy*. More recently, another group ran advertisements in several of America's major newspapers with the following headline:

EARTH'S FINAL WARNING
CHAOS AWAITS MAJOR CITIES . . . RESULTING IN
THE ENFORCEMENT OF A NATIONAL SUNDAY LAW
LIBERTY OF CONSCIENCE DENIED
EVERY PRINCIPLE OF THE CONSTITUTION WILL BE RE-
PUDIATED
ALTHOUGH SHOCKING, IT IS IMPERATIVE THE INFOR-
MATION CONTAINED HEREIN
BE SHARED. THOUGH THE TRUTH HAS BEEN IGNORED
AND NEGLECTED
FOR MANY YEARS, IT MUST NOW BE EXPOSED OUT OF
LOVE
FOR THOSE WHO KNOW IT NOT.[1]

The advertisement, in the form of a full-page newspaper article, goes on to identify the Catholic Church as the harlot of Revelation 17. It also quotes a number of Ellen White statements from *The Great Controversy* and *The SDA Bible Commentary* that warn of Sunday laws and the persecution that will follow for those who refuse to obey them.

This is a prime example of the misuse of Ellen White's view of the papacy in *The Great Controversy* that I spoke about in the previous chapter. Even in their context, these statements sound inflammatory in today's culture. And to take them out of their context and throw them at people who have no background for understanding them is horribly unwise.

I have not talked with the people who prepared these advertisements, but if I were to do so, I suspect I would learn that they took as their guiding principle statements such as the following by Ellen White:

The truth must not be muffled now. Plain statements must be made. Unvarnished truth must be spoken, in leaflets and pamphlets, and these must be scattered like the leaves of autumn.[2]

The truth in all its pointed severity must be spoken.[3]

"Make plain statements." "Scatter the message like the leaves of autumn." "Speak the unvarnished truth" "in all its pointed severity." Thoughts such as these probably motivated those who placed these antichrist advertisements in America's newspapers. They stated in the introduction to their article that "the truth . . . must now be exposed out of love for those who know it not." Unfortunately, in spite of their professed love for souls, I must call this zeal without knowledge, for several reasons. First, it stems from a very unbalanced view of the message that Seventh-day Adventists have to share with the world. Second, it overlooks the examples of Jesus and the apostles in dealing with people. And finally, it is based on a very one-sided view of Ellen White's counsel.

I would like to consider each of these with you in that order.

Misunderstanding our message

First, those who make these public statements condemning the Catholic Church assume that this is our primary message. But it's not! Our primary message is God's love for a lost world and His appeal for people to repent and turn to Him for salvation. Even at the height of the final crisis, when the conflict between good and evil is raging at its most white-hot intensity, our message will not be to condemn the forces of evil in the world. It will be to proclaim God's love to a dying world. Ellen White said that "the last message of mercy to be given to the world, is a revelation of [God's] character of love."[4]

This does not mean we will never call attention to the deceptive and destructive forces of evil during the final crisis. We will, of course. But even then, our motive will be a burden for souls who are rushing toward an eternal grave because of the deceptions of the forces of evil.

The example of Jesus

Another reason why I object to the form of "evangelism" we are discussing here is the example of Jesus that I quoted in the previous chapter: " 'I have much more to say to you, more than you can now bear' " (John 16:12). The general public has absolutely no background for understanding truth that is stated on billboards and in one-page newspaper advertisements. Regardless of the truthfulness of the message, if people perceive it as offensive, they will reject it.

Ellen White said that dealing with minds is "the nicest work"[5] that has ever been given to human beings. She was using the word *nice* in one of its then-current meanings of "requiring precision or discrimination." Our task is not merely to throw the truth indiscriminately before the masses, but to find ways to proclaim it that will most likely entice people to listen to it and accept it. Casting Ellen White's strongest statements about the papacy before the public in an indiscriminate fashion guarantees that the vast majority of the people who read them will be turned off by them, and once turned off by a blunt presentation, they will be far less likely to listen to a more judicious presentation in the future.

I propose that those who want to throw around our most controversial truths, with no consideration for the ability of those who hear to understand, are operating out of their need to condemn rather than from a genuine love for souls. But our mission is not to condemn Catholics or anyone else. It's to win souls. To do that, we must show as much respect as possible even to those with whom we disagree. The gifts of the Spirit are love, joy, peace, patience—and I would add respect, even if Paul didn't mention it. Except in certain very special circumstances, condemnation shows disrespect. And when we disrespect people, we are not operating out of a true love for souls. Jesus said that " 'God did not send his Son into the world to condemn the world, but to save the world through him' " (John 3:17). Our mission is not to condemn, but to save. And to do that we need to show as much respect as we possibly can.

The example of John and Paul

A third reason why I oppose the confrontational form of evangelism reflected in these billboards and newspaper advertisements is that it is contrary to the approach adopted by the New Testament writers.

John's method of sharing harsh truth in Revelation is a good example. John could have condemned the Roman government point blank, in very literal terms. Instead, he couched his words in symbolic language so that it would not arouse the hostility of the authorities.[6] We need to learn this lesson. If John needed to be careful how he stated the truth about the forces that opposed Christ and His truth in his day, certainly we should strive to be as discreet as possible in stating the more controversial aspects of our message in these closing days of history, when the conflict between good and evil is about to throw God's people into the worst crisis in world history. If we aren't careful, our injudicious words can create a crisis before the time for the final crisis and hinder our work rather than advance it.

Paul is another New Testament example of wise evangelistic methods. Notice what he said:

> To the Jews I became like a Jew, to win the Jews. To those under the law I became like one under the law . . . so as to win those under the law. To those not having the law I became like one not having the law . . . so as to win those not having the law. To the weak I became weak, to win the weak. I have become all things to all men so that by all possible means I might save some (1 Corinthians 9:20-22).

111

Paul did everything he possibly could, without compromising principle, to identify with those he was trying to reach. We also should identify as much as possible with those we are trying to reach. But we can't do that and at the same time fly in the face of their cultural perceptions of propriety. We can't do that and at the same time condemn them. The day will come when circumstances will demand that we proclaim our message in spite of cultural perceptions, but that time is still future.

In the following statement, Ellen White gives us a significant insight into Paul's method of labor. She says that he

did not at first make prominent the birth, betrayal, crucifixion, and resurrection of Christ, *notwithstanding these were the special truths for that time.* He first brought them down step by step over the promises that had been made of a Saviour, and over the prophecies that pointed Him out. After dwelling upon these until the specifications were distinct in the minds of all, and they knew that they were to have a Saviour, he then presented the fact that this Saviour had already come. . . . This was the "guile" with which Paul caught souls. He presented the truth in such a manner that their former prejudice did not arise to blind their eyes and pervert their judgment.[7]

Notice that, even though the truth about Jesus as the Messiah was "present truth" for Paul's time, he first gave the people the background they would need in order to understand that truth. Then he introduced them to Jesus. To do otherwise would have aroused their prejudice, blinded their eyes, and perverted their judgment. It would have closed their minds to *ever* listening to the special truths for that time again.

Unfortunately, that's exactly what billboards and newspaper advertisements that condemn Catholics will do in the minds, not only of Catholics, but of the majority of other readers as well.

The advice of Ellen White

Finally, any Adventist who has given serious thought to Ellen White's counsel—as those who throw out these statements for public consumption claim to do—will be very careful how he or she presents the more controversial aspects of our message to the public. Ellen White was very specific on this point, as the following statement shows:

Let not those who write for our papers make unkind thrusts and allusions that will certainly do harm and that will hedge up the way and hinder us from doing the work that we should do in order to reach all classes, the Catholics included. It is our work to speak the truth in love and not to mix in with the truth the unsanctified elements of the natural heart and speak things that will savor of the same spirit possessed by our enemies. All sharp thrusts will come back upon us in double measure when the power is in the hands of those who can exercise it for injury. Over and over the message has been given to me that we are not to say one word, not to publish one sentence, especially by way of personalities, unless positively essential in vindicating the truth, that will stir up our enemies against us and arouse their passions to a white heat.[8]

Several points are important in this statement. First, Ellen White cautioned us to be careful how we speak lest we "hedge up the way and hinder [ourselves] from doing the work that we should do to reach all classes, *the Catholics included.*" Surely, throwing the most controversial features of our faith into the public arena the way these billboards and full-page newspaper advertisements did is a violation of that counsel. Ellen White warned that these "sharp thrusts" will come back to haunt us. And she said that God had warned her "over and over" about this matter.

On the positive side, notice what Ellen White said is our true work: "To speak the truth in love." She warned against mixing in with our presentation of truth "the unsanctified elements of the natural heart." Love for souls is the only valid motive for presenting the truth, even its most controversial aspects. When the unsanctified elements of the natural heart are mixed in with our presentation of the truth, then even if the presentation itself is doctrinally correct, it will do more harm than good. I can understand the desire of those who published these advertisements to see "the work finished so we can go home." But if we aren't careful, this can become a very selfish motive that is so anxious to "go home" that it fails to consider the impact of the message on the listener.

A genuine love for souls will lead us to set aside our own anxiety about "getting home" and to think instead of the best way to reach our readers and listeners. It will lead us to be patient; it will give us a willingness to wait for "homecoming" just a little longer. In fact, I suspect that in the long run, patient waiting will turn out to be the fastest way to get home!

Here are several other paragraphs from the pen of inspiration:

There are strong statements often made by our brethren who bear the message of mercy and warning to our world, that would better be repressed. . . . Let not one word be expressed to stir up the spirit of retaliation in opposers of the truth. Let nothing be done to arouse the dragonlike spirit, for it will reveal itself soon enough, and in all its dragon character, against those who keep the commandments of God and have the faith of Jesus.[9]

The time will come when unguarded expressions of a denunciatory character, that have been carelessly spoken or written by our brethren, will be used by our enemies to condemn us. These will not be used merely to condemn those who made the statements, but will be charged upon the whole body of Adventists. Our accusers will say that on such and such a day one of our responsible men said thus and so against the administration of the laws of this government. . . . Many will be surprised to hear their own words strained into a meaning that they did not intend them to have. Then let our workers be careful to speak guardedly at all times and under all circumstances. Let all beware lest by reckless expressions they bring on a time of trouble before the great crisis which is to try men's souls.[10]

Do not make prominent the objectionable features of our faith, which strike most decidedly against the practices and customs of the people, until the Lord shall give the people a fair chance to know that we are believers in Christ, that we do believe in the divinity of Christ and in His pre-existence. . . .

If the Majesty of heaven guarded *His* every word lest *He* should stir up the spirit of Satan and the fallen angels, how much more careful should *we* be in all things![11]

[We are] not to provoke those who have accepted the spurious Sabbath, an institution of the Papacy, in place of God's holy Sabbath. Their not having the Bible arguments in their favor makes them all the more angry and determined to supply the place of arguments that are wanting in the Word of God by the power of their might. The force of persecution follows the steps of the dragon. Therefore *great care should be exercised to give no provocation.*[12]

These statements are so plain that they hardly need my help to clarify their meaning. Every Seventh-day Adventist needs to study them carefully and apply them generously in all their soul-winning efforts. If we must err, it's always better to err on the side of mercy and respect for the feelings of others. Any "soul winning" that does not follow that principle is not genuine soul winning.

Questions to ask

Following are several questions I suggest that we ask ourselves any time we are preparing to share our controversial teachings:

- Is this the most important truth that Adventists have to share with the world?
- Do the people I plan to approach with this truth have the background to understand it?
- Will sharing this truth at this time in people's experience cause them to reject our entire message, whereas they might accept other more important truths if we avoid turning them off by an unwise presentation of this truth?
- Can I share this truth at this time with genuine love, or am I motivated by antagonism toward other religious groups?
- Am I more interested in getting the message "out there" than in the spiritual well-being of the people who will read or hear what I have to say?

Those last two questions are the most important of all, because if we are motivated by a genuine love for souls we will be sensitive to the right answers to each of the other questions, and our witness will be in harmony with those answers. On the other hand, if we do not truly love souls, nothing we say will come out right.

An example of bigotry

You remember Matthew Shepherd, don't you? The young man up in Wyoming who was tied to a fence by anti-homosexual bigots and beaten to death? I don't happen to approve of homosexuality, but I am outraged that anyone would brutalize a homosexual in this way. And I am equally incensed at the crude use that one Christian preacher made of this unfortunate incident to further his anti-homosexual cause. Fred Phelps, pastor of the Westboro Baptist Church in Topeka, Kansas, picketed Matthew Shepherd's funeral with signs that read "God Hates Fags," "No Tears for Queers," and "Execute Homosexuals." Phelps has also created a Web site called <godhatesfags.com> to further his anti-homosexual cause.

Regardless of your view of homosexuality—even if you hold the most conservative, traditional views on the subject—I hope you can recognize the utter impropriety of that kind of "witnessing" for what you believe to be truth.

Now let me share with you the aftermath of Fred Phelps's method of evangelism. Another group has created a Web site on <geocities.com> to "make people aware of the actions of Baptist zealots all over the world." And below that is a picture of Jesus with the words "Baptist Watch" written on His garment. So this Web site now characterizes all Baptists by the actions of one unwise Baptist preacher.

Ellen White said we should "make every exertion to place [ourselves] in a proper light before the people."[13] Unfortunately, unwise methods such as those we've been discussing in this chapter accomplish exactly the opposite. They paint the entire Adventist Church with the brush of bigotry, and the vast majority of readers are unaware that the bigotry was sponsored by only a handful of people who in many cases were not even members of the Seventh-day Adventist Church.

That's why we need clear spiritual thinking about Catholics—and about people of all religious faiths for that matter—as we approach the end time.

----

1. The *Fresno Bee* (California), Tuesday, April 4, 2000, A8. Similar advertisements were published in the *St. Louis Dispatch* (November 28, 1999), the *Miami Herald* (December 1), the *Dallas Morning News* (December 2), the *Greenville News* (South Carolina, December 5), the *Indianapolis Star* (December 10), the *Los Angeles Times* (December 14), and the *Tallahassee Democrat* (December 20). According to the magazine *Catalyst* (the journal of the Catholic League for Religious and Civil Rights), the Catholic League obtained an apology from most of the newspapers that published these advertisements together with a promise never to publish such anti-Catholic bigotry again. The *Catalyst* also noted that "The Eternal Gospel Church of Seventh-day Adventists is currently being sued by the Seventh-day Adventists for misuse of their name" (*Catalyst*, January–February 2000, 5).

2. *Testimonies*, 9:231.

3. Ibid., 5:187.

4. *Christ's Object Lessons*, 415.

5. "To deal with minds is the nicest work in which men ever engaged" (*Testimonies*, 3:269).

6. I am aware, of course, that the beasts of Revelation 13 refer to end-time powers that did not exist 2,000 years ago when John wrote his prophecy. However, scholars generally recognize that John and his readers 2,000 years ago understood these beast powers to refer to Roman emperors.

7. *Evangelism*, 141, italics added.

8. *Testimonies for the Church*, 9:240, 241.

9. *Selected Messages*, 3:403.

10. *Testimonies for the Church*, 6:394, 359.

11. *Testimonies to Ministers*, 253, italics in the original.

12. *Selected Messages*, 3:284, italics added.

13. *The Great Controversy*, 616.

a Changing Catholic Church

In this chapter I want to discuss with you a very complex issue. Clarifying the various aspects of this issue will require that we go back hundreds of years in history and examine a number of ancient documents in some detail. Then we will compare these documents with several of more recent origin to see what similarities, if any, exist between the ancient and the modern. The basic question we will address is this: Has today's Roman Catholicism changed from what it was during the Middle Ages, when it was such a persecuting power? The documentation required to define the problem and provide the answers will make this by far the longest chapter in the book. To make the chapter easier for you to follow, I have divided it into four major parts.

PART I
THE PROBLEM AND INITIAL CONCLUSIONS

An article by Reinder Bruinsma that appeared in the Summer 1999 issue of *Spectrum* puts the question in sharp focus. The article, titled "Adventists and Catholics: Prophetic Preview or Prejudice?" describes the development of the Adventist understanding of Catholicism, especially its role in end-time events, and the author points out that this prophetic interpretation reached its definitive form among Adventists during the late 1800s. Large numbers of Catholics were pouring into America from Europe at this time—a fact that caused great apprehension among Protestants who feared a revival of the Inquisition. Sunday laws were also being agitated in the Congress of the United States during the late 1880s and early 1890s, and since Adventists see the papacy as primarily responsible for the change of the Sabbath to Sunday, we expressed great apprehension toward this combination of insurgent Catholicism and potential Sunday laws. Bruinsma concludes that the Adventist interpretation of Catholicism and end-time prophecy is rooted in this nineteenth-century worldview.

He goes on to point out that Ellen White developed this view at length in her book *The Great Controversy*, which was published in 1888, at the height of the tension between Catholics and Protestants in America and at the very time when Sunday laws were being agitated in the U.S. Congress. And, since Adventists view Ellen White as a divinely inspired author, we have tended to set her nineteenth-century interpretation in cement. As Bruinsma states it, "Once she codified those views, it became virtually impossible to reevaluate them critically without questioning her prophetic authority."[1]

Bruinsma notes, however, that great changes have taken place in Roman Catholicism during the hundred-plus years since Ellen White wrote *The Great Controversy*, particularly as a result of Vatican II in the early 1960s. Nevertheless, Bruinsma says that the Adventist interpretation of Catholicism and its role in the final crisis remains virtually unchanged. In other words, Catholicism has changed, but Adventism's view of Catholicism has not.

Bruinsma points to two significant evidences of this nineteenth-century interpretation of Catholicism and prophecy that continued through twentieth-century Adventism and has now entered the twenty-first. One is the fact that Adventists still rely heavily on nineteenth-century sources to support their interpretation of the end-time role of the Catholic Church. The other is Ellen White's statement in *The Great Controversy* that "the Roman Church now presents a fair front to the world, covering with apologies her record of horrible cruelties. She has clothed herself in Christlike garments; *but she is unchanged*."[2] Bruinsma comments:

> The basic premise in Adventist reports of developments in Catholicism was that "Rome" would never change. Any seemingly positive development was explained as a matter of expediency and was not considered genuine, or was interpreted as part of a vast conspiracy. Even in the momentous days of Vatican II (1962-65), when Catholicism underwent enormous change, the Adventist view

remained constant, even though B. B. Beach, the chief Adventist correspondent at all four sessions, had relatively positive appraisals of the proceedings.[3]

Initial conclusions

Bruinsma has raised significant issues that deserve a fair hearing. Unfortunately, some Adventists feel that it's a compromise of principle even to *ask* questions such as those raised by Bruinsma. I propose, however, that the problem is not with the questions. It's with the answers and with our willingness to examine the evidence with open minds. So let's look at the questions along with the evidence to see what kinds of answers we find.

A nineteenth-century worldview. Ellen White's comments on Catholicism and its prophetic role admittedly reflect a nineteenth-century worldview. It could hardly be otherwise. Read Genesis, Exodus, Leviticus, Numbers, and Deuteronomy. You'll discover that they were written from the perspective of a worldview that existed somewhere between the thirteenth and the fifteenth centuries B.C.[4] Isaiah reflects an eighth-century B.C. worldview. The four Gospels, the letters of Paul, and John's Revelation reflect a first-century A.D. worldview. All prophets write from the perspective of the times in which they live because they are writing to their contemporaries, not to generations that will live centuries or even millenniums later. Much as we might wish that the Bible were written from a twentieth-century perspective (wouldn't it be nice to have clear prophetic statements about such issues as TV and women's ordination?), this would not have made sense to the Israelites of Moses' time or Isaiah's time or to Christians during the time of Christ and the apostles.

In the same way, Ellen White's understanding of the role of Catholicism during the final crisis reflects, not only the Catholicism that existed in her day, but even more importantly the *perception* of Catholicism that existed among Protestants in her day. However, I don't know of anyone other than the most liberal Protestant interpreter who would say that Moses, Isaiah, Matthew, and Paul have no relevance to our day simply because they were written at a time when people's view of the world was much different than ours.

Similarly, the fact that Ellen White's understanding of the role of the papacy during the final crisis was written from a nineteenth-century perspective should not make it invalid for those of us living in the twenty-first century. The question is how to interpret Ellen White's expression of Catholicism in a way that both acknowledges its nineteenth-century Protestant expression and applies it appropriately to the twenty-first century. Given the hundred-plus years since *The Great Controversy* was written, should we change our understanding of the papacy? And if so, in what ways? Will the findings of an objective inquiry into today's papacy harmonize with, or contradict, Ellen White and our traditional Adventist view?

Has Ellen White set us in cement? Bruinsma says that once Ellen White codified the nineteenth-century prophetic interpretation, it became difficult (he says "virtually impossible") for Adventists to reevaluate this interpretation critically without questioning her prophetic authority.[5]

That is in fact a very true statement—and it should be. We must always be careful how we reinterpret inspired writings. A great deal of damage has been done to the Christian faith over the centuries because of misguided reinterpretations of the Bible, and more recently for Adventists, because of misguided reinterpretations of the writings of Ellen White. This does not mean that we should refuse to reinterpret the Bible and the writings of Ellen White. It's precisely because these inspired writings reflect a worldview that is different from ours that each generation *must* reapply them to its own situation.

Our prophetic understanding. The real issue in this entire discussion has to do not so much with Ellen White or with our present view of Catholicism. It has, rather, to do with Scripture. For 150 years, Adventists have understood the little horns of Daniel 7 and 8 to refer to the papacy of the Middle Ages, based on the historicist we had of interpreting prophecy. This view did not arise, however, out of late nineteenth-century Adventism. It was the common interpretation of the Reformers 350 years earlier, and it was the view of William Miller and his associates in the mid-1800s. In addition, from the beginning of our movement in the late 1840s, we have also understood the first beast of Revelation 13 to refer to both the papacy of the Middle Ages and the papacy of the end time this is also based on the historical method.

The little horns of Daniel 7 and 8 are clearly in rebellion against God, and they are persecutors of His people. The same is true of the first and second beasts of Revelation 13. As historicists, we have always understood the little horns in Daniel 7 and 8 to be the medieval papacy, and the similarity between these two horns and the first beast of Revelation 13 is sufficient to identify the latter as representing the same power of religious apostasy during the end time.

The issue is not so much whether this interpretation arose from Ellen White and nineteenth-century Adventism. The issue is whether our historical interpretation of these prophecies is correct. If it is—and I believe that it is—then our view of the papacy can truly be said to arise out of these prophecies and not merely out of the prejudices of nineteenth-century Adventism. I find it significant that nearly all of today's Protestant bodies have abandoned the historical interpretation, which is why many Protestants today have largely embraced the papacy—if not doctrinally, at least as a sympathetic fellow-traveler—while Adventists have not.

Nineteenth-century sources. One of Bruinsma's major concerns is that we still tend to use nineteenth-century sources to support our end-time view of the papacy. I must confess to a certain agreement with Bruinsma on this point. For years I have felt that too often we have cited very dated evidence in these discussions. I would frankly not be very impressed with a physician who turned to a nineteenth-century medical textbook for information on how to treat my disease. He probably would not be my physician much longer! Neither should we in the early twenty-first century expect our non-Adventist readers and listeners to accept the validity of our interpretation of the papacy when we use mostly nineteenth-century evidence.

That's one of the major reasons I wrote the book *The Antichrist and the New World Order* back in the early 1990s. That book is a modern-day look at the conflict between Christ and Satan that uses contemporary language, evidence, and quotations. I intended it to be a late twentieth-century version of the chapters in *The Great Controversy* dealing with the final crisis.

However, for two reasons, I must also take exception to Bruinsma's statement that Adventists still rely heavily on nineteenth-century sources to support their end-time view of the papacy. First, while there may be Adventists who do this, as I read today's Adventist literature I find us citing many *very* contemporary sources in both our books and our magazines. Malachi Martin's 1990 book *The Keys of This Blood* is one excellent example of a source that has been widely cited by Adventists, as is John Paul's Apostolic Letter *Dies Domini*.[6] I continually receive magazine articles and newspaper clippings from readers of *Signs of the Times*® and *Signswatch*® with information about both religious right Protestants and the papacy. One *Signswatch*® reader even sent me a subscription to the Catholic magazines *Inside the Vatican* and *The Pope Speaks*. Obviously, many Adventists are using very contemporary sources in their effort to understand Bible prophecy.

The second reason I take exception to Bruinsma's charge that Adventists tend to use nineteenth-century evidence is that, to a certain extent, there's nothing wrong with that. Every organization has its history, and every organization, regardless of how old, is influenced by its history. For example, a careful examination of the views of our pioneers in the late 1840s toward the Great Disappointment makes it very clear that their understanding of that event and its aftermath is significantly different from ours. The "shut door" theory is one obvious example. Nevertheless, the events of October 22, 1844 continue to have a very important influence on our Adventist self-understanding.

The same is true of Catholicism. Catholics, too, are influenced by their history. Thus, the issue should not be whether we use nineteenth-century— or ninth-century—evidence in our evaluation of Catholicism today. The issue is whether we use that evidence in a way that is fair and that reflects the actual situation in today's Catholicism rather than what we want to believe about Catholicism.

Has Catholicism changed? The major question Bruinsma raises is whether Catholicism has changed in the hundred-plus years since Ellen White wrote *The Great Controversy*. And the short answer is Yes, of course. Everything around us is constantly changing. Nothing earthly or human ever remains the same—certainly not for one hundred years. Therefore, we should *expect* the Catholic Church to change.

Then what are we to make of Ellen White's statement in *The Great Controversy* that Rome "is unchanged"?[8] I propose that the issue is not so much *whether* Rome has changed, but *how*. And, more importantly, in what ways has Rome *not* changed?

Bruinsma is certainly correct that the most dramatic changes in the Roman Catholic Church during the last century came about as a result of the Vatican II Council. Among other things, Vatican II allowed the Mass to be said in the vernacular language (the language of the people), it brought a great increase in the Catholic Church's ecumenical outreach, and it affirmed the right of every human being to his or her own religious beliefs.

Mass in the vernacular is largely a Catholic matter that doesn't concern Adventists a great deal. We have been quite willing to recognize the increase in the Catholic Church's ecumenical outreach. That, after all, fits with our end-time scenario! However, the Catholic Church's affirmation of the principle of religious freedom probably leaves some of us puzzled. Because it does *not* fit with our end-time scenario, it's very easy for us to treat it as mere window dressing. Nevertheless, the Catholic Church's affirmation of the principle of religious freedom since Vatican II is a far cry from the Inquisition of the Middle Ages, when the whole idea of the freedom of the individual to live in harmony with his or her own conscience was anathema to the Church.

So, yes, Catholicism *has* changed in significant ways during the past hundred years. However, of greatest interest to Adventists are the ways in which Rome has *not* changed. I will mention two. The first is Catholic doctrines that remain the same, and the second is Catholic political theory that remains the same. I will conclude Part I with a discussion of Catholic doctrines. Catholic political theory will take up most of the rest of the chapter.

Doctrines that remain the same. In the area of basic doctrine, the papacy is still the same church that it was a hundred and even 500 years ago. It could hardly be otherwise for a church that claims never to have erred. There's a long list of doctrines over which Protestants, including Adventists, disagree with Catholics. Among these are the veneration of saints, indulgences, purgatory, images in the church, Mary's role in salvation, the Mass (especially transubstantiation), apostolic succession and the primacy of the pope, and the teaching that salvation is available only through the Catholic Church and its sacraments. In addition to these teachings, which Protestants in general dispute, are several which Adventists are largely alone in disagreeing with. These include Sunday observance, the state of the dead, and the eternal punishment of the wicked.

My point is that all of these Catholic teachings remain the same as they were during the nineteenth century, and in most cases far back beyond that. I do not hesitate to state that *Rome is not about to change these doctrines.* Therefore, in these areas it is very accurate and very fair to say that today's Roman Catholicism is the same as it was a hundred years ago. It has not changed.

Political theory that remains the same. Another way in which Catholicism remains much the same today as it was in the nineteenth century is in its political theory regarding church-state relationships. And that discussion brings us to Part II of this chapter.

PART II
HISTORICAL BACKGROUND OF CATHOLIC POLITICAL THEORY - A.D. 300-1850

Today's Catholic political theory, especially its understanding of church-state relationships, has a long history that began almost 1,700 years ago and developed by stages over the next 1,500 years. I will review four of these stages in the next few pages.

First stage: Constantine
To understand the political thought of the Roman Catholic Church, we must go back to the reign of the Roman emperor Constantine in the early fourth century. Constantine, as you are no doubt aware, converted to Chris-

tianity and by the Edict of Milan in 313 established freedom for the Christian religion. This brought to an end the nearly 300 years of on-again, off-again persecution of the church by the empire.

At first, the empire dominated the church. Constantine called the Council of Nicea, at which he presided and over which he had a major influence. For a number decades Christianity and paganism were both "approved religions," but eventually the church's influence grew to the point that paganism was outlawed and Christianity became the official religion of the empire.[9] This put the church into a direct relationship with the Roman government, and as the Barbarian invasions of the fourth and fifth centuries brought the empire to its knees, the church stepped in to fill the power vacuum. Now it was the church's turn to dominate the state, and Augustine provided the theological rationale.

Second stage: Augustine

Next to the apostle Paul, Augustine (A.D. 354-430) was the most influential theologian of the first millennium, and his thinking continues to exert a dominant influence in both Catholic and Protestant theologies.

The early Christian church anticipated the return of Christ "at any time." As we noted in the chapter "How to Think About the Delay," most of the apostles who wrote books in the Bible affirmed that the coming of Christ was near, and this attitude continued to be prominent in Christian thinking for a couple of centuries following the death of the apostles. However, by Augustine's time nearly 400 years had passed without the anticipated Second Advent, and the Christian church was ripe for a reinterpretation of that hope.

Augustine provided that reinterpretation, and its impact on church-state relationships was profound.

In his book *On the City of God*, Augustine proposed that the kingdom of God was the Christian church, not some future eternal kingdom during a 1,000-year reign of Christ on the earth. Augustine reinterpreted the millennium to be, not a future event with a resurrection of the righteous at its beginning and a resurrection of the wicked at its conclusion, but an indeterminate period of time that began with Christ's resurrection. According to Augustine, the first resurrection of the saints (Revelation 20:4-6) is the experience of conversion that comes to each believer when he or she accepts Christ, and the second resurrection (Revelation 20:5) refers to the resurrection of both righteous and wicked that will take place at Christ's second coming. The thrones of judgment during the millennium (Revelation 20:4) Augustine interpreted to mean the ecclesiastical courts in the larger cities of the empire.

Augustine also reinterpreted Nebuchadnezzar's vision of the great image in Daniel 2. The stone that struck the image he understood to be the Christian church rather than the second coming of Christ. Thus, the church would be the one to destroy the kingdoms of this world and replace their dominion with its own. In other words, *the church would control the world's political systems.*

Augustine's prophetic reinterpretation, both of the millennium and of Nebuchadnezzar's great image, laid the theological foundation for the medieval church's theory of church-state union.

Third stage: 1000-1500

The next major development in Catholic thought on church-state relations came during the first half of the second millennium. We will consider views expressed by several of the most prominent thinkers of this period.

Pope Gregory VII. The first of these was Pope Gregory VII, whose papacy extended from 1073 to 1085. Gregory wrote a document called "Dictates of the Pope,"[10] which included the following propositions:

9. "That of the pope alone all princes shall kiss the feet."

12. "That it may be permitted to him [the pope] to depose emperors."

22. "That the Roman church has never erred; nor will it err to all eternity."

27. "That he [the pope] may absolve subjects from their fealty [loyalty] to wicked men [including rulers]."

These propositions clearly set the authority of the Catholic Church over that of secular governments. And Gregory knew how to put this philosophy into practice, for he is the pope who put King Henry IV under the ban, deposed him from his kingdom, and forced him to cross the Alps in the middle of the winter to stand barefoot in the snow for three days at Canossa awaiting absolution.

Bernard of Clairveaux. One of the most influential Catholics of the twelfth century was the mystic Bernard of Clairvaux (1090-1153).[11] To provide you with the background to Bernard's thinking, allow me to take you on a journey back to the time of Christ, and specifically to a rather minor incident that occurred in the Garden of Gethsemene at the time of Christ's arrest.

According to John, when the mob came to arrest Jesus, Peter drew his sword and cut off the ear of a man named Malchus, who was the servant of the high priest. Jesus immediately ordered Peter " 'Put your sword away! Shall I not drink the cup the Father has given me?' " (John 18:11). By this Jesus clearly meant that His kingdom was not to be established by force of arms but by spiritual persuasion. Anyone who might doubt this needs only to turn to Jesus' response to Pilate when the governor asked Him if He was a king. " 'My kingdom is not of this world,' " Jesus said. " 'If it were, my servants would fight to prevent my arrest by the Jews. But now my kingdom is from another place' " (John 18:36).

Christ stated very clearly that His church should refuse to maintain its position in society through political power. Rather, He intended that a distinct separation should exist between the church and the state. However, Bernard of Clairveaux isolated Christ's brief statement to Peter in Gethsemene and used it to turn His meaning around 180 degrees:

> He who would deny that the sword belongs to thee [the pope] has not, as I conceive, sufficiently weighed the words of the Lord, where he said, speaking to Peter, "Put up *thy* sword into the scabbard" (John 18:11). For here it is plainly implied that even the material sword is thine, to be drawn at thy bidding, although not by thy hand. Besides, unless this sword also appertained to thee in some sense, when the disciples said to Christ, "Lord, behold, here are two swords" (Luke 22:38), he would never have answered as he did, "It is enough," but rather, "it is too much." We can therefore conclude that both swords, namely the spiritual and the material, belong to the Church, and that although only the former is to be wielded by her own hand, the two are to be employed in her service. It is for the priest to use the sword of the word, but to strike with the sword of steel belongs to the soldier, yet this must be by the authority and will of the priest and by the direct command of the emperor. . . . For the two swords are Peter's, to be drawn whenever necessary, the one by his own hand, the other by his authority.[12]

This statement provides the key to understanding the Catholic view of church-state relationships that continues to the present time. According to Bernard of Clairveaux, the authority of the church, being spiritual, is superior to that of the state, which is only temporal. Therefore, the church has the right—indeed the obligation—to dictate the moral principles that the state will enforce upon the population.

Popes Innocent III and IV. In 1198 Pope Innocent III wrote: "Ecclesiastical liberty is nowhere better cared for than where the Roman church has full power in both temporal and spiritual affairs."[13] Innocent used the analogy of the sun and the moon to argue that the authority of the spiritual realm supercedes the authority of the political realm: "As the Moon receives its light from the Sun, . . . so the royal power derives from the pontifical authority the splendor of its dignity."[14]

And Innocent IV, who was pope from 1294-1303, said "The emperor is the protector of the pope and takes an oath to him and holds the empire from him."[15]

Pope Boniface VIII. Reiterating the concept of two swords first expressed by Bernard of Clairvaux, Pope Boniface VIII[16] wrote the encyclical *Unam Sanctam* in 1302, in which he said:

> We are informed by the texts of the gospel that in this Church and in its power are two swords; namely, the spiritual and the temporal. . . . Both, therefore, are in the power of the Church, that is to say, the spiritual and the material sword, but the former is to be administered *by* the Church but the latter *for* the Church; the former in the hands of the priest; the latter by the hands of kings and soldiers, but at the will and sufferance of the priest.[17]

Thomas Aquinas. The outstanding Roman Catholic theologian and philosopher of the fourteenth century, and arguably one of the two foremost Catholic theologians of all time,[18] was Thomas Aquinas. Thomas shared the views of his predecessors regarding the relationship of the spiritual and secular powers. He wrote, for example, that "secular power is subject to the spiritual power as the body is subject to the soul,"[19] and "in the pope the secular power is joined to the spiritual. He holds the apex of both powers."[20]

Thus, by the time of the Reformation, the idea was firmly entrenched in Catholic thinking, both theologically and in practice, that the church should dominate the secular government, especially in matters of doctrine and morals. And this religio-political theory was confirmed by one of the foremost church councils in Roman Catholic history—the Council of Trent, which extended from 1545 to 1563.

Fourth stage: The Council of Trent and after

The Council of Trent. The Council of Trent was called primarily to respond to the "heresies" of the Protestant Reformation. It declared that "all temporal power is his [the pope's]; the dominion, jurisdiction, and government of the whole Earth is his by divine right. All rulers of the Earth are his subjects and must submit to him."[21] Thus, the Council of Trent put a cap on nearly 500 years of Catholic thinking about the relationship of the church to the state.

Pope Gregory XVI. Pope Gregory XVI, whose papacy extended from 1831 to 1846, opposed the separation of church and state, which has been one of the foundational principles of Western governments for 200 years. In his Encyclical Letter "On Liberalism," Gregory wrote:

> Nor can We predict happier times for religion and government from the plans of those who desire vehemently to separate the Church from the State, and to break the mutual concord between temporal authority and the priesthood. It is certain that that concord which always was favorable and beneficial for the sacred and civil order is feared by the shameless lovers of liberty.[22]

This brief discussion of the development of Catholic political theory, and especially the Catholic understanding of church-state relationships, spans a period of 1,500 years. And my point is that it's simply not possible for today's Catholic Church to suddenly divest itself of these ideas or to be unaffected by them.

PART III
CATHOLIC POLITICAL THEORY IN THE MODERN ERA
1850 to 2000

It is now time to examine the Catholic understanding of church-state relationships in the modern era, beginning about 1850, which is the period during which our own Adventist Church has existed. The question we want to answer is whether the Catholic Church's understanding of the relationship of the church and the state in our day has changed from what it was during the 1,500 years prior to 1850.

Pope Pius IX

In 1864 Pope Pius IX issued a "Syllabus of Errors" that lists eighty "principal errors of our time." Among these errors are pantheism, rationalism, modern liberalism, etc. Of special interest to our discussion are what Pius considered to be errors with regard to religious freedom and the relationship of church and state. Keep in mind that Pius and his church considered each of the seemingly positive statements below to be a serious error:

15. Every man is free to embrace and profess that religion which, guided by the light of reason, he shall consider true.

23. Roman Pontiffs and ecumenical councils have wandered outside the limits of their powers, have usurped the rights of princes, and have even erred in defining matters of faith and morals.

24. The Church has not the power of using force, nor has she any temporal power, direct or indirect.

34. The teaching of those who compare the Sovereign Pontiff to a prince, free and acting in the universal Church, is a doctrine which prevailed in the Middle Ages.

54. Kings and princes are not only exempt from the jurisdiction of the Church, but are superior to the Church in deciding questions of jurisdiction.

55. The Church ought to be separate from the State, and the State from the Church.

57. The science of philosophical things and morals and also civil laws may and ought to be kept aloof from divine and ecclesiastical authority.

77. In the present day it is no longer expedient that the Catholic religion should be held as the only religion of the State, to the exclusion of all other forms of worship.[23]

This document clearly opposes anything that would contradict the philosophy of the subordination of the state to the church that prevailed during the Middle Ages—namely, that the Catholic Church has authority over the state.

Pope Leo XIII

My research in Catholic literature has not been exhaustive, so I cannot be sure, but Pius IX appears to be one of the last of the popes to declare boldly that the Catholic Church has the power of employing force and of exercising temporal power and that kings and princes are subordinate to the Church. The popes who followed Pius IX were much more subtle in their language, but a careful reading shows that they held the same philosophy of church-state relations as their forebears.

A good example of this is an encyclical letter "On the Christian Constitution of States,"[24] which was published by Pope Leo XIII, who was pope from 1878 to 1903. It was during this very time that Ellen White wrote *The Great Controversy*. Leo published his encyclical letter "On the Christian Constitution of States" in 1885. Near the beginning of this document he said:

> Many, indeed, are they who have tried to work out a plan of civil society based on doctrines other than those approved by the Catholic Church. . . . But as no society can hold together unless some one be over all, directing all to strive earnestly for the common good, every body politic must have a ruling authority, and this authority, no less than society itself, has its source in nature, and has, consequently, God for its author.

The statement that "every body politic must have a ruling authority" means that every civil government must have an authority that is superior to it to rule over it. Leo then said that this authority has "God for its author." While he did not *say* it, Leo can be understood to mean that since God is not personally present on the earth to exercise that authority, it must be exercised by the church, which is His personal representative on the earth. This conclusion is fully in harmony with Catholic Church-state philosophy of the preceding 1000 years.

Leo also made it clear that Catholicism is the only true religion, and that:

> it is a sin for the State not to have care for religion as something beyond its scope, or as of no practical benefit; or out of the many forms of religion to adopt that one which chimes in with the fancy; for we are bound absolutely to worship God in that way which He has shown to be His will.

And, of course, for Leo, it was God's will that men should worship according to the Catholic religion. Thus, it was an absolute moral duty for government to make Catholicism the religion of the state and for the state to submit to church authority.

Leo also condemned that "harmful and deplorable passion for innovation which was aroused in the sixteenth century [and which] threw first of all into confusion the Christian religion." This is an obvious reference to the Protestant Reformation. He also longed for a time past "when States were governed by the philosophy of the Gospel." At that time, he says,

> the religion instituted by Jesus Christ, established firmly in befit-

ting dignity, flourished everywhere, by the favor of princes and the legitimate protection of magistrates; and Church and State were happily united in concord and friendly interchange of good offices.

Leo obviously considered the ideal relationship between church and state to be that which existed during the Middle Ages, prior to the Protestant Reformation, when the state was the servant of the church. While he does not come right out and say so, the thrust of Leo's document is clearly that differences of opinion between church and state must be resolved by the spiritual authority.

Vatican II

The Catholic Church has held numerous general councils during the past 1,500 years. The first, which I mentioned earlier, was the Council of Nicea, which was held in A.D. 325 to resolve the Arian controversy.[25] The most recent is Vatican II, which was held from 1962 to 1965. Several statements in the Vatican II "Declaration on Religious Freedom" are quite surprising in view of the Catholic Church's history of intolerance. I will quote two:

This Vatican Council declares that the human person has a right to religious freedom. This freedom means that all men are to be immune from coercion on the part of individuals or of social groups and of any human power, in such wise that no one is to be forced to act in a manner contrary to his own beliefs, whether privately or publicly, whether alone or in association with others within due limits.

All men should be at once impelled by nature and also bound by a moral obligation to seek the truth, especially religious truth. They are also bound to adhere to the truth, once it is known, and to order their whole lives in accord with the demands of truth. However, men cannot discharge these obligations in a manner in keeping with their own nature unless they enjoy immunity from external coercion as well as psychological freedom. Therefore the right to religious freedom has its foundation not in the subjective disposition of the person, but in his very nature. In consequence, the right to this immunity continues to exist even in those who do not live up to their obligation of seeking the truth and adhering to it and the exercise of this right is not to be impeded, provided that just public order be observed.

Coming from an institution with such a long history of persecution of dissenters, these statements are truly remarkable affirmations about religious freedom. Thus, Reinder Bruinsma is correct when he says that Vatican II brought a major change in Catholic thinking. However, a closer look shows that these positive statements in the Vatican II document on religious freedom include qualifying phrases and sentences that could, under certain circumstances, be used to negate what they appear so clearly to affirm.

The first statement begins with the declaration that "the human person has a right to religious freedom," but it concludes by stating that this freedom is "within due limits." Of course, the idea that there are limits to religious freedom is not necessarily bad. The United States Supreme Court has also taken the position that under certain circumstances government is justified in preventing people from acting in harmony with their religious beliefs. To use a common hypothetical example, a person cannot act upon the religious belief that it is his duty to punch other people in the nose. An actual example is the practice of handling poisonous snakes during religious services,[26] which U.S. courts have consistently held that the government can forbid.

Thus the question relative to the phrase "within due limits" in the Catholic document on religious freedom is not whether this is a wrong principle. Rather, the question is Who will set those limits? In a democratic, secular government that is uncontrolled by religious presuppositions about moral right and wrong, the chances are fairly good that those limits will be defined very narrowly, and religious freedom will be largely protected. However, in a state where the Catholic philosophy of church-state relationships prevails, the church will be the entity that defines those limits, and the religious freedoms of those who disagree could very easily be curtailed.

The second statement above begins by affirming that all men are "bound by a moral obligation to seek the truth, especially religious truth," and "they are also bound to adhere to the truth, once it is known." However, it goes on to say that, "men cannot discharge these obligations in a manner in keeping with their own nature unless they enjoy immunity from external coercion as well as psychological freedom." Furthermore, "the right to this immunity continues to exist even in those who do not live up to their obligation of seeking the truth and adhering to it." In other words, people have a right to be wrong! Coming as it does from a Catholic Church-wide council, that is indeed a remarkable statement, which we can surely applaud!

The qualifying phrase in the second statement is the one that says, "provided just public order be observed." This can be understood to mean simply that no one has the religious right to punch others in the nose. The real question, as with the previous statement, is Who gets to define what constitutes a "just public order"? And on that question, a statement later in the Vatican II declaration on religious freedom is sobering:

> Furthermore, society has the right to defend itself against possible abuses committed on the pretext of freedom of religion. It is the special duty of government to provide this protection. However, government is not to act in an arbitrary fashion or in an unfair spirit of partisanship. Its action is to be controlled by juridical norms which are in conformity with the objective moral order. These norms arise out of the need for the effective safeguard of the rights of all citizens and for the peaceful settlement of conflicts of rights, also out of the need for an adequate care of genuine public peace, which comes about when men live together in good order and in true justice, and finally out of the need for a proper guardianship of public morality.

Notice that "it is the special duty of government" to defend society against "possible abuses committed on the pretext of freedom of religion." Again, that's fine, as long as we understand it to mean that nobody has a religious right to harm another person. But the Vatican statement goes beyond that. It says that the government's action in defending society against abuses committed on the pretext of religious freedom is to be "controlled by juridical norms which are in conformity with the objective moral order," and which "arise out of . . . the need for a proper guardianship of morality."

If the Catholic Church is the higher of the two authorities of church and state, then in situations where the Catholic Church is favored by government, the Church is responsible for defining the moral principles of the "objective moral order" that the state is to protect. This is a major qualification to the very positive statements about religious freedom that we read a moment ago. Given the proper circumstances, it could easily be interpreted to give the Church the same authority over civil government that it had during the Middle Ages.

The Catholic catechism

The *Catechism of the Catholic Church*, which was published in 1994, contains a statement that is relevant to our discussion:

> The teaching of the [Catholic] Church has elaborated the principle of *subsidiarity*, according to which "a community of a higher

order should not interfere in the internal life of a community of a lower order, depriving the latter of its functions, but rather should support it in case of need and help to co-ordinate its activity with the activities of the rest of the society, always with a view to the common good."[27]

This statement is quite in harmony with the Church's medieval philosophy of church-state relationships. It describes two communities—one of a higher order, which in the case of our discussion would be the church, and the other of a lower order, the state. The word *subsidiarity* in the opening sentence is a sociological term. It means that those functions that a subordinate organization can perform effectively should not be assumed by a higher organization, since the subordinate organization is closer to its local situation.

Roman Catholic church-state philosophy, of course, considers the state to be subordinate to the church. Thus, the principle of subsidiarity means that those functions which the state (the lower organization) can best perform should be left to it. That sounds good at first glance, especially the statement that "a community of a higher order [the church] should not interfere in the internal life of a community of a lower order [the state], depriving the latter of its functions." However, the statement goes on to say that the community of a higher order (the church) should "support it [the community of a lower order—the state] in case of need and help to co-ordinate its activity with the activities of the rest of society, always with a view to the common good."

This could be understood to mean that the community of the lower order (the state) is still dependent on the "support" and "coordination" of the community of the higher order (the church). Interpreted in this way, the church would be free to intervene in the affairs of the state "in case of need."

Malachi Martin

Malachi Martin, a former Jesuit priest and one-time professor at the Vatican's Pontifical Biblical Institute, is a best-selling Catholic writer who caught the attention of many Adventist readers during the 1990s. Many Adventists have read all or parts of his book *The Keys of This Blood*,[28] which was published by Simon and Schuster in 1990. This book is of major significance for our discussion.

Martin begins his book with the bold statement that "willing or not, ready or not, we are all involved in an all-out, no-holds-barred, three-way global competition." The competition, Martin says, is about who will control the coming one-world government, which anyone under forty in 1990 would live to see, according to Martin. He then says that "the chosen purpose of John Paul's pontificate . . . is to be the victor in that competition, now well underway."[29] Please notice: According to Malachi Martin, John Paul's highest ambition is to rule the coming one-world government. And given the global influence that John Paul developed for himself and his church during his pontificate, it's easy to believe that Martin knew what he was talking about.

Later in his book Martin makes a number of other statements that help us to understand the Catholic philosophy of church-state relationships in the late twentieth century. He says that:

> it is axiomatic for John Paul that no one has the right—democratic or otherwise—to a moral wrong; and no religion based on divine revelation has a moral right to teach such a moral wrong or abide by it.[30]

The key question, of course, is Who has the right to decide what's morally right and wrong? Here is Martin's answer:

> The Roman Catholic Church has always claimed—and under John Paul claims today—to be the ultimate arbiter of what is morally good and morally bad in human action.[31]

Notice that the Catholic Church claims to be "the ultimate arbiter," not of what's morally good and bad for Catholics, but for the entire human race. So what does John Paul's church propose to do about people who choose to teach and abide by a moral wrong? Martin's answer and his church's answer to that question is sobering to contemplate:

> The final prerequisite for georeligious capability [translate: religious domination of the world] is authority. The institution [Roman Catholic Church], in its organizational structures and undertakings, must have unique authority: an authority that is . . . *autonomous* vis-à-vis all other authority on the supranational plane; an authority that carries with it such *sanctions* as are effective in maintaining the unity and aims of the institution [Roman Catholic Church] as it goes about its business of serving the greatest good of the community as a whole and in its every part.[32]

On careful analysis, these words have somber implications. Martin said at the beginning of his book that John Paul wants to rule the coming world government. Then he tells us that in order for any organization to have this "georeligious capability" it must have an authority that is "*autonomous* vis-à-vis all other authority on the supranational plane." What he means is that the Roman Catholic Church must have authority that is independent of, and superior to, any other authority in the world so that it cannot be overruled.

He says further that the Roman Catholic Church must have the ability to put in place "such *sanctions* as are effective in maintaining the unity and aims of the institution as it goes about its business of serving the greatest good of the community as a whole and in its every part." What he means is that the Roman Catholic Church must have the authority to stop anyone who interferes with its global ambition of serving what *the Church* perceives to be for "the greatest good of the community as a whole and in its every part." So the Church wants control over every element of society. That's the same philosophy of church-state relationships that existed during the Middle Ages!

Some Catholics would no doubt argue that Malachi Martin, who died in 1999, represented a very conservative element in Catholicism that is not accepted by the majority of Catholics today, especially in North America and Western Europe. That certainly is true, which is why we must recognize that there truly is, within a large segment of today's Catholicism, a radical break with the medieval philosophy and practice of church-state relationships.

My point still stands, however. Malachi Martin may represent a minority view in Western Catholicism, but it's a view that is alive and well in a significant segment of Catholicism. And given the right conditions, it could regain dominance.

Thus, it is fair to say, as we enter the twenty-first century, that the medieval Catholic view of church-state relationships is still alive and well in the minds of a significant number of Catholics and their church leaders.

PART IV
HOW TO THINK ABOUT A CHANGING CATHOLICISM

So how should we think about Ellen White's statement in *The Great Controversy*, that the papacy "is unchanged"?[33] First, as I noted near the beginning of this rather long chapter, everything always changes, and the Catholic Church *has* changed from what it was a hundred years ago. Furthermore, many of those changes, even from an Adventist perspective, have been for the better. Certainly we can rejoice that the Vatican II "Declaration on Religious Freedom" recognizes the right of every human being not only to choose his or her own religion, but also the right to be wrong.

However, in the one area that counts most—the relationship of the Church to the state—Catholic philosophy and theology remain much as they were 1,000 years ago; at least in the minds of some Catholics. And that is precisely the point Ellen White made in her statement in *The Great Controversy*:

> The Roman Church now presents a fair front to the world, covering with apologies her record of horrible cruelties. She has clothed herself in Christlike garments; but *she is unchanged*. The doctrines devised in the darkest ages are still held. . . . She possesses the same pride and arrogant assumption that lorded it over kings and princes, and claimed the prerogatives of God.[34]

Notice the two areas that Ellen White said have remain unchanged: Catholic doctrine and the Catholic teaching of the Church's superiority to the state, what she called "pride and arrogant assumption that lorded it over kings and princes." And these are the very characteristics of the papacy that we have examined in this chapter and found are indeed unchanged, even today.

However, I believe we need to be careful how we think about this reality. It's unfortunately true that some Adventists use Ellen White's statement as an excuse to continue holding on to their bigotry and prejudice toward Catholics. While Protestants of the nineteenth century were justified in their fear of the Catholic threat to religious freedom, their blind prejudice, which led to instances of severe persecution of Catholics, was absolutely wrong. In the name of preserving their own freedom they prevented others from having theirs. Adventists today should avoid that kind of bigotry like we would avoid contracting AIDS. We must look for the very best in everyone.

This same principle applies with respect to recent requests by John Paul II for forgiveness for Catholic errors of the past, including the Inquisition. You may find it strange that I should say this in view of Ellen White's statement that "the Roman Church now presents a fair front to the world, covering with apologies her record of horrible cruelties." Indeed, following the publication of John Paul's apologies, I received a number of letters from readers of *Signs of the Times*® questioning John Paul's sincerity in light of Ellen White's statement. However, I believe John Paul's apologies are genuine. I believe he truly regrets the cruelties of the Inquisition, and I don't think he has any desire to institute a twenty-first century version. I don't think he wants to persecute anyone.

Of course, Bible prophecy as we understand it points to a much different role for the Catholic Church during the final crisis. So how does that fit with my statement that John Paul is sincere in his apologies for the Inquisition? Keep in mind that the situation during the final crisis will be vastly different from what it is today. As I described it in chapter 2, the final crisis will be brought on by natural disasters so severe that they will threaten the survival of the human race. Crises of this magnitude cause all of us to think and act in ways we would not normally think and act, and this will be as true of the Catholic Church at that time as it is for any of the rest of us.

The issue is not whether John Paul is sincere in his apology for the Inquisition today. We can acknowledge that he is and that he has no desire at the present time to persecute anyone, yet at the same time recognize that the underlying philosophy of church-state relationships that brought on the Inquisition several hundred years ago is still alive and well in a significant segment of Catholicism. This could lead to a future Inquisition in spite of John Paul's best sentiments at the present time.

I find it extremely significant that four times in Revelation 13 we are told that the world will *give* authority to the beast powers, which will enable them to control the world and enforce their brand of false worship:

- "The beast was *given* a mouth to utter proud words and blasphemies and to exercise his authority for forty-two months" (Revelation 13:5, italics added).
- "He was *given* power to make war against the saints and to conquer them" (Revelation 13:7, italics added.)
- "He was *given* authority over every tribe, people, language and nation" (Revelation 13:7, italics added).
- "He was *given* power to give breath to the image of the first beast, so that it could speak and cause all who refused to worship the image to be killed" (Revelation 13:15, italics added).

I propose that during the final crisis a desperate world will easily give authority to an organization that can bring order out of the global chaos. Many people will gladly surrender freedom in exchange for food, shelter, and security. And the Vatican, with its present worldwide influence, will be in a prime position to fill that role. Indeed, global chaos is precisely how Malachi Martin says John Paul *expects* to gain global control:

John Paul is waiting . . . for an event . . . on public view in the skies, in the oceans, and on the continental landmasses of this planet . . . [that] will particularly involve our human sun. . . .

[This event] will immediately nullify all the grand designs the nations are now forming and will introduce the Grand Design of man's Maker. John Paul's . . . ministry as the servant of the Grand Design will then begin.[35]

Given the rapid moral degeneration of society today, it's entirely plausible to suppose that when this global chaos erupts, the majority of people in the world will say "God is trying to tell us something; we've got to restore moral order." And who will define the moral order to be restored? The beast power that is "given [political] authority over every tribe, people, language and nation" (Revelation 13:7).

So while Reinder Bruinsma is very correct in pointing out the major changes that have occurred in Catholicism during the hundred-plus years since Ellen White wrote *The Great Controversy*, I don't believe that we are justified in completely reinterpreting her words in light of those changes. Rather, we must understand her statement that Rome "is unchanged" to mean that it is unchanged in its doctrine, and among some Catholics it is unchanged in those underlying principles of church-state relationships that can lead to persecution when the conditions are right. All that is needed is a circumstance that will restore medieval church-state relationships, and it will be very easy, in the name of bringing order out of chaos and maintaining public morality (which the Catholic Church claims the right to define), for the Church to become a persecuting power again.

1. Reinder Bruinsma, "Adventists and Catholics: Prophetic Preview or Prejudice?" *Spectrum*, Summer 1999, 50.

2. *The Great Controversy*, 571.

3. Bruinsma, op. cit., 51.

4. For an extended discussion of the date of the Exodus from Egypt, see *The SDA Bible Commentary*, 1:184-195.

5. Bruinsma, op. cit., 50, 51.

6. *Dies Domini* was published May 31, 1998.

7. *Signswatch*® is a quarterly publication by *Signs of the Times*® that examines contemporary evidence for our prophetic end-time scenario. It is available free of charge to anyone who sponsors six or more subscriptions to *Signs of the Times*®. It's also available

for a subscription price. For information call (208) 465-2500 and ask to speak to a customer service representative.

8. *The Great Controversy*, 571.

9. After Constantine's death.

10. In Latin, *Dictatus Papae*; see <www.fordham.edu/halsall/source/g7-dictpap.html>. Some authorities argue that the Dictates were written by another author after Gregory's death. However, the principles stated in the document clearly reflect Gregory's views.

11. He was canonized in 1174.

12. Cited in Brian Tierney, *The Crisis of Church and State, 1050-1300* (Englewood Cliffs: Prentice-Hall, 1964), 21, 22.

13. Cited in Tierney, op. cit., 132.

14. Cited in *Readings in Church History*, C. J. Barry, editor (Westminster, Md.: The Newman Press, 1960), I:438.

15. Cited in Tierney, 153.

16. Boniface VIII was pope from 1294 to 1303.

17. See <www.newadvent.org/docs/bo08us.htm>.

18. The other being Augustine.

19. Cited in *The Political Ideas of St. Thomas Aquinas*, Dino Bigongiari, editor (New York: Hafner Publishing Company, 1953), xxiv.

20. Ibid.

21. Cited by John W. Robbins in *Ecclesiastical Megalomania: The Economic and Political Thought of the Roman Catholic Church* (Dallas: The Trinity Foundation, 1999), 131.

22. Pope Gregory XVI, "On Liberalism" (*Mirari Vos*). See *The Popes Against Modern Errors* (Rockford, Ill.: Tan Books and Publishers, Inc., 1999), 11.

23. Pope Gregory XVI, "Syllabus of Errors." See *The Popes Against Modern Errors* (Rockford, Ill.: Tan Books and Publishers, Inc., 1999), 15-26.

24. Pope Leo XIII, "On the Christian Constitution of States" (*Immortale Dei*). See <www.newadvent.org/docs/le13id.htm>.

25. Arius (256-336), a bishop in what is now Lybia, proposed that Christ was not co-eternal with the Father and that He was a created Being. This contradicted the church's traditional Trinitarian teaching.

26. Snake-handling is practiced by certain primitive Christian groups in the U.S. These groups base their practice on Mark 16:18, which says that believers " 'will pick up snakes with their hands; . . . [and] it will not hurt them at all.' "

27. *Catechism of the Catholic Church*, page 460, paragraph 1883, italics in the original.

28. Malachi Martin, *The Keys of This Blood: The Struggle for World Dominion Between Pope John Paul II, Mikhail Gorbachev, and the Capitalist West* (New York: Simon and Schuster, 1990).

29. Ibid., 15-17.

30. Ibid., 287.

31. Ibid., 157.

32. Ibid., 158, italics added.

33. *The Great Controversy*, 571.

34. Ibid.

35. Martin, op. cit., 639.

HOW TO THINK ABOUT

the
Final Crisis

the
Close of Probation

The close of probation is potentially one of the scariest doctrines of the Seventh-day Adventist Church. I think most Seventh-day Adventists understand what the terms "probation" and "close of probation" mean. However, let's spend a few moments examining these terms, and then I'll talk about the scary part.

What is probation?

In everyday legal terms, probation refers to the period of time that a person who has been paroled from prison must spend under the supervision of an officer of the law. Judges also sometimes sentence first-time criminals to a period of probationary supervision in lieu of a prison term. Probation provides the criminal an opportunity to demonstrate his ability to live within the law. Often, the terms of probation place certain restrictions on the criminal's activities, such as the people he is allowed to visit or the distance from home that he can travel. When the probationary period has expired—usually anywhere from several months to several years—the individual is released from the supervision of the law, and also, in most cases, from its restrictions on his or her activities.

Probation in the biblical sense is similar, but there are significant differences. Biblical probation began in the Garden of Eden. God had warned Adam and Eve that the day they ate of the fruit of the Tree of the Knowledge of Good and Evil, they would die. As we all know, they did eat the fruit of the tree, but they didn't die that day. Instead, God came to them with a promise, recorded in Genesis 3:15, that the woman would bruise the serpent's head. This symbolic statement meant that Christ, the ultimate seed of the woman, would defeat Satan. In plain English, God instituted a plan whereby those who chose to do so could come back into favor with Him. And He put a moratorium on the death penalty so that all humans (not just Adam and Eve) could have time in which to accept His offer. *Probation* is the word we use to refer to this time that God has provided for us to accept His offer of salvation.

Christ's mediatorial ministry is closely bound up with probationary time. The purpose of this ministry is to make available to His people on earth the benefits of His sacrifice on the cross. Probationary time provides the opportunity for each of us to take advantage of those benefits.

The "close of probation" refers to the time when this period of grace[1] ends. And when probation closes, God's offer of salvation and Christ's mediatorial ministry will end. The question is: When will that happen?

When will probation end?

At first glance, the most logical time for probation to close would seem to be at the second coming of Christ. According to the Bible, that is the time when God will give eternal rewards to both the righteous and the wicked and separate them from each other. However, Seventh-day Adventists believe that probation will close a short time *before* Christ's return. This is very obvious from a careful study of Revelation 14, 15, and 16.

Revelation 14 tells of a time when God will inflict wrath unmixed with mercy upon all rebellious sinners. This outpouring of wrath is graphically described in chapter 16 as "seven last plagues." A careful reading of this entire chapter shows that these plagues will occur just before Christ's second coming. And Revelation 15 makes it clear that probation will close just before this manifestation of God's wrath. In verses 5 and 6 God's temple in heaven—the place of Christ's mediatorial ministry—is opened, and the seven angels with the seven last plagues emerge. Verse 7 shows one of the four beasts that surround God's throne giving these angels the bowls of God's wrath. The climax of the chapter comes in verse 8, *when the temple fills with smoke from the glory of God, and no one can enter the temple until the seven last plagues have been poured out.*

This interesting imagery is drawn from two Old Testament passages, both having to do with the dedication of Solomon's temple. The Bible says that the ark of the covenant was brought to the Most Holy Place, following which "the temple of the Lord was filled with a cloud, and *the priests could not perform their service* because of the cloud, for the glory of the Lord filled the temple of God" (2 Chronicles 5:13, 14, italics added). Again, following Solomon's dedicatory prayer, "the glory of the Lord filled the temple. And the *priests could not enter the temple of the Lord* because the glory of the Lord filled it" (2 Chronicles 7:1, 2, italics added).

A comparison of these two Old Testament passages with the description in Revelation makes it clear that Revelation is speaking of the close of probation:

Solomon's Temple	God's Temple in Heaven
•Is filled with a cloud.	•Is filled with smoke.
•Is filled with God's glory.	•Is filled with God's glory.
•The priests cannot enter the temple.	•No one can enter the temple.
•The priests cannot serve.	

My conclusion is that, just as the cloud and glory of God prevented the priests in the Old Testament type from entering Solomon's temple to perform their service, so the smoke and glory of God will prevent Christ from performing His service in heaven's temple. That is what I understand the words in Revelation 15:8—"no one could enter the temple"—to mean. And since this momentous event in heaven will immediately precede the seven last plagues, it is evident that probation will close shortly *before* rather than *at* the second coming of Christ.

Ellen White clearly supports the view that Christ's mediatorial ministry in the heavenly sanctuary will conclude at the beginning of the seven last plagues. In her book *The Great Controversy*, at the very beginning of the chapter "The Time of Trouble,"[2] she says:

> When the third angel's message closes, mercy no longer pleads for the guilty inhabitants of the earth. . . . Jesus ceases His intercession in the sanctuary above. He lifts His hands and with a loud voice says, "It is done;" and all the angelic host lay off their crowns

as He makes the solemn announcement: "He that is unjust, let him be unjust still: and he which is filthy, let him be filthy still: and he that is righteous, let him be righteous still: and he that is holy, let him be holy still." Revelation 22:11. Every case has been decided for life or death.[3]

And on the next page Ellen White says that "when [Jesus] leaves the sanctuary, . . . the righteous must live in the sight of a holy God without an intercessor."[4]

Unfortunately, the idea that there will be no mediator in the heavenly sanctuary after the close of probation has caused some Seventh-day Adventists a great deal of anxiety: They're afraid they may not be "good enough" to live without a mediator.

Living without a mediator

What will it mean to live "without a mediator"? What will be the consequence to God's people? To the wicked? Before answering these questions, we need to ask another: What is Christ doing as our Mediator in the heavenly sanctuary now, while probation is open? I'm sure the list below is quite incomplete, but it suffices to make my point:

1. He continually sends His Holy Spirit throughout the world to influence those who are not His people to give their lives to Him, and He commissions the Spirit to transform the minds and hearts of those who surrender to Him. This transformation is called conversion.
2. The Spirit dwells in the minds and hearts of God's people throughout their Christian life.
3. When His people confess their sins, He writes "forgiven" beside the record of those sins in heaven's record books.
4. He continually covers His people with the robe of His righteousness so that they appear sinless before God even though they still have many character defects.
5. He gives His people power to overcome sin.
6. He responds to all the prayers of His people.
7. He defends His people against Satan's accusation that they are unworthy of salvation.

Let's examine these various aspects of Christ's mediatorial ministry, asking one simple question about each of them: Will this benefit still be available to God's people after the close of probation?

1. *Influencing those who are not His people to surrender their lives to Him.* Will Jesus continue this activity after the close of probation? The answer is clearly No. When Jesus makes the solemn announcement "He that is unjust, let him be unjust still: . . . and he that is holy, let him be holy still" (Revelation 22:11, KJV), every case will have been decided for life or death. There will be no more changing sides. Thus, the ones who need to fear the close of probation are the wicked, not the righteous, for they will have missed their last opportunity to obtain eternal life.

2. *Indwelling the minds and hearts of His people.* I have heard some Adventists express the fear that they will have to live without the presence of the Holy Spirit after the close of probation. Fortunately, I can assure you that this is not true.

Allow me to explain.

Shortly before His death Jesus announced to His disciples that He would soon be leaving them. Naturally, they expressed great concern,[5] so Jesus assured them, " 'I will not leave you as orphans; I will come to you' " (John 14:18). And He explained how He would do that: " 'I will ask the Father, and he will give you another Counselor to be with you forever—the Spirit of truth' " (verses 16, 17).

Please notice carefully what Jesus said: "*I will ask the Father,* and he will give you another Counselor." So asking God to send the Holy Spirit into the minds and hearts of His people is one of the important aspects of Jesus' intercessory ministry. And how long did Jesus say that He would be with His disciples through the Holy Spirit—and by extension, with you and me?

Forever!

In His Great Commission, Jesus promised His disciples, " 'Surely I am with you always, to the very end of the age' " (Matthew 28:20). By "the end of the age" Jesus meant His second coming. Notice that He did not say to His disciples, "I'll be with you till the close of probation, but between probation's close and My second coming you'll have to make it on your own." He said, "I will be with you *until* My second coming."

Jesus would break this promise if He were to remove His Holy Spirit from His people after the close of probation!

There's another extremely important reason why the Holy Spirit *has* to remain with God's people after the close of probation: It's absolutely impossible for anyone to live the Christian life without the presence of the Holy Spirit. Jesus told Nicodemus, "You must be born again" (John 3:7) in order to see the kingdom of God. Are we to suppose that after the close of probation God's people will somehow make it "on their own," when no one has ever been able to make it "on his own" without the converting power of the Holy Spirit at any other time in the history of the world? Of course not! You can search your Bible and the writings of Ellen White from beginning to end, and you won't find so much as a *hint* anywhere that God will remove the Holy Spirit from His people after the close of probation. The only people who will lose the Spirit's power in their lives at that time will be the wicked. Here's how Ellen White stated it:

> When He [Jesus] leaves the sanctuary, darkness covers the inhabitants of the earth. . . . The restraint which has been upon the wicked is removed, and Satan has entire control of the finally impenitent. God's long-suffering has ended. The world has rejected His mercy, despised His love, and trampled upon His law. *The wicked have passed the boundary of their probation; the Spirit of God, persistently resisted, has been at last withdrawn.* Unsheltered by divine grace, they have no protection from the wicked one.[6]

3. *Forgiving sin.* We can be sure that there will be no forgiveness available for the wicked after the close of probation, and the righteous may not need it. Why do I say *may* not need it? There's a fairly widespread understanding among Seventh-day Adventists that God's people will be perfect after the close of probation, which is usually understood to mean that they will not sin. If this is true, then logically, forgiveness won't be necessary. We should be careful, though, about reaching that conclusion too quickly. Logic can sometimes get us in trouble when doing theology. Let's just say that if God's people need forgiveness in any sense after the close of probation, it will surely be available.

4. *Covering us with the robe of Christ's righteousness.* Some Adventists may be tempted to believe that because there will be no mediator in the heavenly sanctuary after the close of probation, God's people will have to get along without the robe of Christ's righteousness. However, that idea is just as incorrect as the idea that God's people will have to get along without the Holy Spirit between the close of probation and Christ's second coming. As long as we are on this earth, even if we are living perfectly sinless lives, we will need Christ's righteousness to cover us. The idea that our own righteousness will be sufficient following the close of probation is totally contrary to the gospel.

5. *Power to overcome sin.* Some people may also be tempted, based on a perfectionist theology, to suppose that we won't need God's power to overcome sin after the close of probation. Why would we need God's power to overcome sin when we are no longer sinning? That's like asking why a car needs gasoline since the engine is already running. If anything, because of the severity of the trials that will confront us during the time of trouble we will need *more* of the Spirit's power, not less.

6. *Responding to our prayers.* Do I really need to comment on this one? Does any Adventist seriously believe that the cessation of Christ's ministry in the heavenly sanctuary means that He won't be responding to the prayers of His saints during the time of trouble?

7. *Defending us against Satan's accusations.* Revelation 12:10 describes Satan as " 'the accuser of our brothers, who accuses them before our God day and night.' " Defending His people against these accusations is one of the most important functions of Christ's mediatorial ministry,[7] and I believe that too will be available to all God's people during the time of trouble. If anything, given the fact that Satan has such a very short time left, his accusations will almost certainly grow in intensity during that crucial period, which will make Christ's response to them even more imperative than it is now.

There are no doubt other aspects of Christ's mediatorial ministry in the heavenly sanctuary that we could talk about, but a careful examination of this list is enough to make my point: All the benefits that God's people receive from Christ's mediatorial ministry today will still be available to them after the close of probation. Since Christ will no longer be a Mediator in the heavenly sanctuary, these benefits will obviously have to come through some other means, but *they will be available.*

What if I'm not "good enough"?
Now for the scary part.

Over the years, many Seventh-day Adventists have worried that they may not be "good enough" for the close of probation. This question is clearly suggested by the following Ellen White statements:

> Those who are living upon the earth when the intercession of Christ shall cease in the sanctuary above are to stand in the sight of a holy God without a mediator. Their robes must be spotless, their characters must be purified from sin by the blood of sprin-

kling. Through the grace of God and their own diligent effort they must be conquerors in the battle with evil.[8]

Now, while our great High Priest is making the atonement for us, we should seek to become perfect in Christ. Not even by a thought could our Saviour be brought to yield to the power of temptation. Satan finds in human hearts some point where he can gain a foothold; some sinful desire is cherished, by means of which his temptations assert their power. But Christ declared of Himself: "The prince of this world cometh and hath nothing in Me." John 14:30. Satan could find nothing in the Son of God that would enable him to gain the victory. He had kept His Father's commandments, and there was no sin in Him that Satan could use to his advantage. This is the condition in which those must be found who shall stand in the time of trouble.[9]

The big question is this: What if God is ready to close probation, and I still haven't overcome all my sins? This concern has fostered a great deal of unhealthy perfectionism in the Adventist Church during the last hundred or so years, which I will discuss in chapter 14. Here I would like to respond to the question from the standpoint of the close of probation itself.

Seventh-day Adventists have typically thought of the close of probation as a particular point in time—which it is, of course. However, it's more than that. The close of probation will actually be a process that happens over a rather significant period of time—perhaps as much as several years. Why do I say that? Because of the following statement by Ellen White:

The time of God's destructive judgments is the time of mercy for those who have had no opportunity to learn what is truth. Tenderly will the Lord look upon them. His heart of mercy is touched; His hand is still stretched out to save, *while the door is closed to those who would not enter.*[10]

Notice that God's hand will "still be stretched out to save" those "who have had no opportunity to learn what is truth" while the door will already be closed "to those who would not enter." In other words, probation's door will be open to some, closed to others. Thus, it's obvious that probation will not end for everyone at the same time. I understand this to mean that probation will close over a period of time.

The idea that the close of probation will take place over a period of time is good news for those who are concerned that they may not be quite "good enough." For if you need a little more time in which to get ready, Jesus will give it to you. If you're earnestly doing everything you know to get ready for the close of probation, He's *not* going to slam the door in your face a few hours or days before you're ready. To the contrary, He has a plan for helping you to get ready even more quickly than usual. It's called "the latter rain," which comes shortly before the close of probation to push your character development and mine into fast forward. During this powerful latter rain we will be able to develop a level of character in a matter of weeks or even days that would take months or even years under present circumstances.

So please don't worry about whether you're good enough for the close of probation. If you're serious about being ready, Jesus will see to it that you are, and He absolutely *will not* close the door *until* you are.

How God will bring probation to a close

One final question before concluding this chapter: How is God going to bring probation to a close? The problem I refer to is illustrated by an explanation some people give for the delay in Christ's return that I commented on in chapter 6. Jesus is waiting, they say, for a few more people to accept Him. While this sounds very generous on God's part, it's an argument that has no end. As long as life continues the way we know it today, *there will always be a few more people to accept Jesus.*

So how does God plan to bring probation to a close? One of these days He's going to bring a crisis on the world of such incredible intensity that every human being will be forced to make a final choice. Ellen White often referred to this as "the final crisis."

Adventists have traditionally understood that there will be two times of trouble—a "little time of trouble"[12] just before the close of probation and a "great time of trouble" just after, which we associate with the seven last plagues. Please don't allow the word *little* to fool you. This "little" time of trouble before the close of probation is when the dragon's attack on the woman will reach its most savage intensity. Revelation 13 describes the struggle through the symbol of two great beast powers that dominate the whole world, threatening with death anyone who refuses to submit to their spiritual authority.

The immediate cause of this crisis, as I pointed out in chapter 2, will be terrible natural disasters. In response to the horrendous emergency these calamities create, the world's leaders will enact spiritual solutions that will conflict with God's laws. Into this utterly chaotic situation Satan will inject his masterful deceptions. And it is precisely at this time that God's people, under the power of the latter rain, will proclaim the final warning, urging men and women everywhere to take their stand for truth. Thus, every human being will be forced to make a final choice for or against God and His truth. Probation will close when every decision is final.

How to think about the close of probation

So how should you and I think about the close of probation?

Most important, we need to understand that God had a reason for informing us of it—so we could prepare for it. My book *Conquering the Dragon Within* provides a number of practical suggestions for making that preparation. However, we should do so free of anxiety and fear. As I pointed out earlier, God will not slam probation's door shut in your face if you aren't quite ready. He won't close the door until *every one* of His people is ready. That's one of the important reasons why the close of probation is a process—to give anyone who needs it the time to prepare.

Of course, we must not wait till the process of closing probation begins to start preparing. That process will especially provide time for the *final* preparation that is needed by those who accept the truth shortly before the close of probation. That's precisely how Ellen White viewed the matter. She said, "The time of God's destructive judgments is the time of mercy *for those who have had no opportunity to learn what is truth.*"[11]

Neither should you worry about discovering some sin or character defect *after* probation has closed that you should have dealt with *before*. If you're coming close to Jesus each day and working to overcome your character defects as He reveals them to you, He isn't going to close the door until He has revealed each defect that He knows you need to deal with.

I don't know when I'll be "good enough" for the close of probation, and you don't know when you'll be "good enough." But God does! And if we truly love Jesus and are cooperating with Him each day to deal with the sins and character defects He reveals to us, then we can be sure of one thing: He will reveal to us everything we need to know before the close of probation, and He'll do it in time for us to make the necessary changes in our lives before the close of probation. There will be no such thing as one of God's true people going a little beyond the close of probation and then discovering some sin he or she should have dealt with before the close of probation. *He simply won't allow that to happen.*

Now that's good news! And that's how I like to think of the close of probation.

1. In some languages probation is called "time of grace" and the close of probation is called "end of the time of grace."

2. Seventh-day Adventists understand that the time of trouble will be caused by the seven last plagues. Thus, the two will run concurrently.

3. *The Great Controversy*, 613.

4. Ibid., 614.

5. John 13:33-37.

6. *The Great Controversy*, 614, italics added.

7. Ibid., 484.

8. Ibid., 425.

9. Ibid., 623.

10. *The SDA Bible Commentary*, 7:979, italics added.

11. Ibid., italics added.

12. See *Early Writings,* 33, 85.

the
Time of Trouble

I can still remember the first time I heard about the time of trouble. I cried.

I was about seven years old at the time, living in Argentina with my parents, who were missionaries to Latin America. As I recall, it was either a Friday evening or a Sabbath afternoon, and my mother read the chapter on the time of trouble from *The Great Controversy* to my sister and me. I don't remember my sister's reaction. Since she's a couple of years younger than I am, she probably didn't understand that much about what she heard. But I was quite frightened by it all. My mother handled my fears very gently. She wiped away my tears and assured me that Jesus would be with us during that time.

Since then I've met a number of Adventists who told me they were terrified of the time of trouble as children. Some heard about it in church school, others in Sabbath School, others, like me, from their parents. Wherever they heard it, it upset them terribly. And some have never lost this fear. I suspect that anxiety about the time of trouble has actually caused some people to leave the Adventist Church.

There's no question that the biblical teaching about the time of trouble is, shall we say, troubling! While I've never felt traumatized by it (since that first exposure), I don't look forward to it with any degree of enthusiasm. There's no way to make it seem like a Sunday afternoon picnic. It *is* frightening. Always has been. Always will be. So how should we think about the time of trouble?

Fortunately, we're not the only ones who have gone through a "time of trouble." For one thing, there are the saints during the Middle Ages who endured the Inquisition. There are also Daniel and his three friends who were persecuted for their faith.[1] However, our greatest example of One who endured a time of trouble is Jesus, and it's to His life and example that I'd like to turn your attention.

Jesus' anticipation of His time of trouble

We don't know exactly when Jesus became fully aware of His mission and all that it implied. We do know that He had a good idea of it by the age of twelve, when He talked to the Jewish leaders in the temple, because when His mother asked Him why He had failed to tell them where He was, He said, "Didn't you know that I must be about My Father's business?"(Luke 2:49).[2] And speaking of Jesus' temple visit, Ellen White says:

> For the first time the child Jesus looked upon the temple. He saw the white-robed priests performing their solemn ministry. He beheld the bleeding victim upon the altar of sacrifice. With the worshipers He bowed in prayer, while the cloud of incense ascended before God. He witnessed the impressive rites of the paschal service. Day by day He saw their meaning more clearly. Every act seemed to be bound up with His own life. New impulses were awakening within Him. Silent and absorbed, He seemed to be studying out a great problem. The mystery of His mission was opening to the Saviour.[3]

Thus, by the age of twelve, Jesus had a beginning awareness of His own time of trouble—the sacrifice He was to make for the human race on the cross. Ellen White says that "new impulses were awakening within Him," but she doesn't describe those impulses. Was there fear? Perhaps.

We know that by the time Jesus was an adult He had a very clear understanding of His role as a sacrifice for the sins of the world. He surely heard John the Baptist's inspired words " 'Look, the Lamb of God, who takes away the sin of the world!' " (John 1:29). And early in His ministry He said to Nicodemus " 'Just as Moses lifted up the snake in the desert, so the Son of Man must be lifted up, that everyone who believes in him may have eternal life' " (John 3:15). But again, there's no clue as to how Jesus *felt* about His approaching time of trouble.

This doesn't mean we're left with no idea of Jesus' feelings about what He knew would happen to Him. Satan's third temptation in the wilderness[4] provides us with that. Satan offered Jesus the kingdoms of the world on condition that " 'you will bow down and worship me' " (Matthew 4:9). Why was this such a temptation? Because Jesus' mission was to wrest those kingdoms back from Satan through suffering, and Satan offered Him a way to obtain them without having to go to the Cross. What an attractive offer! The fact that the Bible calls it a temptation shows that Jesus had the normal feelings that any human being would have as He contemplated His death by crucifixion.

We have a similar clue in Matthew 16. The Bible says that following Peter's confession, " 'You are the Christ, the Son of the living God' " (Matthew 16:16), Jesus "began to explain to his disciples that he must go to Jerusalem and suffer many things at the hands of the elders, chief priests and teachers of the law, and that he must be killed and on the third day be raised to life" (verse 21).

The Jewish people in Christ's time expected the Messiah to deliver them from the Romans, and Jesus' disciples held this misunderstanding. The idea of a suffering Messiah simply did not fit their agenda of "the end time." So when Jesus began talking about His coming trial and death it didn't make sense to them. The Bible says that Peter took Jesus aside "and began to rebuke him. 'Never, Lord!' he said. 'This shall never happen to you!' " (verse 22). It's important to understand that Peter's motive was perfectly innocent. He had no intention of tempting Jesus. He probably thought Jesus was a bit depressed that particular day and needed a bit of encouragement.

But the strength of this temptation is evident in Jesus' response. His words were almost violent: " 'Get behind me, Satan! You are a stumbling block to me; you do not have in mind the things of God, but the things of men' " (verse 23).

Why did Jesus address Peter as Satan? He didn't. His words were directed at Satan himself, who had put these words in Peter's mouth to try to get Jesus to back away from the Cross. And the swiftness and intensity of Jesus' response tells us that His coming trial was extremely painful for Him to think about. He didn't relish the thought of His approaching time of trouble any more than you and I do ours. He was a human being, after all, just like you and me!

Finally, there's Gethsemane, where Jesus pleaded three times with His Father, " 'If it is possible, may this cup be taken from me' " (Matthew 26:39). The struggle was so intense that He actually sweat blood! At one point God even sent an angel to strengthen Him for the conflict (Luke 22:43, 44).

Jesus did not want to go through His time of trouble!

Jesus' "time of trouble"—physical abuse[5]

After His arrest in Gethsemane, Jesus was taken to the home of Annas, the "high priest emeritus," who was the father-in-law of Caiaphas, the actual high priest at the time. However, Annas's interview was probably more a formality that acknowledged the older man's status. The real Jewish trial began when Jesus was interrogated by Caiaphas. Caiaphas demanded to know if Jesus claimed to be the Messiah. When Jesus responded affirmatively, Caiaphas charged Him with blasphemy, which, according to Jewish law, was punishable by death. He was then given a night trial before a partial meeting of the Sanhedrin—something comparable, perhaps, to our grand jury.

From this "grand jury" Jesus was taken to a guardroom, where He was beaten by an angry mob. The people spat on Him, struck Him with their fists, and slapped Him in the face, demanding that He tell them who struck Him. Next, He was taken to a trial during daylight hours before the full Sanhedrin, which condemned Him to death. However, because the Romans reserved to themselves the right to impose the death penalty, the Sanhedrin had to send Jesus to Pilate for ratification of their sentence. But before sending Him to Pilate, the Jewish leaders allowed the crowd to beat Him again, this time within the judgment hall itself. Ellen White says that "had it not been for the Roman soldiers, Jesus would not have lived to be nailed to the cross."[6]

When Jesus finally reached Pilate's palace, the governor gave Him a hearing. But upon learning that Jesus was a Galillean, Pilate passed Him off to Herod, the governor of Galillee, who was in Jerusalem for the Passover. Herod demanded that Jesus perform a miracle, but Jesus refused. Enraged, Herod personally mocked Christ, and the mob lunged forward and beat Him so severely that again He would have been torn in pieces had the soldiers not intervened.

Since Herod could not get what he wanted out of Jesus, he sent Him back to Pilate. Pilate granted Jesus a second hearing, and then pronounced Him innocent. However, fearing the displeasure of the Jewish leaders, the governor washed His hands of responsibility for Jesus' death and turned Him over for crucifixion.

The death sentence called for a scourging—forty lashes with a whip made of leather strips that were tipped with sharp pieces of metal. The pain of these leather strips and their metal tips raking across a condemned person's back was so intense that the victim of scourging often died before it was over. However, Jesus actually survived two scourgings!

Finally, He was led off to be crucified. I hardly think I have to describe the pain that He must have endured as the nails were driven through His hands and feet![7] He was nailed to the cross while it was lying on the ground. It was then picked up and dropped into the hole that had been dug for it. Kim Johnson, in his book *The Gift*, describes how it would have happened:

> Jesus gritted His teeth and glanced around wild-eyed as He felt Himself and His cross being rudely lifted upward by several careless soldiers then suddenly thrust violently downward into position. As the end of the upright hit the bottom of the drilled hole with a body-jolting thud, the wounds in His wrists gaped open, tearing flesh and causing a fierce spasm of pain. Blood continued to flow from the four beatings, from each area of flesh mangled by the scourge, from each puncture wound made by the thorns, and from the injuries created by the nails. Frankly, Christ was a bloody mess. Flies gathered, crawling and picking at the many wounds. The scene was nothing at all like the sanitized crucifixion paintings of the Middle Ages.[8]

By now you may be shuddering at the thought of what Jesus went through. So let's ask: What was the cause of this terribly inhumane treatment? What drove the people around Him to this frenzy of persecution? The answer is simple: It was Satan. For three-and-a-half years Satan had tried to get Jesus to give up His allegiance to His Father and turn it over to him (Satan). However, so far *he had failed every single time*. This was Satan's last chance, and he was determined to make very good use of it. As Kim Johnson stated in his book, *"The devil planned to torture Christ into giving up or sinning."*[9]

Jesus' "time of trouble"—psychological abuse

In addition to all this physical persecution, Jesus also endured intense psychological persecution. We all want to be well liked. That's why ridicule is one of the most common forms of persecution that we humans perpetrate against each other, and it's one of the most effective forms of intimidation. When others make fun of us, the temptation is to yield our convictions. And Satan used intense ridicule against Jesus in his effort to get Him to yield the conflict.

158

Because Jesus looked like any other human being, His claim to be the Messiah and the Son of God brought forth howls of laughter from His enemies. The Bible says that "they slapped him and said, 'Prophesy to us, Christ. Who hit you?' " (Matthew 26:67). After Pilate had turned Jesus over for crucifixion,

> the governor's soldiers took Jesus into the Praetorium and gathered the whole company of soldiers around him. They stripped him and put a scarlet robe on him, and then twisted together a crown of thorns and set it on his head. They put a staff in his right hand and knelt in front of him and mocked him. "Hail, king of the Jews!" they said. They spit on him, and took the staff and struck him on the head again and again. (Matthew 27:27-30)

And the ridicule continued on the cross:

- "Those who passed by hurled insults at him, shaking their heads and saying, 'So! You who are going to destroy the temple and build it in three days, come down from the cross and save yourself!' " (Mark 15:29, 30).
- "The chief priests and the teachers of the law mocked him among themselves. 'He saved others,' they said, 'but he can't save himself! Let this Christ, this King of Israel, come down now from the cross, that we may see and believe' " (Mark 15:31, 32).
- "The soldiers also came up and mocked him. They offered him wine vinegar and said, 'If you are the king of the Jews, save yourself' " (Luke 23:36, 37).

All of this persecution—both physical and psychological—was perpetrated by Satan, who was putting forth the most intense effort to defeat Jesus, to get Him to yield the great controversy to him, that is, to Satan. Now we need to inquire how Jesus was able to endure His "time of trouble" without yielding. Because when we understand that, we will also have some good clues as to how we can endure our time of trouble without yielding our allegiance to God.

How Jesus endured His "time of trouble"
 I'm sure we could say many things about how Jesus endured His "time of trouble," the most important of which would surely be that He had maintained a close, day-by-day relationship with His Father prior to that time.

You would expect me to say that, of course, and that is a very true answer. However, there's more, and here I would like to focus on one point of utmost importance: *Jesus understood that reality was not what it appeared to be from the perspective of everyone else around Him,* including His own disciples. He understood that issues of consequence to *the entire universe* were at stake in the choices He made during those crisis hours. In recounting the events between Gethsemane and the cross, the Gospel writers give us several glimpses into the fact that Jesus understood the events transpiring around Him in the context of this universal conflict.

In Gethsemane. Our first glimpse comes from Jesus' prayer to His Father in Gethsemane. As I pointed out a moment ago, Jesus knew very well what was about to happen, and in His human nature He shrank from it just as forcefully as you and I would. Recall what He said: " 'My Father, if it is possible, may this cup be taken from me. Yet not as I will, but as you will' " (Matthew 26:39). These words show clearly that Jesus understood the issue that He was about to face—that the salvation of the human race was at stake in the events of the next few hours, not just His own life.

The arrest. Our next glimpse comes from something Jesus said to the soldiers who came to arrest Him: " 'Do you think I cannot call on my Father, and he will at once put at my disposal more than twelve legions of angels? But how then would the Scriptures be fulfilled that say it must happen in this way?' " (Matthew 26:53, 54).

The mob that approached Jesus saw a mere human being. An ordinary man. A carpenter's son who had managed to distinguish himself as something of a teacher for a few years. Perhaps you noticed that I did not capitalize words such as Man, Son, and Himself in the previous three sentences, as we ordinarily do in English to indicate Deity. That was deliberate, a way to emphasize that all the crowd saw was a human being just like themselves. But Jesus' statement that His Father would have sent twelve legions of angels to deliver Him shows that He knew He was the divine Son of God, and it hints at the fact that a conflict beyond this world was transpiring at that very moment.

The mob didn't understand this. *Jesus did.*

Before the Sanhedrin. As I said a moment ago, the Romans did not allow the Jews to carry out an execution on their own authority. In order to enforce a sentence of death, they had to persuade the governor that the criminal had committed a crime worthy of death under Roman law. So the Sanhedrin's job that night was not to find Jesus worthy of death by their standards, but to come up with a capital offense that would pass muster with the governor. Matthew says that "the chief priests and the whole

Sanhedrin were looking for false evidence against Jesus so that they could put him to death. But they did not find any, though many false witnesses came forward" (Matthew 26:59, 60). Two witnesses even testified that Jesus had said He could destroy the temple and rebuild it in three days, but everyone knew that was a purely religious charge, which the governor would reject out of hand.

Then there was another major problem. They couldn't get Jesus to talk. He wouldn't defend Himself. Matthew says that "Jesus remained silent" in spite of intense questioning by Caiaphas (Matthew 26:63). Finally, in utter frustration and probably out of a good bit of anger, the high priest charged Jesus " 'under oath by the living God: Tell us if you are the Christ, the Son of God' " (Matthew 26:63).

" 'Yes, it is as you say,' Jesus replied. 'But I say to all of you: In the future you will see the Son of Man sitting at the right hand of the Mighty One and coming on the clouds of heaven' " (Matthew 26:64).

Here was a charge they could take to the Roman governor. This is evident when we compare Jesus' response with the words of the prophet Daniel in his vision of chapter 7. Please note especially the italicized words:

> "In my vision at night I looked, and there before me was one like a *son of man, coming with the clouds of heaven.* He approached the *Ancient of Days* and was led into his presence. He was given authority, glory and sovereign power; all peoples, nations and men of every language worshiped him. His dominion is an everlasting dominion that will not pass away, and *his kingdom is one that will never be destroyed"* (Daniel 7:13, 14, italics added).

When Jesus said to Caiaphas "In the future you will see the Son of Man sitting at the right hand of the Mighty One and coming on the clouds of heaven," He was claiming to be the Son of Man in Daniel's vision, who would rule over every nation on earth, and whose kingdom would never be destroyed. The Jews, of course, understood the "son of man" in Daniel's prophecy to refer to the Messiah, and they understood the Son of Man's eternal kingdom to refer to the Messiah's overthrow of the Roman Empire. Numerous messiahs had arisen in Judea in those times, causing the Roman government no end of grief. If these messiahs had thought of themselves as mere pious religious figures, the Romans could hardly have cared less. But the Jews' belief that the Messiah would cast the Romans out of Judea, give the Jews their independence, and eventually give them control of the whole world, was grounds for the charge of treason against the Roman government, and that *was* punishable by death.

Jesus' claim to be Daniel's "son of man" also explains why Caiaphas pronounced Him a blasphemer; it explains what was going on in the Sanhedrin that night; *and it provides unmistakable evidence of the difference between Jesus' understanding of those events and that of the Jews.* They saw a man on trial for blasphemy and sedition. Jesus saw a vast universe watching the conflict between good and evil being played out in a Jewish court of law! The point is that *Jesus refused to view reality from the perspective of the crowd.* He stuck to His view of who He was—the Son of God. He stuck to His view of what was going on—that He was to give His life as a sacrifice for the sins of the world and to vindicate God in the eyes of the universe. And He stuck to His view of the end of the conflict between good and evil when He, the Son of man, would come with the clouds of heaven.

The Jews saw the little picture. Jesus saw the big picture.

In Pilate's court. Predictably, when the Jewish leaders brought Jesus before Pilate, they accused Him of claiming to be the King of the Jews. However, Pilate was smart enough not to take their word alone. He went back into the palace and had Jesus brought to him where he could interview Him in private. When the two were alone, Pilate asked " 'Are you the king of the Jews?' " Jesus replied, " 'My kingdom is not of this world. If it were, my servants would fight to prevent my arrest by the Jews. But now my kingdom is from another place' " (John 18:33-36).

Again, Jesus' point of view stands out clearly. He held a universal perspective on the events transpiring in Pilate's court that night. It would have been so easy for Him, after the beatings He had already suffered and knowing what lay ahead, to view matters from the standpoint of the mob. After all, aren't all of us to some extent swayed by the popular view of things? Don't we tend to think the way our culture thinks? Especially when everyone around us is criticizing us, isn't it easy to think "Well, maybe I *am* wrong. Maybe the crowd is right"? That was the great temptation for Jesus, and Satan was right there to press it home upon His mind! After all, from a human point of view, wasn't it better to accept the popular explanation of things and spare Himself the agony that lay ahead?

But Jesus refused to be moved from the perspective of the universal conflict between good and evil that He knew was going on around Him right then, even if no one else understood it.

On the cross. Finally, Jesus' last words before He died reveal His understanding of the conflict between good and evil that was raging around

Him. In a loud voice—Ellen White described it as "clear, trumpetlike tones, that seemed to resound throughout creation"[10]—Jesus cried, " 'It is finished' " (John 19:30). He meant that He had met Satan on his own ground and defeated him. The war was won! The conflict between good and evil had been decided!

Each of these incidents during Jesus' trial, arrest, and crucifixion reveal to us that He understood what was happening in the context of the great controversy. Had He viewed those events as nothing more than the persecution of the Jews against Himself, a mere man, He would almost certainly have given up from the beginning. What would have been the point of allowing Himself to be treated in such an inhumane manner when there was no reason for it?

And how easy it would have been to take that point of view! *That's exactly what Satan was so desperately trying to get Him to do.*

How we can endure the coming time of trouble

I wish there were a way I could make our coming time of trouble seem easier, less fearful for you and me to anticipate. Unfortunately, there isn't a way. Like Jesus, we're human, and humans don't relish looking forward to trials of that magnitude. Daniel called the world's final conflict " 'a time of distress such as has not happened from the beginning of nations' "[11] (Daniel 12:1). And Ellen White said, "It is often the case that trouble is greater in anticipation than in reality; but this is not true of the crisis before us. The most vivid presentation cannot reach the magnitude of the ordeal."[12] God in His wisdom has chosen to give us a fairly clear understanding of what lies ahead.

So how do we handle it?

I'm sure there are many things I could tell you, such as "Stay close to Jesus," "Learn to be completely submissive to His will," etc. And all of this would be true, of course. But it's what you would expect me to say. It's what you've already been told time and again by preachers and Sabbath School teachers. I'll return to these suggestions at the close of the chapter, but right now I'd like to focus on other ways we can prepare.

Adopt Jesus' universal outlook. The first is to view our conflict the way Jesus viewed His—as part of the great controversy that has been raging in the universe since Satan's original rebellion. From Gethsemane to the cross, Jesus was locked in the *decisive* battle in the conflict between good and evil. Our coming time of trouble will be the *final* battle in this conflict.

As I pointed out in chapter 2, during the final crisis the world will be in utter chaos from horrible natural disasters that threaten the survival of the human race. I propose that the world's political, scientific, and religious leaders will meet to solve the crisis, and one of the solutions they will recommend is spiritual. However, because God's people refuse to cooperate with the world's spiritual solution to the crisis, they will be accused of treason, of standing in the way of efforts to restore order and save the human race from extinction.[13] From a human perspective, it will seem that God's people are simply dupes in a conflict on this earth. People will ridicule them and call them names. Thus, yielding to popular demands and the efforts of the world's governments to solve the crisis will appear to be the most reasonable thing to do. And those who take this earthbound view of the crisis *will* yield their faith.

In order to remain true to God during this time, we will have to adopt the same universal outlook to our trial that Jesus adopted to His. We will have to understand that what's happening to us, what's going on around us, is the final conflict between Christ and Satan that involves the entire universe, not just our little world. This perspective will be apparent only by faith because *everything in the world around us would lead us to believe that we are stupid, obstinate rebels against law and order*.

However, we aren't going to have that universal outlook if we wait till that time to get it. We must be cultivating it today. That's why I recommend that you familiarize yourself with books by Ellen White such as *Early Writings*, *The Great Controversy*, and *Last Day Events*. I also recommend that you read some of the recent books by Adventist authors on end-time events. I have written four, all of which are still in print as I write these words: *The Crisis of the End Time*, *The Antichrist and the New World Order*,[14] *The Coming Great Calamity*, and *How to Think About the End Time*, which you are reading right now.[15] A number of other authors have written books on the end time in recent years, including Jon Paulien, Clifford Goldstein, Dwight Nelson, Don Mansell, and Ed Reid.[16]

I also recommend that you familiarize yourself with the various teachings of the Adventist Church and the biblical evidence that supports them. When we are called before kings and rulers to answer for our faith (see Matthew 10:18), the enemies of truth will understand very well the so-called weak points in our teachings, and they will exploit these to the fullest in their effort to get us to yield our faith. The better we understand the scriptural foundation for our teachings, the easier it will be for us to hold firmly to our faith in the face of intense persecution.

All of this will help you to adopt the universal outlook when everything and everyone around you is pressuring you to view matters from a purely earthbound perspective.

Let today's trials be stepping stones to preparation. Jesus endured His final conflict because He was fully submissive to His Father's will. In Gethsemane, after asking God, if possible, to take this cup from Him, He said, " 'Yet not as I will, but as you will' " (Matthew 26:39).

You may ask: How can I become fully submissive to God's will like that? And the answer is simple, if not particularly welcome: Endure today's trials patiently, submitting to them as part of God's plan for your life. I don't mean that God necessarily *brings* these trials on you. I don't think He creates them. He doesn't have to. Satan initiates some of them. The imperfect world we live in creates others. And some we bring on ourselves because of our own foolishness and sinfulness. Nevertheless, God *allows* us to experience these trials, and He uses each of today's trials to strengthen us for tomorrow's greater trials.

Our tendency, when faced with these painful situations, is to become angry with God or to complain or to just plain give up. However, each of today's trials is an opportunity for growth, to develop a deeper trust in God, till eventually we become spiritually strong enough to pass through earth's final conflict on God's side. We need to think of our trials that way, and then with God's help learn the lessons each one has for us.

Develop a character that can stand through the final crisis. In the next chapter, I will share with you a number of statements by Ellen White in which she makes it very clear that God's people must reach a high level of character development in order to pass through the time of trouble successfully. In addition to living without a Mediator in the heavenly sanctuary, one of the very important reasons why character development will be necessary is that it will take this very high level of character development to withstand the pressures of the time of trouble. Many of God's people will be confronted with death in the same way that Daniel and the three Hebrews were when they stared into a lions' den and a roaring fiery furnace. This kind of pressure is not for character weaklings!

Commenting on the experience of the ten virgins when they heard the cry " ' "Here's the bridegroom! Come out to meet him!" ' " (Matthew 25:6), Ellen White says, "It is in a crisis that character is revealed." She then goes on to apply this principle to the final crisis:

> So now, a sudden and unlooked-for calamity, something that brings the soul face to face with death, will show whether there is any real faith in the promises of God. It will show whether the soul is sustained by grace. The great final test comes at the close of human probation,[17] when it will be too late for the soul's need to be supplied.[18]

Today's life in North America and other developed parts of the world is fairly easy. We can coast along without having a high level of character development. But the strength of character that we are developing today— or that we fail to develop today—*will be revealed by the final crisis and the time of trouble*. Notice that it is during the "quiet time," before the final crisis breaks, that the 144,000 are sealed (Revelation 7:1-4). This means we must be making that preparation *now*. The question is: How? Again, I have written two books that can help you: *Conquering the Dragon Within* and *The Coming Global Crisis*.[19]

Understand the gospel. Finally, I urge you to obtain a clear understanding of the plan of salvation, and specifically of righteousness by faith, by which I mean both justification and sanctification.[20]

As you are no doubt aware, the third angel's message of Revelation 14 is God's scathing rebuke against those who yield to the popular pressure and accept the mark of the beast. However, the third angel's message closes with a brief word to God's own people: "Here is the patience of the saints: here are they that keep the commandments of God, and the faith of Jesus" (Revelation 14:12, KJV). We learn to keep the commandments of God through the process of sanctification, and I think it's reasonable to understand Revelation's command to keep "the faith of Jesus" as a reference to justification by grace alone through faith. Thus, God is telling us, not only that those of us who stand firm during the final crisis will have a clear understanding of the gospel of righteousness by faith, but that we will have learned by experience the correct relationship between faith and works, grace and obedience.

In a nutshell, here is my understanding of the gospel:

- We receive salvation—the assurance of eternal life in God's kingdom—as a gift through God's act called *justification,* whereby we are forgiven of our sins and placed in a right standing with God through Christ's righteousness that is credited to us (Romans 3:21-24, 28). This justification qualifies us to be accepted by God "just as if we had not sinned."[21]
- Nothing we *do*—no amount of obeying the commandments or keeping church standards—can qualify us for this acceptance by God (Romans 3:20; Ephesians 2:8, 9).
- However, those of us who experience justification also receive the power of the Holy Spirit through conversion or the new birth, which enables us to begin obeying God's commands. This is the ultimate goal of the gospel (Ephesians 2:10). Our continued growth in obedience is called *sanctification.*[22]

•True obedience can be developed only *after* we have *been* saved. It can never be counted as merit *toward* our salvation.

If my understanding of Revelation 14:12 is correct, then we *must* understand as much as possible about the gospel as I summarized it above, not only theoretically but experientially. We will be overwhelmed as we search our lives during the time of Jacob's trouble[23] if we don't understand that our righteousness, our acceptance by God, is based on justification, not sanctification.

Some may object that we must have a perfect character in order to live without a Mediator, because justification will cease to be available to God's people during the time of trouble. I consider this to be a terrible heresy. Never, as long as we live on this sinful planet, will we be acceptable to God on any basis other than through Christ's righteousness attributed to us as a free gift, completely apart from our own works. I will comment further on this in the next chapter.

Develop a relationship with Jesus. Following are the ways to prepare for the final crisis that we've examined up to this point:

•Adopt Jesus' universal outlook.
•Let today's trials be stepping stones to preparation.
•Develop a character that can stand through the final crisis.
•Understand the gospel.

Developing a relationship with Jesus is surely as important as any of these others. I have kept it till the last, not because I think it's less important, but because these other ways are *how* we develop our relationship with Jesus. If you follow through carefully on each of these other suggestions, you *will* develop a very strong relationship with Jesus.

I have good news for you: Ellen White assures us that all of God's people will be ready for the time of trouble:

> When the third angel's message closes, mercy no longer pleads for the guilty inhabitants of the earth. The people of God have accomplished their work. They have received "the latter rain," "the refreshing from the presence of the Lord," and *they are prepared for the trying hour before them.*[24]

Notice that Ellen White tells us *how* we will become ready for the time of trouble: Through the latter rain, which is the special outpouring of God's Holy Spirit shortly before the close of probation.

However, we mustn't wait for the latter rain to begin preparing our-selves spiritually for the time of trouble. In fact, we dare not wait. The Spirit is available to us today, and through the Spirit we need to culti-vate each day our relationship with God. We need to have the commit-ment to His will that Jesus had. That's how we prepare to endure the time of trouble. If we are cultivating that relationship with God today, we can trust that whatever preparation we are lacking as we approach the final crisis, God will provide through the latter rain when it comes.

1. Revelation 13 adopts the experience of the three Hebrews before the fiery fur-nace as a metaphor of the world's persecution of God's people during the final crisis (see Revelation 13:14, 15).

2. I've combined the King James Version and the New International Version render-ing of Jesus' reply to His mother. The KJV says, "Wist ye not that I must be about my Father's business?" The NIV says, " 'Didn't you know I had to be in my Father's house?' " Either response shows that Jesus understood at this early age that He had a unique rela-tionship with God.

3. *The Desire of Ages*, 78.

4. Or the second temptation, depending on which Gospel you're reading. Matthew places Satan's offer of the kingdoms of the world third, and Ellen White follows that order in her discussion of Christ's temptations in the wilderness in her book *The Desire of Ages*. However, Luke presents Satan's offer as the second temptation.

5. For this discussion, I am indebted to Kim Johnson's thorough review of the final events in Christ's life—Gethsemane to the cross—as he recounts them in his book *The Gift* (Pacific Press®, 2000).

6. *The Desire of Ages*, 715.

7. The nails were almost certainly driven through the upper part of His wrists rather than through the palms, as is typically portrayed in illustrations of the Crucifixion. Ac-cording to the dictionary, the hand includes the wrist.

8. Kim Johnson, *The Gift* (Nampa, Idaho: Pacific Press®, 2000), 55.

9. Ibid., 47, italics in the original.

10. *The Desire of Ages*, 756.

11. Genesis 10 lists the nations that were formed after the Flood. Thus, Daniel is telling us that the world's final conflict will be the worst time of distress since the Flood.

12. *The Great Controversy*, 622.

13. In His famous sermon on signs of the end, Jesus said the coming time of distress will be so severe that if God didn't cut it short, " 'no one would survive' " (Matthew 24:21, 22)—that is, the human race would become the next extinct species.

14. *The Antichrist and the New World Order* may be out of print by the time you read this book.

15. You may also find my book *How to Prepare for the Coming Global Crisis: A Spiritual Survival Guide* to be helpful. Only two chapters deal with the final crisis. The rest of the book is about how to prepare for the crisis.

16. I have some concerns about Ed Reid's time-setting tendency, but in most other ways his books are helpful in understanding what lies ahead and how to prepare for it.

17. We should not understand Ellen White's words "*at* the close of probation" to mean that the "great final test" will happen simultaneously with the close of probation, because if it did it would not be a test. It must obviously occur enough prior to the close of probation that people will have time to decide one way or the other. Her point is that we must be preparing for the crisis and for the close of probation now, because it will be too late to prepare for the close of probation when the crisis comes.

18. *Christ's Object Lessons*, 412.

19. I wrote *Conquering the Dragon Within* for Adventist readers. However, since *The Coming Global Crisis* was the missionary book of the year (also called the sharing book of the year) for 2001, I wrote it with a secular, non-Adventist audience in mind.

20. I am aware that some in the Adventist Church consider the term *righteousness by faith* to be synonymous with *justification* and thus to exclude *sanctification*. This is obviously not the place to debate that issue. I am including both *justification* and *sanctification* under the general term *righteousness by faith* for practical reasons, not because I am taking a particular side in this debate.

21. *Steps to Christ*, 62.

22. In the Bible, *sanctification* means "set apart for a special, holy use." However, John Wesley used *sanctification* to refer to growth in obedience, and Adventists generally use the term in the same way, as have numerous other denominations that followed in the Wesleyan tradition, such as the Methodists, the Nazarenes, and the various Pentecostal groups.

23. *The Great Controversy*, 616.

24. Ibid., 613, italics added.

End-time
Perfection

On September 4, 1999, I received the following email from a former Seventh-day Adventist pastor who is now serving in a church of another denomination:

> After reading Clifford Goldstein's article "When God Sorts Out His Own," I was pleased to see that some in the Adventist Church have finally come to the conclusion that it is by grace we are saved and not by works.
>
> I was also pleased to see that many of the fine writers for your magazine are using the Scriptures as their source of reference rather than Ellen White. This deeply pleases me and many other persons who have left the Adventist denomination years ago because of the overkill counsel by Ellen White espoused in many pulpits that we were to become "perfect" prior to Christ's second coming. That doctrine drove many of us away after twenty or thirty years of struggling to do just that. NEVER being able to even come close, we thought we were failures, and walked away.
>
> Although no longer an Adventist, I am saved, filled with the Holy Spirit, and am joyfully awaiting the return of my Lord.

Contrast that email message with another that I received on March 28, 2000:

Having just the experience and the knowledge of justification will never bring Christ's physical return. There has to be a body of sanctified believers, bond servants of God, dressed in white, that serve Him day and night. I left the church because I felt that most Adventists needed Adventism more than they needed Christ, and I was one of them. Living a luke-warm spiritual life. Oh well, I could go on and on. I do apologize if I sounded critical. I just get frustrated with something God has placed heavily on my heart and people are quite content as they are.

Each of these individuals left the Adventist Church for the same reason, but also for opposite reasons. In each case, the immediate cause of their departure was the Adventist teaching about end-time perfection. But it's the differences that I want you to notice.

The first person—the former Adventist pastor—believed the Church's teaching about end-time perfection and struggled for twenty or thirty years to be perfect, but never came even close. He finally got so frustrated from trying and failing that he left. Now, having discovered the biblical teaching about God's grace, he's given up the teaching about end-time perfection.

The second person also believed the Church's teaching about end-time perfection—and obviously still does. He left the Church because no one else was interested in striving for that perfection. They're "living a luke-warm spiritual life," he said, "quite content as they are."

The first person left because *he* couldn't achieve perfection, the second because *no one else* was trying to reach perfection. The first person eventually gave up his belief in end-time perfection. The second person still believes it.

Where did these people come up with this idea about end-time perfection that caused them to leave the Adventist Church? The former pastor said he got it from Ellen White, and I suspect the second writer was also strongly influenced by what she said. But is the idea of end-time perfection, that they got from Ellen White, also biblical? Some people (probably including our first letter writer) would say No. But do they understand her correctly? Even more importantly, have *we* understood her correctly? It's essential that we find the answers to these questions in order to have a correct understanding about end-time perfection.

Sinless perfection

One of the most common views of perfection among Adventists is reflected in the two letters I shared with you earlier. I'm tempted to call

171

this the "traditional" view because it's had such widespread acceptance among us for such a long time—at least one hundred years. According to this explanation, God's people must be sinlessly perfect in order to live successfully through the time of trouble after the close of probation. This idea is derived from statements by Ellen White such as the following, which I quoted in the previous chapter:

> Those who are living upon the earth when the intercession of Christ shall cease in the sanctuary above are to stand in the sight of a holy God without a mediator. Their robes must be spotless, their characters must be purified from sin by the blood of sprinkling. Through the grace of God and their own diligent effort they must be conquerors in the battle with evil. While the investigative judgment is going forward in heaven, while the sins of penitent believers are being removed from the sanctuary, there is to be a special work of purification, of putting away of sin, among God's people upon earth.[1]

Ellen White made another statement in *The Great Controversy*, this one from the chapter "The Time of Trouble," that also is frequently used by those who advocate sinless end-time perfection:

> Now, while our great High Priest is making the atonement for us, we should seek to become perfect in Christ. Not even by a thought could our Saviour be brought to yield to the power of temptation. Satan finds in human hearts some point where he can gain a foothold; some sinful desire is cherished, by means of which his temptations assert their power. But Christ declared of Himself: "The prince of this world cometh, and hath nothing in Me." John 14:30. Satan could find nothing in the Son of God that would enable him to gain the victory. He had kept His Father's commandments, and there was no sin in Him that Satan could use to his advantage. This is the condition in which those must be found who shall stand in the time of trouble.[2]

Another statement that is frequently used in support of sinless end-time perfection is the following:

> When the character of Christ shall be perfectly reproduced in His people, then He will come to claim them as His own.[3]

Traditionally, this statement has been understood to mean that Jesus can't return until His people have developed a character like Christ's. And since Jesus was without sin,[4] His people obviously must also be sinless in order to have perfect reproductions of His character.

Is it biblical?

Adventists claim to base all their teachings on the Bible. Ellen White may confirm these teachings once we've developed them, and she may also expand on them, but the basic teaching must be biblical. As significant as our traditional teaching about end-time perfection is, we need to ask: Is it biblical? Revelation 6:12-16 describes the wicked crying for the rocks and the mountains to fall on them at the second coming of Christ, and it concludes with the words " 'For the great day of their wrath has come, and *who can stand?' "* (italics added). Chapter 7:1-4 follows immediately with what is surely John's answer to the question: The 144,000 can stand because they have received the seal of God in their foreheads.

The 144,000 are further described in chapter 14:1-5, and here the statement is made that "they follow the Lamb wherever he goes. . . . No lie was found in their mouths; *they are blameless"* (italics added).[5]

From the evidence we have examined thus far, we can safely say that both Scripture and Ellen White affirm that, at the very least, God's people who live through the end time must reach a very high level of character development. The Bible describes them as "blameless," and Ellen White uses expressions such as "their robes must be spotless"; "their characters must be purified from sin"; "they must be conquerors in the battle with evil." She also says there was nothing in Jesus that Satan could use to his advantage and that "this is the condition in which those must be found who shall stand in the time of trouble." We may disagree over exactly what perfection means, but the inspired evidence leaves us in no doubt that those who live during the end time must attain to it, whatever it is.

Other definitions of perfection

Theologians generally define perfection in one of three ways. The first is sinless perfection, which we just reviewed. The others are "maturity" and "the robe of Christ's righteousness."

Maturity. Usually, when the Bible speaks of perfection for Christians it has in mind maturity. For example, in Philippians 3:12-14 Paul says that he is not already perfect, but forgetting what is behind he presses on toward the goal "to win the prize for which God has called me heavenward in Christ Jesus." Then in verse 15 he urges each of his readers to do the same. Here is how his advice reads in the King James Version and in the New International Version:

King James Version
"Let us therefore, as many as be *perfect,* be thus minded" (italics added).

New International Version
"All of us who are *mature* should take such a view of things" (italics added).

A similar example is found in Ephesians 4:11-13. In verse 11 Paul mentions several spiritual gifts—apostles, prophets, pastors, and teachers. In verses 12 and 13 he explains the purpose of these gifts: to build up the body of Christ "until." It's in this word "until" that we find, again, the two ways of understanding perfection:

King James Version
"Till we all come in the unity of the faith, and of the knowledge of the Son of God, unto a *perfect* man, unto the measure of the stature of the fulness of Christ" (italics added).

New International Version
"Until we all reach unity in the faith and in the knowledge of the Son of God and become *mature,* attaining to the whole measure of the fulness of Christ" (italics added).

Sinless perfection obviously means coming to the point in our Christian experience that we no longer sin, and this must include both overcoming all sinful deeds and also having sinless minds and hearts. The mature Christian, on the other hand, is not necessarily sinless. While he won't be sinning carelessly and continually, he may sin on occasion, either in deed or in thought.

"The Robe of Christ's righteousness." Another biblical definition of perfection is in the sense of Christ's perfection that is attributed to us as a gift through justification. Ellen White says, for example, that if you accept Jesus as your Savior, "Christ's character stands in place of your character, and you are accepted before God just as if you had not sinned."[6] We sometimes speak of this perfection as "being covered with the robe of Christ's righteousness."

So how should we think of the perfection we will need in order to stand through the time of trouble without a Mediator in the heavenly sanctuary? Is it "the robe of Christ's righteousness" covering our character defects? Is it maturity? Or is it sinlessness?

Surely after the close of probation we will continue to be covered with the robe of Christ's righteousness! And I think we can all agree that end-time Christians will be very mature spiritually. So the question is whether they will be sinless. The idea that they will be sinless is quite strongly rooted in Adventist thinking. And I frankly don't have a problem with the idea that it's *possible* for human beings to be so totally devoted to Christ that they come to the place of having overcome all sin. Nor do I have a problem with the idea that this is the level of perfection that God wants His end-time people to reach. That conclusion, as I pointed out earlier, has strong support in both the Bible and the writings of Ellen White.

A balanced view of perfection

However, having said that victory over all sin is *possible* and perhaps *necessary* for God's end-time people, I must also hasten to point out a couple of major problems that this idea easily creates. First, the concept of end-time perfection can be very frightening to sinners this side of the close of probation who are struggling desperately with character defects that seem to them impossible to overcome. And second, the idea of end-time perfection easily lends itself to a very unhealthy perfectionism and fanaticism. Thus, I would like to add a number of qualifications that can help us to think about end-time perfection in a rational and balanced way rather than in a fearful and extremist way.

Evidence on the other side of the question. I just cited several statements from both the Bible and Ellen White supporting the idea of sinless end-time perfection. However, Ellen White also makes a statement in her chapter "The Time of Trouble" in *The Great Controversy* that suggests that God's people may not be entirely sinless during that time:

> God's love for his children during the period of their severest trial is as strong and tender as in the days of their sunniest prosperity; but it is needful for them to be placed in the furnace of fire; *their earthliness must be consumed* that the image of Christ may be perfectly reflected.[7]

A couple of points need to be noted in this statement. First, is the fact that Ellen White says "their earthliness must be consumed." Obviously, some form of imperfection will remain in God's people after the close of probation that must be removed during the time of trouble. The advocates of sinless perfection argue that earthliness does not mean sinful imperfection. That's an admirable "explanation" for those who need God's people to be sinless after the close of probation, but that's about as far as we can carry it. We really do not know enough about the meaning of either "earthliness" or "sinfulness" to distinguish between them in a way that would make sense.

A second consideration is Ellen White's statement that "their earthliness must be consumed *that the image of Christ may be perfectly reflected.*" Earlier in this chapter I shared with you a statement by Ellen White that some Adventists use to support the idea of sinless end-time perfection: "When the character of Christ shall be perfectly reproduced in His people, then He will come to claim them as His own."[8] While the wording in *The Great Controversy* is different, the idea of the image of Christ being "perfectly reflected" is quite similar to the idea in *Christ's Object Lessons* that "the character of Christ" must be "perfectly reproduced in His people." If this comparison is correct, then some of the work of perfection that is necessary to bring God's people to the point of perfectly reflecting His character or His image will go on during the time of trouble. The trials that God's people experience during the time of trouble will be a necessary part of the preparation they must have in order that Christ can "come to claim them as His own."

Again, one might argue that this part of the preparation of God's people for His return won't involve the removal of sinfulness. But I would respond again that the primary usefulness of such an argument is in upholding a particular theology of end-time sinlessness for those who need it. We don't understand the differences between sinful and nonsinful character traits enough for the distinction to be meaningful.

The subtlety of sin. A second consideration we need to keep in mind before we rush to adopt a theology of sinlessness for God's end-time people is the difficulty of defining sin and sinlessness. If we adopt an exclusively behavioral definition of sin—that sin is the wrong things we *do*—then sinlessness may not be too hard to define or to recognize. That was the definition of sin in the mind of the Pharisee who prayed " ' "God, I thank you that I am not like other men" ' " (Luke 18:11). This man fasted twice a week and paid tithe, and he didn't rob or commit adultery. That was his notion of sinlessness. I'm sure this is the definition of sin in the mind of the occasional person we hear about who claims not to have sinned in six months.

It goes without saying, of course, that wrong behavior is sin. However, all sin arises out of our sinful hearts, out of character defects that take time—often a very long time—to correct. The problem with sin is not so much with our behavior as with our inner sinfulness. After giving a long list of sins, Jesus said, " 'All these evils come from *inside* and make a man "unclean" ' " (Mark 7:23, italics added). Sinlessness obviously has to do with the condition of our mind and heart, with our defective and impure desires and motives: Pride, fear, anger,[9] and selfishness, to name a few.

I'm aware of some deeply ingrained and unhealthy emotions within myself, and I know that they sometimes prompt me to do wrong things. And any sinless perfection that may be required of God's people in order to live without a Mediator after the close of probation will have to include perfection of the mind and heart, not just of behavior. This is the perfection we must be developing today. And for that we need God to point out to us our defects of character, our sins of the heart. The good news is that this help is available, as the following statement by Ellen White shows:

> To men whom God designs shall fill responsible positions, He in mercy reveals hidden defects, that they may look within and examine critically the complicated *emotions* and *exercises of their own hearts,* and detect that which is wrong. The Lord in His providence brings men where He can test their *moral* powers and reveal their *motives* of action. God would have His servants become acquainted with the *moral* machinery of their own *hearts.*[10]

I'm glad that God is continually trying to reveal my wrong motives to me, and I'm grateful for those times when I've actually recognized some of them so that I could cooperate with Him in ridding my life of them. I think it goes without saying that I can't be sinless until they're all gone.

But I do not understand enough about my mind and heart to ever be able to say that I have no wrong motives.

That's the subtlety of sin. And my point is that we really cannot define sinless perfection in such a way that we can recognize it in either ourselves or anyone else. We will never know when we have reached sinless perfection at the level of our minds and emotions. That's why John said "If we claim to be without sin, we deceive ourselves and the truth is not in us" (1 John 1:8). So if we will never *know* when we are sinlessly perfect and if we can never *claim* to be sinlessly perfect, what's the point of making a huge issue out of end-time sinless perfection?

Allow me to elaborate with a parable. One day I'm sitting in my living room watching the news, and the TV anchor reports a strange new skin disease that's spreading rapidly to people all over the world. While at the present time it's not life-threatening, it has scientists and health experts very worried. They're frantically searching for a cure that can stop its advance. Something clicks in my mind at that point. I remember that the first plague is a skin disease—the Bible calls it "ugly and painful sores"—that afflicts those who have received the mark of the beast. I know, of course, that probation will close before the plagues begin to fall, and the unsettling thought crosses my mind that maybe probation has closed!

Just then there's a knock at my door, and when I open it, my friend Bill is standing there. I invite him in, and after we're both comfortably seated we start talking about the news. I mention my question about the close of probation, and Bill says "You know, I've been wondering the same thing." Then Bill turns to me and says, "Do you feel *good enough* for the close of probation?"

What do think my response will be? Will I clench my fists and pump my arms in the air and say, "Yes! I'm perfect! I'm ready for the close of probation!"

Is that what I'll say?

Of course not!

Whether God has in mind the mature kind of perfection for His end-time people or the sinless variety *really doesn't matter,* because either way, you and I won't know we've got it, and we will never be able to claim it. So, I repeat, why make an issue out of it? What's the point of worrying about it?

Perfection doesn't come by striving for it. I know that in 1 Corinthians 9:25 Paul says we must strive for victory over temptation. Nevertheless, it's also true that perfection doesn't come by striving for it. I realize that this statement may surprise and perhaps offend those who make a major issue out of end-time perfection. After all, how are we going to achieve even the "mature" definition of perfection, to say nothing of the "sinless" definition, if we don't strive for it?

True enough. But allow me to use an analogy. The ultimate goal of all human beings is happiness. "But our ultimate goal should be to know Jesus," you say. True enough again, but that's simply stating where the most genuine happiness is to be found. It doesn't do away with the fact that our ultimate goal as humans is to be happy. It's our unhappiness that often drives us to Jesus as the Source of happiness.

And I propose that happiness doesn't come by striving for it. The most miserable people are often those who are striving the most diligently to be happy. Happiness comes by forgetting about happiness and doing things that lead to happiness—things like serving others, working hard at a project we enjoy, or taking time out for recreation and even an occasional bit of wholesome entertainment. Happiness is most easily achieved as a by-product of other activities rather than as an end in itself.

In the same way I propose that perfection is a by-product. We achieve it, not by striving for it as such, but by doing other things that develop it within our minds and hearts. Thus, while theologically I can grant the possibility of sinless end-time perfection for God's people, an overemphasis on that idea leads *very easily* to an unhealthy striving for perfection for its own sake that leaves Christians nervous and afraid of their standing with God. The word for this is perfection*ism*. I'm all for perfection. I'm totally opposed to perfection*ism.*

Jesus will get me there. As I pointed out earlier, I don't know what perfection is in any way that would make it possible for me to recognize it within myself or anyone else, so why worry about it? It's a waste of time to make too much of an issue over end-time perfection, and it's a waste of emotional and spiritual energy to worry about whether "I'm good enough" for the close of probation.

The truth is that Jesus *will* know—and He and God are the *only* Ones who will know—when I'm ready for the close of probation. I don't know whether the "sinless" definition of perfection is what God is looking for in my life before probation closes or whether the "maturity" definition will be adequate. But I know this: If I stay close to Jesus and, to the best of my ability, cooperate daily with Him in my character development, He'll get me as good as I need to be for the close of probation, and He promises to do it before probation closes. And that's really all I need to know.

Thus, the basic issue for me isn't perfection or striving for perfection. The basic issue is faith—trusting Jesus to be even more concerned about my preparation for the close of probation and the time of trouble than I am. And the basic issue is striving each day to overcome the character deficiencies He brings to my attention. (I do believe in striving against sin!) The kind of perfection I'll need in order to live through the time of trouble without a Mediator is Jesus' problem. When I stay close to Him and cooperate with Him in my character development, I can trust that He'll get me ready with whatever definition He has in mind.

And that sure does relieve me of a lot of worry about whether I'm "good enough" for the close of probation!

---

1. *The Great Controversy*, 425.
2. Ibid., 623.

3. *Christ's Object Lessons*, 69.

4. See for example 1 John 3:5; John 8:46. Ellen White wrote "Never, in any way, leave the slightest impression upon human minds that a taint of, or inclination to corruption rested upon Christ, or that He in any way yielded to corruption. He was tempted in all points like as man is tempted, yet He is called that holy thing. It is a mystery that is left unexplained to mortals that Christ could be tempted in all points like as we are, and yet be without sin" (Baker Letter, published in *Manuscript Releases*, 13:19).

5. It could, with some merit, be argued that the "blameless" perfection ascribed to the 144,000 in chapter 14 is after they get to heaven, since John's vision of them in this chapter shows them in heaven, not on earth.

6. *Steps to Christ*, 62.

7. *The Great Controversy*, 621, italics added.

8. *Christ's Object Lessons*, 69.

9. I don't mean that all fear and anger are wrong. They do have their place in our lives, but we easily misuse them in sinful ways.

10. *Counsels to the Church*, 54, 55, italics added.

the Mission of God's End-Time People

the
Final Generation

Closely related to the issue of end-time perfection that we discussed in the previous chapter is a variation on that theme that I call "the final generation theology." This concept probably began with A. T. Jones and E. J. Waggoner, who were two of the principle players at the 1888 General Conference session. However, its chief proponent since then was M. L. Andreasen, who developed the theory much beyond the concepts of Jones and Waggoner. Andreasen was for many years one of our most respected and brilliant theologians. During his ministerial career he was, among other things, the president of two conferences, the president of Union College, and a professor at the Adventist Theological Seminary in Washington, D. C. from 1938 to 1949.

Dr. Andreasen wrote a book titled *The Sanctuary Service*, in one chapter of which he expounded at length on his theology of the final generation. The title of the chapter, appropriately enough, is "The Last Generation."[1] This final-generation theology has had a significant reception, especially among conservative Adventists. However, I have serious reservations about it, and I will explain why in this chapter. While a number of Adventist students of prophecy have written on the final-generation theology since 1950, I will restrict my comments to Andreasen's explanation of it in *The Sanctuary Service*. I will begin with a brief summary of his understanding of the final generation, and then I will elaborate on it with quotations from his book and my comments.

Andreasen proposed that God has been waiting 6,000 years for a community of saints who can demonstrate to the universe that His law can be kept by the very weakest human being, and He will finally achieve that objective in the final generation. And this demonstration must be made before Jesus can return, because should it not be made, Satan would be proven correct in his claim that God's law cannot be kept, and he would emerge victorious in the great controversy. However, God is fitting up a people—the 144,000—to be sinlessly perfect ambassadors for Him during the time of trouble. By their perfect lives during the most intense time of distress the world has ever known, they will prove that God's law *can* be kept. Thus, they will disprove Satan's claim and thereby defeat him. This will vindicate God, and then Jesus can come. The opening paragraph of Andreasen's chapter "The Last Generation" introduces this view:

> The final demonstration of what the gospel can do in and for humanity is still in the future. Christ showed the way. He took a human body, and in that body demonstrated the power of God. Men are to follow His example and prove that what God did in Christ, He can do in every human being who submits to Him. The world is awaiting this demonstration. (Rom. 8:19.) When it has been accomplished, the end will come. God will have fulfilled His plan. He will have shown Himself true and Satan a liar. His government will stand vindicated.[2]

Here are two other statements in which Andreasen made a similar point:

> Thus it shall be with the last generation of men living on the earth. Through them God's final demonstration of what He can do with humanity will be given. He will take the weakest of the weak, those bearing the sins of their forefathers, and in them show the power of God. They will be subjected to every temptation, but they will not yield. They will demonstrate that it is possible to live without sin—the very demonstration for which the world has been looking and for which God has been preparing. It will become evident to all that the gospel really can save to the uttermost. God is found true in His sayings.[3]

> God will have in the last days a remnant, a "little flock," in and through whom He will give to the universe a demonstration of His

love, His power, His justice, which, if we exempt Christ's godly life on earth and His supreme sacrifice on Calvary, will be the most sweeping and conclusive demonstration of all the ages of what God can do in men.[4]

In the first statement Andreasen said that "men are to follow His [Christ's] example and prove that what God did in Christ, He can do in every human being who submits to Him"; and in the second statement he said that this final generation "will be the most sweeping and conclusive demonstration of all the ages [apart from Jesus' life and death] of what God can do in men." I don't have a problem with the statement that God wants to prove that He can do through every human being who submits to Him what He did in Christ, namely, bring total victory over sin. I do have a problem with the idea that God will not achieve this in any human being until the final generation that lives after the close of probation. While God alone knows who they are, there have almost certainly been many examples of God working with this kind of power in human lives during the millenniums of Judeo-Christian history.

Andreasen also said that "the world is awaiting this demonstration." I don't think so, if by "the world," we are to understand nonbelievers. The world *hates* the perfection of believers. John said that Cain killed his brother Abel "because his [Cain's] own actions were evil and his brother's were righteous" (1 John 3:12). Andreasen refers to Romans 8:19 to support his view that "the world is awaiting this demonstration," but that verse says only that "the creation waits in eager expectation for the sons of God to be revealed." Paul understood "sons of God" to be all Christians, not just the final generation of saints who achieve sinless perfection.

In the second statement above, Andreasen said that through this final generation of saints "it will become evident to all that the gospel really can save to the uttermost. God is found true in His sayings." Andreasen alludes here to Hebrews 7:25, which says that Jesus is "able also to save them to the uttermost that come unto God by him" (KJV). However, even a casual reading of Hebrews makes it clear that *every* Christian in *every* generation is a demonstration that God is able to save to the uttermost those who come to Him through Christ.

Andreasen claims that it is up to the final generation to defeat Satan. Here is what he says:

In the last generation God is vindicated and *Satan defeated*.[5]

[Satan] had failed in his conflict with Christ, but he might yet succeed with men. So he went to "make war with the remnant of her seed, which keep the commandments of God, and have the testimony of Jesus Christ." Rev. 12:17. *If he could overcome them he might not be defeated*.[6]

Through the last generation of saints God stands finally vindicated. *Through them He defeats Satan and wins His case.* They form a vital part of the plan of God.[7]

I have a *major* problem with the idea that God will not defeat Satan until the final generation demonstrates its loyalty to His law. *Jesus already defeated Satan by His life and by His death!* John proclaimed:

"Now have come the salvation and the power and the kingdom of our God and the authority of his Christ. For the accuser of our brothers, who accuses them before our God day and night *has been hurled down*" (Revelation 12:10, italics added).

Satan was defeated at the cross. It was *Jesus'* perfect life that defeated Satan once and for all. He doesn't need to be defeated again by the final generation. *Jesus* demonstrated that God's law can be kept, and once He made that demonstration the battle was won. *Jesus* demonstrated Satan's claims to be false. There's nothing left for the final generation to prove. *Jesus* vindicated God. The final generation doesn't have to.

Or, perhaps it would be more correct to say that *every generation of saints vindicates God before the universe.* Paul said that "through the church,"—the saints in his day, not just those in the final generation— "the manifold wisdom of God [is] made known to the rulers and authorities in the heavenly realms" (Ephesians 3:10). He said that "we"— he and his fellow apostles—"have been made a spectacle to the whole universe, to angels as well as to men" (1 Corinthians 4:9). Every generation of Christians is a demonstration to the universe of what the gospel can do in human hearts. However, note that neither of the two verses I just quoted says that we humans vindicate God. While there may be some limited ways in which our lives can do that, the *only* Person who vindicated God for the purpose of bringing the plan of salvation to a close was Jesus.

The idea that Satan will not be defeated until the final generation proves its loyalty to God by perfect obedience to His law puts the burden on sinful human beings to complete the plan of salvation, and *I have a huge problem with that idea!* Jesus is the *only* One on whom God placed the responsibility to defeat Satan. Jesus' righteousness is the *only* righteousness and His obedience is the *only* obedience that could defeat Satan. To say that God must await the righteousness of the final generation to defeat Satan is to make *our* righteousness effective in bringing the plan of salvation to a final conclusion, and *that simply cannot be true.* Jesus' righteousness is the only righteousness that could accomplish that. If God must await the righteousness of the final generation to defeat Satan and complete the plan of salvation, then Jesus' life and death were inadequate, and again, *that simply cannot be true.*

Finally, Andreasen suggests that after the close of probation the Holy Spirit will be removed from God's people, and they will have to battle the powers of darkness on their own:

> God's people in the last days will pass through an experience similar to Job's. They will be tested as he was; they will have every earthly stay removed; Satan will be given permission to torment them. In addition to this the Spirit of God will be withdrawn from the earth, and the protection of earthly governments removed. God's people will be left alone to battle with the powers of darkness.[8]

The idea that after the close of probation God will remove His Spirit from His people, leaving them to battle Satan alone, is *simply not true.* It is the wicked who will suffer the loss of His presence. A statement by Ellen White that I quoted in a previous chapter is worth repeating here:

> When He [Christ] leaves the sanctuary, darkness covers the inhabitants of the earth. In that fearful time the righteous must live in the sight of a holy God without an intercessor. *The restraint which has been upon the wicked is removed,* and Satan has entire control of the finally impenitent. . . . *The Spirit of God, persistently resisted, has been at last withdrawn.*[9]

It is strange theology indeed that suggests on the one hand that victory over sin is impossible without the aid of the Holy Spirit and on the other hand that the final generation must live perfect lives *without* the presence of the Spirit!

In preparing this chapter, I took the time to read carefully through Ellen White's entire chapter in *The Great Controversy* on "The Time of Trouble." This chapter covers the whole period during which Andreasen's final generation of saints will live; and, with the exception of the first page of the following chapter, it is the only one in the entire book that deals with any part of this time. I read this chapter very carefully, but I did not find the faintest suggestion that God's people who live during the time of trouble must vindicate God, must defeat Satan, or must make a demonstration of perfect obedience to the universe. There is not the slightest hint that God is waiting on them to accomplish anything to bring the plan of salvation or the great controversy to a close. The emphasis, rather, is their total dependence on God to make it through that fearful time without yielding their faith.

Please do not misunderstand me. I believe that during the time of trouble God's people will be a demonstration to the universe of what God can accomplish in the lives of those who surrender fully to Him. But this has been true of God's people in all ages. While neither the Bible nor Ellen White say so, it's possible that God's people during the time of trouble will in some way be a *unique* demonstration to the universe, though I don't know what that might be. My objection to Andreasen's theology is the idea that God is in any way depending on the sinless witness of that generation to vindicate God, defeat Satan, and bring the conflict between good and evil to a final close. Jesus is the only One who could have accomplished all that, and once He did it, there's nothing left for any other generation to do.

I will also point out several other problems I see with Andreasen's final-generation theology. First, if God is waiting for the final generation to prove that God's law can be kept, then Jesus failed to prove the point 2,000 years ago. On the other hand, if Jesus proved the point, then there's nothing left for a final generation to prove.

Furthermore, God's people will be *sealed* after the close of probation. While I don't understand all that this implies, it apparently closes up their characters in such a way that they cannot be changed and they will not sin. That being the case, how can it be said that God has been waiting thousands of years for a generation of saints to demonstrate a point that only the final generation will have the "sealing" experience to demonstrate? Will the final generation have an experience that goes beyond what Jesus had? I hardly think so! They will no doubt have a relationship with God that is *like* the relationship Jesus had with His Father, but the sealing work will simply make that experience permanent in their lives. It won't give them an experience beyond what Jesus had.

Dr. Andreasen was probably introduced to his final-generation theology through his reading of Jones and Waggoner, or perhaps through hearing them speak, since he was a contemporary of theirs during his early life. However, I suspect that certain statements about perfection in the writings of Ellen White together with the biblical evidence about the 144,000 formed the foundation on which he built his theology. Unfortunately, without realizing it, I'm sure, he extrapolated far beyond what the inspired evidence actually allows.

That's why it's so important that we think very carefully about the end time. We must be sure that all our conclusions are based on inspired evidence and not what we read *into* the inspired evidence, which its language does not actually *support*. There's a great tendency for Christians who are anxious for Jesus to come to do that. *We must guard against this temptation,* for if we don't, we can be led astray without even realizing it. The deceptions of the end time will be so subtle that only by God's Word will we be able to distinguish the counterfeit from the true.[10] But we must be sure the Word actually says what we think it says. Satan will have plenty of false theories to attract those who are given more to interpreting the Bible according to what they *want* it to say than to examining each word carefully for what it *actually* says. Now is the time when we must learn to do this kind of careful study of both the Bible and Ellen White. Now is the time to be absolutely certain that every one of our beliefs has a firm basis in the inspired evidence.

My conclusions in this chapter differ sharply from those of Dr. Andreasen. I first went to the seminary ten years after he retired, so I never had the privilege of meeting him. However, I know that he was a very respected theologian in the Adventist Church. I also know that he was a sincere Christian, and I am certain that for the most part his doctrinal understandings were correct. I want to make it clear that in disagreeing with him in this chapter it has not been my intention in any way to malign his character. We all have incorrect doctrinal ideas. I'm sure I have mine, which a later generation may disagree with as strongly as I have disagreed with Dr. Andreasen. Fortunately, God saves us in spite of our doctrinal misconceptions. I expect to meet Dr. Andreasen in the kingdom someday, and I hope to have the privilege of spending many hours with him studying more deeply into God's marvelous plan to save sinners.

1. M. L. Andreasen, *The Sanctuary Service* (Washington, D. C.: Review and Herald, 1947), 299-321.

2. Ibid., 299.

3. Ibid., 302.

4. Ibid., 303.

5. Ibid., 303, 304, italics added.

6. Ibid., 310, italics added.

7. Ibid., 319, italics added.

8. Ibid., 314, 315.

9. *The Great Controversy*, 614, italics added.

10. Ibid., 593.

the
Remnant

One of the more fascinating aspects of my job as editor of *Signs of the Times*® is reading the letters to the editor that people send. I learn all kinds of things about people's attitudes and how they think on a variety of theological and spiritual topics. I've already shared several of these letters in this book. Here are several paragraphs from an undated letter that I received in late 1999 or early 2000:

> The vast majority of Christians, including most Seventh-day Adventists, perceive D. L. Moody, who was active from 1873 until his death in 1899, to be a great man of God. This perception is erroneous. D. L. Moody was not of God. That is not to say that he was a bad man with evil motives. I am simply saying that he was not a messenger of God. He was a counterfeit.
>
> It is not for us to judge D. L. Moody's character, his motives, or his heart. The Lord will take care of that. Our role is to try the spirits (teachings) to see whether or not they are of God. We are commanded to do this. We should obey.
>
> Never at any time did Moody correctly preach the Adventist doctrine of the Sabbath, the state of the dead, the sanctuary, the judgment, or the Spirit of prophecy. He was a rejecter of these truths.
>
> If we claim that Moody was of God, then what is to prevent

us from claiming that the yet future antichrist, who will look and act like Jesus, is also of God? The Lord does not call us out of Babylon and then turn right around and raise up another messenger from out of the midst of Babylon that we are supposed to listen to. God simply does not work that way. Those who believe that Moody was a man of God are at the very least, already partially deceived.

My correspondent said that Moody "was not a messenger of God," suggesting that whatever preaching he may have done was of no value. If not a false prophet, Moody was at least an irrelevant prophet.

So what do you think? During the years of his ministry, was Moody a genuine servant of God, doing God's work as he understood it? Or was he a counterfeit who only claimed to lead people to Christ but never really did and whose work contributed nothing toward building up God's kingdom on the earth? If the person who wrote that letter is right, then neither has God worked through Billy Graham to win souls for His kingdom, nor is He working through any other Protestant minister or lay person other than Seventh-day Adventists.

I happen to disagree strongly with that letter. There is no doubt in my mind that God *did* use Dwight Moody, and more recently He *has* used Billy Graham and a host of other Protestants to advance His kingdom on the earth. Who's to say that even a Catholic can't lead someone to enough of an understanding of the plan of salvation that God can use this knowledge to justify that person and give him or her the new birth? Ellen White did say, after all, that "there are real Christians in the Roman Catholic communion."[1]

My correspondent said "God simply does not work that way," meaning that God does not work through people who do not preach the Sabbath, the state of the dead, and other teachings that are important to Seventh-day Adventists. With all due respect, I must disagree. God often works in ways that seem very strange to us. How can we say that "God never works that way"? Though he did not spell it out in words, the writer of that letter said a *lot* about how he thinks of himself and his Seventh-day Adventist Church. And his ideas are the result of a particular interpretation of what it means to be "the remnant."

I'm sure you are aware that Adventists have historically thought of themselves as "the remnant." Seventh-day Adventists today hold at least three views of what it means to be the remnant. The first is that God raised up our Church to fulfill a unique mission, but we are not the only Christians He is using to accomplish His work on the earth. I think I'm safe in saying that the large majority of us believe this view of what it means to be the remnant. However, two other views exist—one at either extreme of this position. One is the view held by my correspondent, who believes that once God raised up *this* Church with *its* truths for the world, He cannot work through anyone else who does not proclaim all of these truths. At the other extreme are those who deny that the word *remnant* applies to Seventh-day Adventists in any special sense at all. We are arrogant to think of ourselves as "the remnant," say those who hold this view, because we are no different than any other denomination.

Obviously, it's important how we think of "the remnant"! So let's examine the two extremes.

The exclusive remnant

The individual who wrote the letter I just quoted thinks of himself and his church as the "exclusive remnant." As he put it, "The Lord does not call us out of Babylon and then turn right around and raise up another messenger from out of the midst of Babylon that we are supposed to listen to. *God simply does not work that way.*" According to this view, no one is doing God's work in the world except Seventh-day Adventists. No one else is preaching the gospel. No one else is winning souls. If they aren't teaching *our* truths, they aren't teaching *any* truth. A small but significant number of Seventh-day Adventists believe this. I know, because I hear from them now and then. And I disagree, for several reasons.

Where are God's people today? Ellen White said that "notwithstanding the spiritual darkness and alienation from God that exist in the churches which constitute Babylon, the great body of Christ's true followers are still to be found in their communion."[2] Please notice two things about this statement. First, "The great body of Christ's *true* followers" are found in the churches that we say constitute Babylon. Now if they are in Babylon, they obviously hold to some teachings that we would consider to be doctrinally incorrect. Nevertheless, they are genuine Christians, for that's what it means to be a *true* follower of Christ. And if they are true followers of Christ, then they have to be bearing a genuine witness for Jesus, because every true Christian does that, by the life he or she lives if in no other way. And a genuine witness for Jesus always results in genuine conversions to Him.

So if Dwight Moody was one of God's true followers in "Babylon," then regardless of his church affiliation, he bore a genuine witness for Jesus. His witness may not have had all the doctrinal refinements that ours has, but does that mean it was no witness at all? Are we prepared to say that God cannot use another Christian's testimony simply because that Christian happens not to agree with all our beliefs? For me, the answer to each of these questions is No!

What is "light"? John said that Jesus was "the true light that gives light to every man" (John 1:9). I understand this to mean that the Holy Spirit works on the heart of every human being. If that's true, then surely some of those human beings will respond to that light. This doesn't mean that everyone has the full-blown light of truth. Adventists are fond of thinking that we have "the light." I propose, however, that even our light is small compared to the total body of truth known to God. Furthermore, some of our own understandings of "truth" are very likely wrong. That surely was true earlier in our history, when a significant number of people in our Church, both leaders and lay persons, were Arians.[3] Does that mean God could not work through us until we gave up that false teaching? Of course not!

In a similar vein, Paul said that "when Gentiles, who do not have the law, do by nature things required by the law, . . . they show that the requirements of the law are written on their hearts" (Romans 2:14, 15). To have the requirements of the law on the heart means to be converted. Paul is telling us that people in his day who knew nothing of either the Jewish or the Christian religion could be converted. And what was true of his day surely is true of ours as well. So if even non-Christians can be converted, then it follows that even non-Christians can witness for God, albeit in only a very limited way. Surely, then, He can use the witness of Christians who don't understand everything we do.

I propose that God is happy to use every possible witness He can find. If it's primitive, *He'll use it.* If it's somewhat incorrect, *He'll use it.* If it can help people to a better understanding of truth than they had before, *He'll use it.* If it can lead people to accept Him and His plan of salvation, *He'll use it,* even if it's imperfect.

Paul's argument against the Jews

Those who claim that God can use only people who have the full light of truth need to read the second chapter of Romans, where Paul talks about the sins of the Jews:

> Now you, if you call yourself a Jew; if you rely on the law and brag about your relationship to God; if you know his will and approve of what is superior because you are instructed by

the law; if you are convinced that you are a guide for the blind, a light for those who are in the dark, an instructor of the foolish, a teacher of infants, because you have in the law the embodiment of knowledge and truth—you, then, who teach others, do you not teach yourself? (Romans 2:17-21).

The Jews at Paul's time believed they had "the truth," and because Gentiles didn't have the truth, they couldn't possibly have God's favor. Jews didn't have anything to *learn* from Gentiles. They were supposed to *teach* the Gentiles. Paul rebuked this attitude. Let's review his words again, with a few minor changes to apply them to ourselves:

> Now you, if you call yourself a Seventh-day Adventist; if you rely on the Spirit of Prophecy and brag about being the remnant; if you know the Sabbath and approve of health reform because you are instructed by the Spirit of Prophecy; if you are convinced that you are a guide for the blind, a light for those who are in the dark, an instructor of the foolish, a teacher of infants, because you have in the Sabbath and other doctrines the embodiment of knowledge and truth—you, then, who teach others, do you not teach yourself? (Romans 2:17-21).

This is a very accurate description of those who claim that none but Adventists are doing God's work.

Paul went on to point out that a mere knowledge of "the truth" and a mere proclamation of it are not enough. We must *experience* the truth. The truth must dwell in our hearts, not just in a list of twenty-seven fundamental beliefs. This is what Paul meant a few verses later when he said, "A man is not a Jew if he is only one outwardly, nor is circumcision merely outward and physical. No, a man is a Jew if he is one inwardly; and circumcision is circumcision of the heart, by the Spirit, not by the written code" (verses 28, 29). Then Paul said something that was utterly shocking to the Jews: "The one who is not circumcised physically and yet obeys the law will condemn you who, even though you have the written code and circumcision, are a lawbreaker" (verse 27).

The Jews, like some Seventh-day Adventists, believed that anyone who was not of their faith and who didn't adhere to their particular doctrines and lifestyle (laws) couldn't possibly have God's approval. But Paul insisted that Gentiles did *not* have to become Jewish proselytes and keep all the Jewish laws in order to be accepted by God. If their hearts were right, then even if they hadn't kept the law in the traditional Jewish sense, they were actually in a better position than the Jew who "kept" the law but did not have a heart that was right toward God. In fact, Paul went so far as to say that Jews who had the law were actually lawbreakers if their heart was not right. He would surely say also that we who have the Sabbath are law-breakers if our hearts are not right.

And if he were alive today, Paul would also surely say that a person doesn't have to become a Seventh-day Adventist to be accepted by God—or to work for God. The primary issue is whether the heart is right with God. If it is, then the fact that certain people do not understand or practice everything we do does not cause them to be outside of God's favor. And if they are within God's favor, then witnessing for Him is an obligation for them as much as it is for anyone. God does not say, "You can witness for Me only if you have all your theology straight." No one would witness for God, including Seventh-day Adventists, if that were the requirement for witnessing!

Before concluding this section on the arrogant remnant, I would like to share with you an example of this attitude. A number of years ago, I was on the board of a church that was entering upon a major building program. We decided to conduct a stewardship campaign, and we invited two professionals to make presentations. One was by an Adventist stewardship department director from another conference who had experienced some success in fund-raising projects for church building programs. The other was by a professional Christian, but non-Adventist, fund-raising organization.

After both individuals had made their presentations, the board met to decide which one to invite to assist us. I will never forget the comment of one older Adventist on the board who obviously favored inviting the Adventist representative from another conference. He said, "Why should we go to the Philistines for help?"

I felt extremely distressed by that statement, because it reveals the arrogant attitude that is so easy for Adventists to take toward Christians of other denominations. We need to be careful of the attitudes we express toward Christians who are not of our faith. The basic principle is respect. And I propose that we can't show that respect and at the same time call other Christians "Philistines," "heathens," or similar derogatory terms.

The nonremnant extreme

I hear the other extreme of "the remnant" debate from the more liberal spectrum of Adventism, some of whom would have us abandon the view that God has called our Church to carry out a unique work for Him in the closing days of earth's history. "Calling ourselves 'the remnant' is arrogant," they say. "We're no better than anyone else." I suspect this view is largely a reaction to the exclusive view of the remnant. The statement that Adventists are no better than anyone else is most certainly true! The problem with the arrogant view of the remnant is that in rejecting the exclusive view it throws out the whole concept of the remnant. Allow me to pose a few questions:

- Did God give Noah a unique call to build an ark? Yes. Was Noah aware of this call? Of course! Was it arrogant of him to say, "God called me to build an ark"? I think all of us, whatever spectrum of Adventism we identify with, would say, "Of course not!"
- Did God give Moses a unique call to lead His people out of Egypt? Yes. Was Moses aware of that call? Yes. Was it arrogant of Him to claim that God had given him this special call? No.
- Did God give John the Baptist a special call to prepare the way for the Messiah? Yes. Did John know that He had received this call? Yes. Was it arrogant of him to claim it? No.

Go through the Bible and name all the great worthies who were called by God to do a special work for Him: Abraham, Samuel, Elijah, Daniel, Paul, John, to name a few. The questions and the answers are all the same. From time-to-time God has called individuals to do a special work for Him. They knew it, and it wasn't arrogant of them to claim it. On occasion, God calls an entire group of people to carry on His work. The most obvious biblical example is the nation of Israel.

I do not have a problem with the idea that God called Seventh-day Adventists to do a special work for Him *so long as we respond to that call with humility.* The problem with the Jews at Christ's time was their assumption that the call to be God's *unique* people meant they were His *exclusive* people. And that's precisely the problem with the letter I shared with you at the beginning of this chapter. Though he does not say it in so many words, the person who wrote that letter claims that Adventists are God's exclusive people because we are supposedly the only ones God is willing to use to carry on His work in the earth. That's arrogant! If that's what is meant by our being "the remnant," then I must side with my liberal Adventist friends. However, I choose to avoid both extremes. I want to accept God's call to this Church with all the grace and humility the Holy Spirit can give me. And then I want to carry out the small piece of work He has given me to do with that attitude.

How should we think about the remnant?

In one of Ellen White's earliest visions, she was given a view of the remnant. In the vision she called them "the Advent people," since the idea of calling them "the remnant" was still future by a number of years. Even though she wrote this description of the remnant more than 150 years ago, it is still very applicable today:

> While I was praying at the family altar, the Holy Ghost fell upon me, and I seemed to be rising higher and higher, far above the dark world. I turned to look for the Advent people in the world, but could not find them, when a voice said to me, "Look again, and look a little higher." At this time I raised my eyes, and saw a straight and narrow path, cast up high above the world. On this path the Advent people were traveling to the city, which was at the farther end of the path. They had a bright light set up behind them at the beginning of the path, which an angel told me was the midnight cry. This light shone all along the path and gave light for their feet so that they might not stumble. If they kept their eyes fixed on Jesus, who was just before them, leading them to the city, they were safe. But soon some grew weary, and said the city was a great way off, and they expected to have entered it before. Then Jesus would encourage them by raising His glorious right arm, and from His arm came a light which waved over the Advent band, and they shouted, "Alleluia!" Others rashly denied the light behind them and said that it was not God that had led them out so far. The light behind them went out, leaving their feet in perfect darkness, and they stumbled and lost sight of the mark and of Jesus, and fell off the path down into the dark and wicked world below.[4]

From her perspective as part of a small band of discouraged believers just coming out of the Great Disappointment, it probably seemed to Ellen White that the fulfillment of that vision—God's people reaching the heavenly city—was only a few short years away. She could not have known that more than 150 years later this same Advent people would number more than ten million souls scattered all over the world. This leads to a significant question: Is her vision still relevant today? And if so what does it mean?

In fact, that vision is *more* relevant today than when she first received it. It has everything to do with how we think about the remnant. The great question is this: Did God raise up a body of people out of the Great Disappointment and commission them to carry an end-time message to the whole world? That question would not have made much sense to Ellen White at the time she wrote the words we just read. It was far too early in the history of the Seventh-day Adventist Church for her and her fellow Adventists to even imagine a global network of institutions that reached to the remotest part of the earth. But today we know that this is exactly what has resulted from that tiny band of believers who staggered out of the Great Disappointment still believing that a divine hand was guiding them.

The angel told Ellen White that "the light behind them" was the "midnight cry," an expression that referred to the power with which the believers proclaimed the soon coming of Jesus prior to October 22, 1844. The issue is this: Was God indeed leading His people during that time? Those who believe that He was will also believe that He led the believers who came through the Great Disappointment with their faith intact. They will believe that out of this small group of people God raised up an end-time movement that was to circle the globe. And "the remnant" is this end-time movement, which we believe to be the Seventh-day Adventist Church.

It's not surprising that for the past 150 years Christendom as a whole has rejected our claim to have been specially called by God to prepare the world for the final crisis and the return of Jesus. "Who are these few people to make such an arrogant claim for themselves?" they ask. Unfortunately, even some Adventists have been asking that question of late. Pointing to some of the incorrect doctrinal views of our earliest pioneers, one Adventist recently asked how the result of our movement today can be correct when it began with such incorrect teachings? That question assumes that a few doctrinal errors at the beginning of a movement invalidates the movement for the rest of its history, as though the movement must have emerged from the very beginning with a perfectly formed set of teachings that would never need correcting.

If that is the criteria for the origin of a movement ordained by God, then the entire Christian church was a sad mistake from its inception on the day of Pentecost. The believers in those earliest years of Christian history worshiped in the temple every day.[5] They offered their sacrifices, circumcised their baby boys, and practiced all the Jewish purification laws.[6] We today consider such practices to be practically heretical.[7] Yet they were standard procedure for the earliest Christians! So how could the earliest Christian church be a divinely ordained movement when it was so flawed with what we today consider to be doctrinal error? It was the core belief of these early Christians that Jesus was the Messiah of Old Testament prophecy. The movement was founded on *that,* and God allowed the doctrinal errors to correct themselves over time.

In the same way, the Seventh-day Adventist movement emerged from the 1844 disappointment with the certainty that God had led, and between 1845 and 1850 these early Adventists hammered out the basic truths that we today still consider to be among our most foundational teachings. And time took care of the doctrinal errors that they still held.

You will find even among Seventh-day Adventists those who question our core teachings such as the Sabbath,[8] the sanctuary, and the judgment. Often these same people will challenge the view that we are the remnant. Now, I can't prove to you in a totally objective sense that God raised up the Seventh-day Adventist Church to be the remnant. It's a matter of faith. Nevertheless, my faith is informed by evidence. The fact that William Miller and his followers were wrong in their conclusion that Jesus would come on October 22, 1844, thus causing a Great Disappointment, is not a problem for me. God works with us in spite of our mistakes and in fact uses them for His own purposes. He certainly did that at the time of the first "great disappointment" in A.D. 33.

So what is the evidence that informs my faith? I see God leading this Church to develop a global presence during the past 150 years that is like none other in Christendom, save for the Roman Catholic Church. Our global health, publishing, and education ministries are an evidence of God's leading. Our global missionary outreach is an evidence of God's leading. To me, the seventy-year ministry of Ellen White is a powerful evidence of God's leading. I am convinced that without her guidance, we would probably have faded away like most of the other half dozen groups that emerged from the Great Disappointment. Most important is the witness she bore for Jesus. In spite of all the questions that have been raised about her during the past few decades, her insights into the great controversy and the plan of salvation have had a powerful impact on my spiritual life. That's evidence that informs my faith, and *I'm not about to give it up.*

In spite of the objections of those who say that claiming to be the remnant is arrogant, I still believe we are a people specially called by God to carry out a special work for Him in these closing days of earth's history. I realize that we are a relatively insignificant group in today's Christian world, and I don't know how God plans to bring this movement to global prominence. But the Bible and Ellen White say it *will* happen, and I trust these sources to know what they're talking about. I plan to stick by this movement to the end and see what happens. And I want to do my little bit to contribute to its success.

I hope you'll join me!

1. *The Great Controversy*, 565.

2. Ibid., 390.

3. Arianism denies the biblical teaching about the Trinity and claims that Jesus Christ was not fully divine.

4. *Early Writings*, 14, 15.

5. See Luke 24:50-53; Acts 2:46; 3:1.

6. The whole controversy between Paul and the Judizers was over the necessity of Gentiles keeping these laws. Twenty-five years later, some of them were still zealously keeping these laws (see Acts 21:17-26).

7. Many Christian parents in America have their baby boys circumcised at birth, but for health reasons, not for religious reasons.

8. Those who question our teaching about the Sabbath seldom remain with us for long. Those who question our teaching of the sanctuary and the judgment often continue to consider themselves Seventh-day Adventists.

God's End-Time Message

When God calls a man or woman, it's always for a special purpose, to accomplish a specific task on His behalf. Consider, for example, the following biblical examples:

- When God called Noah, it was for a purpose: To build an ark that would preserve people and animals from the coming global Flood.
- When God called Moses, it was for a purpose: To lead the Israelites out of Egypt and into their promised homeland in Canaan.
- When God called John the Baptist, it was for a purpose: To prepare the way for the coming of the Messiah.
- When God called Paul, it was for a purpose: To carry the message of salvation through Jesus to the Gentiles.

Seventh-day Adventists claim to be "the remnant," an end-time group of people who have been specially called by God. And just as God called people in the Old and New Testaments to carry out specific tasks for Him, so He has a special purpose in mind for the remnant today. Seventh-day Adventists believe that our unique call is similar to that of John the Baptist. As John was called to prepare the nation of Israel for Christ's first coming, so we have been called to prepare the world for His second coming. Ellen White expressed this thought well:

John the Baptist went forth in the spirit and power of Elijah, to prepare the way of the Lord. . . . He was a representative of those living in these last days, to whom God has entrusted sacred truths to present before the people, to prepare the way for the second appearing of Christ.[1]

Our call to prepare the way for Christ's second coming is also a call to prepare the world for the crisis that will engulf our planet immediately prior to His return. This will be a time of intense demonic activity, as Satan puts forth his final, supreme effort to conquer in the great conflict between good and evil. And deception is one of Satan's chief strategies for winning people over to his side. Thus, our task is especially to proclaim those truths that will unmask his end-time deceptions.

Our unique truths

Seventh-day Adventists advocate many truths taught in the Bible. Our fundamental beliefs list twenty-seven, and we are responsible for proclaiming all of them. However, certain ones are particularly important in order to prepare people to withstand Satan's end-time deceptions.

The Sabbath. I pointed out in the chapter "How to Think About Sunday Laws" that the first angel's message includes a very clear allusion to the fourth commandment:" 'Worship him who made the heavens, the earth, the sea and the springs of water' " (Revelation 14:7). This contrasts sharply with the false worship that will be demanded by the apostate beast powers in Revelation 13. Thus, the conflict between good and evil will revolve around the issue of true versus false worship.

Almost from the beginning of our movement, Seventh-day Adventists have taught that the mark of the beast will be the observance of Sunday when it is enforced by law. The importance of our proclamation of the Sabbath lies in the fact that it exposes this deception. When the final crisis becomes a reality, those who accept the beast and its mark by yielding to the observance of Sunday will suffer the horrible wrath of God, which according to the third angel's message will be poured out unmingled with mercy.[2] The pressure to conform to the popular demand will be intense, and those only who have made a firm commitment to the truth will be able to stand. Hence the importance of our proclaiming the biblical teaching about the Sabbath.

The state of the dead. Another truth that we have been called to proclaim to the world is the condition of human beings in death. Popular theology teaches that the soul continues a conscious existence after the death of the body. This is also the underlying philosophy of spiritualism. Based on this false premise, spiritualism teaches that human beings can communicate with the dead. This is actually a very reasonable conclusion, if in fact the dead continue a conscious existence on another plane after their demise. But if the dead do not continue a conscious existence, then the idea that they do is a perfect opening for Satan's deceptions. And that is precisely why Adventists view the biblical teaching about life after death to be such an important part of our message. It will protect God's people from being swept into Satan's ranks through spiritualism during the final crisis.

The Sabbath and the state of the dead are two of the primary doctrinal teachings that Seventh-day Adventists have been called to proclaim in order to prepare the world for the final crisis. This is underscored by the following well-known statement by Ellen White:

> Through the two great errors, the immortality of the soul and Sunday sacredness, Satan will bring the people under his deceptions. While the former lays the foundation for spiritualism, the latter creates a bond of sympathy with Rome. The Protestants of the United States will be foremost in stretching their hands across the gulf to grasp the hand of spiritualism; they will reach over the abyss to clasp hands with the Roman power; and under the influence of this threefold union, this country will follow in the steps of Rome in trampling on the rights of conscience.[3]

The judgment. The first angel's message is also a judgment-hour message. " 'Fear God and give him glory,' " the angel says, " 'because *the hour of his judgment has come* ' " (Revelation 14:7, italics added). It's obvious from the context in Revelation 14 that the first angel's message is proclaimed to the world *prior* to Christ's second coming. Therefore, the angel's statement that the hour of God's judgment *has* come means that some form of divine judgment will be in progress during the final days of earth's history. Seventh-day Adventists believe that this judgment is revealed in greater detail in Daniel 7. It involves books of record, and when the court has been seated, heavenly beings will examine those records. We also believe that the time for this judgment to begin—1844—is revealed in Daniel 8:14.

What is the significance of this judgment-hour message? What does it have to do with preparing people for Christ's return? Precisely this: A day is coming when the judgment will be over. When that happens probation will close, and the last opportunity for salvation will have passed. A consciousness that God's final judgment is in progress in heaven should motivate us to make a diligent preparation for the critical hour when the proclamation goes forth, "He that is unjust, let him be unjust still: . . . and he that is righteous, let him be righteous still" (Revelation 22:11, KJV).

It is our mission to alert the world to this fearful hour that draws nearer every day that passes.

Righteousness through Christ

I have left the most important message of the Seventh-day Adventist Church till the last: Salvation by grace alone through faith in Jesus Christ. We can proclaim the Sabbath, the state of the dead, the judgment, and every one of our other twenty-seven fundamental beliefs, but if we have failed to lead men and women to know Jesus as a Savior—or if we fail to know Him ourselves—then all our effort will have been in vain. We can tell them all about the beast powers of Revelation 13 and the conflict that God's people must pass through during the end time, but if we have not taught them to have a trust relationship with Jesus, we have accomplished nothing, for we have not given them the most essential preparation for the final crisis.

The whole point of Revelation 13 is that the two beast powers and the image to the beast are doing their best to *break* the relationship that God's people have with Jesus. Obviously, then, we must lead people to *establish* a relationship with Jesus as a Savior and Friend. The first angel's message is above all else "the eternal gospel" that is proclaimed "to every nation, tribe, language and people" (Revelation 14:6). That's why Ellen White could say that justification by faith is "the third angel's message in verity."[4]

Justification and sanctification must become more than doctrines to us. We must learn by experience how these theological concepts help us to overcome sin, and we must teach this to those with whom we labor. I wrote the book *Conquering the Dragon Within* specifically to help Christians understand how to apply justification and sanctification in their daily life. If you don't have that book, I urge you to obtain a copy at your Adventist Book Center. My book *How to Prepare for the Coming Global Crisis* doesn't at first glance sound like a book to help people make a practical application of justification and sanctification, but it is. And because it's what we call a "missionary book of the year" (in this case for 2001), I wrote it with non-Adventists and non-Christians in mind. I encourage you to pick up a number of copies of this book at your ABC and share them with your friends and relatives.

Ellen White wrote in one place that "the last rays of merciful light, the last message of mercy to be given to the world, is a revelation of [God's] character of love."[5] This is the message of righteousness by faith, the third angel's message in verity. This should be the greatest burden of every Seventh-day Adventist soul winner. We have not proclaimed our message unless we set the Sabbath, the state of the dead, the judgment, and all of our other truths in the context of righteousness by faith.

The most important point to keep in mind about the Seventh-day Adventist message is that it's God's message, not ours. Therefore, we must have God's power in our lives in order to proclaim it. Notice Ellen White's description of how the message will be proclaimed during the final crisis:

> As the time comes for [the third angel's message] to be given with greatest power, the Lord will work through humble instruments, leading the minds of those who consecrate themselves to His service. *The laborers will be qualified rather by the unction of His Spirit than by the training of literary institutions.* Men of faith and prayer will be constrained to go forth with holy zeal, declaring the words which God gives them.[6]

So if we need the power of the Holy Spirit in order to proclaim God's end-time message, how do we obtain it? The answer to that question is very simple: When righteousness by faith, both justification and sanctification,[7] becomes a real experience in our lives, we will *have* the Holy Spirit.

The extent of God's end-time message

The first angel's message is to go to "those who live on the earth—to every nation, tribe, language and people" (Revelation 14:6). In other words, it is to be a global message. I find it extremely significant that the Seventh-day Adventist Church is the only Protestant denomination with a global presence. Others such as Lutherans and Baptists have a representation in other countries, but their denomination in each country is independent and thus not accountable to Lutherans and Baptists in other parts of the world in the same way that Seventh-day Adventists are accountable to each other. If we are "the remnant," as we claim to be, then

206

our united global presence is truly a fulfillment of the message of the first angel.

I would like to suggest a specific target that we should have for completing the task God has given us. If you read my book *The Coming Great Calamity*, you know that in it I argued that people are most susceptible to changing their belief system in the aftermath of a major disaster.[8] However, in order for them to do that, the belief system they will adopt must already be in the culture at the time the disaster strikes.[9] We expect that, among other things, the final crisis will be characterized by natural disasters of a magnitude unknown to the world since the Flood.[10] God will use these disasters to open people's minds to new ways of thinking, to accept truths that previously they had scorned and rejected.

Our objective as a Church, then, should be to establish a Seventh-day Adventist presence in every part of the world. We won't reach everyone, of course. God doesn't expect us to. But if we have a *presence* in every part of the world, then we'll *be there* during the final crisis, when we're needed.

That's why I support so strongly the Adventist evangelism strategy called "Global Mission." The specific objective mandated for Global Mission by the General Conference session of 1990 was to establish a Seventh-day Adventist presence in every people group in the world of one million persons or more. *That's exactly what we ought to be doing!*

During the ten years following 1990, the Seventh-day Adventist Church grew by nearly four million members, we established more than 14,000 new churches, and we entered sixteen new countries. In 1990 there were 2,287 people groups in the world of more than a million that we had not reached. By 1999 we had reduced that number to 892. A mere subtraction of 892 from 2,287 would suggest that we entered 1,395 new people groups during that ten-year period. But in fact, it was closer to 2,395, because there were an additional 1,000 people groups of more than a million in 1999 that didn't exist in 1990.[11] Global Mission's original goal was to establish a presence in 180 unentered population segments every year. However, between 1990 and 1999, Global Mission actually entered an average of 240 new people segments per year.

Allow me to give you some additional statistics that should cheer your heart. In 1870 there was one Seventh-day Adventist for every 250,000 people in the world. In 1930 there was one Seventh-day Adventist for every 6,500 people in the world. By 1990 the ratio was one Seventh-day Adventist for every 800 people in the world, and as of this writing (October 2000), that figure is down to one Seventh-day Adventist for every 535 people in the world![12]

I'm sure we could have done our work much more efficiently, and if we had, I'm sure our progress would have been much faster. But under the blessing of God, *something has happened in the world through Seventh-day Adventists these past 150 years.* And for that, with all humility, I praise God.

Who's proclaiming God's end-time message?

In the previous chapter, I shared with you a letter I received from an individual who believes Seventh-day Adventists are God's exclusive people in the world. This person claims that Dwight L. Moody, Billy Graham, and others cannot possibly be spokespersons for God. Thus, he believes Seventh-day Adventists are the only ones doing God's work in the world today.

I disagree. I believe God has millions of genuine Christians all over the world who are working for Him as verily as we are. I'll grant you they aren't proclaiming the important truths about the Sabbath, the state of the dead, the sanctuary, and the judgment. We understand what they do not—that a time is coming when a correct understanding of the Sabbath and the state of the dead will be absolutely imperative in order to avoid being deceived during the final crisis.

But which is the most central of all Adventist teachings? It's not the Sabbath or the state of the dead. It's Christ our righteousness. And that truth *is* being proclaimed by a great many of these other Christians today. They may not be proclaiming it in the most complete sense as we understand it, but they *are* leading millions to accept Jesus as their Savior. Can we say that these conversions are not genuine? Absolutely not! Of course there are false conversions among them, but unconverted people sometimes join our Church, too.

The point is this: A day is coming when God will sort out all those who are true believers from those who are false believers among both them and us. When that day comes, God's people who are outside of our Church today will turn to a correct understanding of the issues in the final conflict, and we will all join hands as God's final remnant people. Ellen White envisioned this. Here is how she described the impact of our message during the final crisis:

> [As] the rays of light penetrate everywhere, the truth is seen in
> its clearness, and the honest children of God sever the bands which

have held them. Family connections, church relations, are powerless to stay them now. Truth is more precious than all besides. Notwithstanding the agencies combined against the truth, *a large number take their stand upon the Lord's side.*[13]

Those in other churches who are true workers for God *are* preparing people for the end time by bringing them a knowledge of Jesus and establishing them in a relationship with Him. This is *the* most essential preparation for the final crisis. And when that crisis strikes, it will simply be a matter of these godly people adding the truths we've been proclaiming to the Christian experience they already have, and they will be as prepared to endure the crisis as we are.

So how should we think about God's end-time message?

It's difficult to separate a discussion of God's end-time *message* from a discussion of His end-time *messengers*—the remnant. So I will close this chapter by bringing these two ideas together.

It's absolutely essential that we have a correct understanding of who we are as "the remnant." People may chide us for supposing that we—a tiny minority in comparison to the size of the world population or even of Christendom as a whole—have been uniquely called by God to prepare the rest of the world for His coming. That's like saying God didn't call Noah because out of the entire world population at that time only eight souls made up His true people. But we must understand that God has indeed raised up the Seventh-day Adventist Church, like He did Noah, to proclaim the imminent end of the world. *The only reason we exist as a remnant is to proclaim God's end-time message.*

A recognition and acceptance of that responsibility is the primary challenge facing the Seventh-day Adventist Church today, especially in North America and other developed parts of the world. I don't mean that massive numbers of our people have given up their faith that God led a people out of the Great Disappointment to finish His work in the earth. The problem isn't mass apostasy. It's massive indifference. It's a loss of a sense of mission on the part of so many Seventh-day Adventists today.

I recognize this dwindling sense of mission in the declining number of churches in North America that still include the weekly mission story as a part of their Sabbath School program. I see it in the fewer and fewer number of pastors who are willing to include a personal ministries period somewhere in the Sabbath morning services. (I agree with those pastors who say that we come to church to worship God. But since when did our *worship of* God become separated from our *witness for* God?) I see the loss of our sense of mission in the declining subscription rates for all Seventh-day Adventist publications since about 1975. I am particularly aware of this as editor of *Signs of the Times*®.

Can you understand how vitally important it is that we have not only a correct *understanding* of ourselves as the remnant but that we have an *urgency* about the message God has called us to proclaim? Of all the ways to think about the end time, this is the most crucial. For if we fail to understand who we are and have a sense of urgency about the work God has given us to do, then none of the other things I've said in this book matters.

That's why I urge you to do everything you can to share our end-time message with as many people as possible. And one of the best suggestions I can offer is to send *Signs of the Times*® to your non-Adventist friends and relatives. We cover each of our twenty-seven fundamental beliefs every year in *Signs*, and the most important ones we deal with at least twice and usually more often than that. *Signs* is actually one of the best ways you can invest your evangelism dollars, because you don't have to *hope* your friends and relatives will *tune in*. When you send in your subscription, you *know* they'll receive twelve exposures to our message every year. And that will continue as long as you maintain that subscription.[14]

It may seem impossible to you right now that God could use our small movement to accomplish a global task. But think back on what He has already accomplished through us. Our earliest pioneers would be shocked to see where we are today. And remember that during the final crisis, we too "will be surprised by the simple means that [God] will use to bring about and perfect His work of righteousness."[15]

Our task today is to continue spreading our message as far and wide as possible. In His own time, and through means that we do not now understand, God will bring this movement and its message to a glorious, global close.

---

1. *Testimonies*, 3:61, 62.

2. See *The Great Controversy*, 449, 450.

3. Ibid., 588.

4. *Review and Herald*, April 1, 1890; cited in *Evangelism*, 190.

5. *Christ's Object Lessons*, 415.

6. *The Great Controversy*, 606, italics added.

7. Some theologians consider righteousness by faith to be synonymous with justification only, but in this nontechnical discussion I'm using it as an umbrella term that includes both justification and sanctification.

8. Marvin Moore, *The Coming Great Calamity* (Nampa, Idaho: Pacific Press®, 1997), 80-83.

9. Ibid., 87, 88.

10. Ibid., 23-39.

11. I obtained these figures from a letter by Michael Ryan, the General Field Secretary of the General Conference who oversees the Global Mission project, which he wrote to all supporters of Global Mission in October 1999. The October 26, 2000 issue of the *Adventist Review* reported that as of that date there remained only 472 unentered people groups numbering a million or more persons (page 15).

12. The figure 535 for October 2000 is from *Adventist Review,* October 26, 2000, 19. The figures for 1870, 1930, and 1990 are from the letter by Michael Ryan mentioned in endnote 11 above.

13. *The Great Controversy*, 612, italics added.

14. To order *Signs* for yourself and your friends, call your Adventist Book Center at 1-800-765-6955.

15. *Testimonies to Ministers*, 300.

an End-Time Relationship With Jesus

My first pastorate after internship in the Southern California Conference back in the early 1960s was in Mojave, out in the desert, about a hundred miles north of Los Angeles. I always think back on those four years as my "wilderness experience"!

In the early 1960s, Robert Brinsmead was making the rounds of Adventism in North America and Australia. Since a physician who was a member of my church happened to be a follower of Brinsmead, I decided it would be a good idea for me to learn what Brinsmead taught. I remember attending at least two of his meetings, and I obtained quite a number of his books and other materials. I spent the next year or so studying Brinsmead's ideas carefully. Eventually, I came to understand his theology quite well, and I disagreed strongly with his main point.

Brinsmead's theology was built on the final-generation theory that I discussed with you in chapter 15, but he carried it a step further. He claimed that the way the final generation will achieve perfection would be through an internal work God performs on the minds and hearts of His people that wipes out their sinful nature. According to Brinsmead, justification, sanctification, and conversion are just fine *in this life,* prior to the close of probation, but they are not enough to qualify God's people for sinless living after the close of probation. For that, they must have an additional experience he called "the blotting out of sin," which will eradicate every trace of their sinfulness, bringing them to the point of absolute perfection. And this will qualify them to live after the close of probation without a Mediator. Brinsmead equated this "blotting out of sins" with the sealing of the 144,000 that is described in Revelation 7:1-4. And he quoted a number of Bible texts and Ellen White statements in support of his theology. Following are some of his texts:

> In those days, and in that time, saith the Lord, the iniquity of Israel shall be sought for, and there shall be none; and the sins of Judah, and they shall not be found: for I will pardon them whom I reserve (Jeremiah 50:20, KJV).

> As far as the east is from the west, so far hath he removed our transgressions from us (Psalm 103:12, KJV).

> I have blotted out, as a thick cloud, thy transgressions, and, as a cloud, thy sins: return unto me; for I have redeemed thee (Isaiah 44:22, KJV).

Following are some statements by Ellen White that Brinsmead used to prove that the sinful nature will be blotted from the minds and hearts of God's people:

> While they [the saints during the time of Jacob's trouble] have a deep sense of their unworthiness, they will have no concealed wrongs to reveal. Their sins will have been blotted out by the atoning blood of Christ, and they cannot bring them to remembrance.[1]

> In the final atonement the sins of the truly penitent are to be blotted from the records of heaven, no more to be remembered or come into mind.[2]

> The righteous [during the time of trouble] will not cease their earnest agonizing cries for deliverance. They cannot bring to mind any particular sins, but in their whole life they can see but little good. Their sins had gone beforehand to judgment, and pardon had been written. Their sins had been borne away into the land of forgetfulness, and they could not bring them to remembrance.[3]

Please help me to analyze these statements. Did you see anything in any of them to suggest a "blotting out of *the sinful nature*" from the mind and heart? It's not there, is it? But Brinsmead thought it was back in the early 1960s. That's what he understood the following sentences to mean, even though none of them even talks about the sinful nature, to say nothing of blotting it out:

- "Their sins will have been blotted out by the atoning blood of Christ, and they cannot bring them to remembrance."
- "In the final atonement the sins of the truly penitent are to be blotted from the records of heaven, no more to be remembered or come into mind."
- "Their sins had been borne away into the land of forgetfulness, and they could not bring them to remembrance."

I haven't heard anyone advocate Brinsmead's theology for at least thirty years. So far as I know, it's a dead issue in the Adventist Church today, for which we can all be grateful. I bring it up here because it's such a classic example of reading into a passage of Scripture or a statement by Ellen White what we *want* it to say rather than what it *actually* says. It's an example of developing a theology and then searching for inspired evidence to prove it instead of allowing our theology to arise out of what the inspired evidence actually says.

I still remember a conversation I had with my physician friend in the Mojave church one Sabbath morning. We were standing on the sidewalk just outside the front door after the worship service discussing these issues, and I pointed out to him that nowhere do either Ellen White or the Bible actually *say* what Brinsmead claimed they said. The doctor said, "Does *everything* have to come from a written statement in the Bible or the Spirit of Prophecy, pastor?" And I said, "Yes, doctor, *everything*." He gave me a puzzled look, and that concluded our conversation.

Our relationship with Jesus

I've also brought Brinsmead's theology to your attention because it's an excellent example of the *spiritual* consequences of misreading the inspired sources. Brinsmead believed that *justification, conversion,* and *sanctification*—the tools God has provided for salvation and character development *in this life*—aren't enough to prepare God's people for the final crisis. In order to live a sinless life after the close of probation without a

Mediator, they must have this additional experience that he called the *blotting out of sin*. But nowhere do either the Bible or Ellen White ever define such an experience, so the person who believes in it is expecting something that will never happen. Worse yet, expecting it to happen opens a door for Satan to provide some warm fuzzy feeling that will *seem* as though that's what happened.

Do you see the tragic spiritual consequences that can result from a failure to read the Bible and Ellen White's writings *carefully?* Do you see why it's so important to reject anything that doesn't have inspired support? It's for a very good reason Ellen White said that by the testimony of Scripture "every statement and every miracle must be tested"![4]

Where he got it

Where did Brinsmead get the idea that God's people must be sinlessly perfect, anyway? From Ellen White. Notice what she says in the following two statements that I shared with you in an earlier chapter, but which bear repeating here:

> Those who are living upon the earth when the intercession of Christ shall cease in the sanctuary above are to stand in the sight of a holy God without a mediator. Their robes must be spotless, their characters must be purified from sin by the blood of sprinkling. Through the grace of God and their own diligent effort they must be conquerors in the battle with evil. While the investigative judgment is going forward in heaven, while the sins of penitent believers are being removed from the sanctuary, there is to be a special work of purification, of putting away of sin, among God's people upon earth.[5]

> Now, while our great High Priest is making the atonement for us, we should seek to become perfect in Christ. Not even by a thought could our Saviour be brought to yield to the power of temptation. Satan finds in human hearts some point where he can gain a foothold; some sinful desire is cherished, by means of which his temptations assert their power. But Christ declared of Himself: "The prince of this world cometh, and hath nothing in me." John 14:30. Satan could find nothing in the Son of God that would enable him to gain the victory. He had kept His Father's commandments, and there was no sin in Him that Satan could use to his

advantage. This is the condition in which those must be found who shall stand in the time of trouble.[6]

That last statement is from the chapter "The Time of Trouble" in *The Great Controversy*, and since the time of trouble follows the close of probation, it suggests that God's people must be sinless at that time. Brinsmead's question, then, was this: If God's people must be sinlessly perfect after the close of probation, *how* will they arrive at that estate? And his answer was the "blotting out of sin" theology that we discussed above. Unfortunately, Brinsmead failed to read the paragraph immediately following that last statement, where Ellen White states very clearly *how* God's people are to arrive at the perfection they'll need after the close of probation:

> It is *in this life* that we are to separate sin from us, through faith in the atoning blood of Christ. Our precious Saviour invites us to join ourselves to Him, to unite our weakness to His strength, our ignorance to His wisdom, our unworthiness to His merits.[7]

Please notice what Ellen White said: "It is in *this life*"—before the close of probation,[8] when even Brinsmead would have agreed that justification, sanctification, and conversion are the only spiritual tools God has provided by which we are to develop character—"that we are to separate sin from us." If Brinsmead had read that sentence and allowed it's meaning to have its full weight in his mind, he would never have suggested that some additional experience beyond the spiritual tools available in this life is necessary in order to reach the level of perfection that will be required to live without a Mediator after the close of probation.

Using God's spiritual tools

That's what Brinsmead taught, and if that were the only issue I had to discuss with you in this chapter, I would never have brought it up in the first place. My reason for introducing it is this: What I learned as a result of working through these issues provided the basis for my understanding of righteousness by faith that I've held ever since. And that's what I want to share with you now.

The question is this: If justification, conversion, and sanctification are the tools God has provided *in this life* for us to develop a character that can stand without a Mediator after the close of probation, how can we use those tools to make that preparation? I assume that most of those reading this book have been Christians for a long time. However, it's easier to describe the Christian experience from the standpoint of a person who is accepting Christ for the first time, so I trust you will pardon me for talking to you as though you were a new Christian. We're going to discuss the spiritual tools that God has provided for us *in this life.*

Justification. Paul said that "when we were God's enemies, we were reconciled to him through the death of his Son" (Romans 5:10). He means that you and I were reconciled to God long before we placed our faith in Jesus. Our justification was a reality before we were even aware of it! So when you come to Jesus, you can claim the justification that already belongs to you! And it's a gift. You can't do anything to earn it. All you can do is accept it. That's what Paul meant when he said, "We maintain that a man is justified by faith apart from observing the law" (Romans 3:28).

Now, when you first come to Jesus, your life is still very imperfect. But the good news is that that's not how God sees you. "Christ's character stands in place of your character, and you are accepted before God just as if you had not sinned."[9] "When it's in the heart to obey God, when efforts are put forth to this end, Jesus accepts this disposition and effort as man's best service, and He makes up for the deficiency with His own divine merit."[10] The moment you come to Jesus, He forgives everything about your past. God accepts Christ's righteousness in place of your sinfulness, and He considers you to be perfect *right then!* And right then you have the assurance of salvation. If you were to die shortly after accepting Jesus, you would spend eternity in His kingdom. You no longer have to feel guilty over the sins you've committed or the defects in your character.

No wonder Paul said, "Since we have been justified through faith, we have peace with God through our Lord Jesus Christ" (Romans 5:1).

Conversion. When you accept Jesus in the way I just described, some wonderful changes begin happening inside of you. You have a new outlook on life. The good things you once hated you now love, and the wrong things you used to love you now hate. Spiritual things used to seem stupid to you, but all of a sudden you discover they make perfect sense! That's what Paul meant when he said, "God chose the foolish things of the world to shame the wise" (1 Corinthians 1:27).

What happened?

It's called conversion, by which God's Spirit begins changing your attitudes and feelings. Jesus compared this experience to birth. He said, " ' "You must be born again" ' " (John 3:7), and Paul said, "Be transformed by the renewing of your mind" (Romans 12:2). The practical result of this is that the wrong things you used to do no longer seem attractive, and you begin laying them aside.

I wouldn't want you to think, though, that your struggle with sin is all over the moment you accept Jesus as your Savior. It's quite the opposite. Your struggle has just begun! The point of conversion isn't that the new Christian is totally transformed into the likeness of Jesus. It's that he or she now has the attitude that makes growth *toward* Christlikeness *possible*. And that leads into the third and final provision God has made for our salvation.

Sanctification. Some people have the mistaken idea that Christians don't have to struggle against their temptations. Let me ask you a question. How long did it take for Arthur Rubinstein to become a concert pianist? Well, I haven't asked him, so I can't say for sure, but I think you'll agree that it took years. Nothing worth achieving in this life comes easily, and that's as true for our character development and overcoming sin as for anything else. It takes time, and it takes effort. And Christians call that process "sanctification."

It's important to understand that sanctification and obedience—your effort to grow in your Christian experience—can never be a part of your assurance of acceptance by God. God is very pleased with your good works. Jesus said that our good works give glory to God (Matthew 5:16). But your acceptance by God depends on His grace, which you appropriate by just believing it.

The mature Christian

I said earlier that I would describe salvation in terms of the person who was just starting out in his Christian walk. But it's important to understand that the same three spiritual tools that got us started—justification, conversion, and sanctification—are also available to us throughout our Christian life. We use them to start the process, and we use them to finish the process. So now let's talk about that.

In a sense, we could say that sanctification is simply a daily re-application of justification, because, as I pointed out earlier, we don't overcome all of our sins at once, which means that we keep falling into them. So we have to keep coming back to Jesus and re-applying justification. And *this is one of the most important parts of the Christian life.* Some people think sanctification happens *after* they are justified, which of course is true. The point is that justification isn't a once-for-all affair that happens at the beginning of the Christian walk. Justification keeps on happening over and over, every day, as long as life on this earth lasts. Understood in this way, justification is an integral *part* of sanctification. To put it another way, if you do not understand and apply justification in your life on an on-going basis, you will not experience sanctification.

Let's get practical. Think of your most besetting sin, the one that keeps getting you into trouble over and over. The one you feel so guilty about each time you fall into it. The one that you wonder if you'll ever overcome.

Now let me ask: How do you feel one minute or perhaps five minutes after you've "done it"? What kind of "self-talk" is going on in your head right then? Because I'm part of the sinful human race, I *know* what's going on in your head. You're giving yourself messages like these:

- I'm nothing but worthless scum. I have no right to call myself a Christian!
- God can never accept me as long as I keep yielding to this temptation!
- I'll never gain the victory if I don't try harder than this!

Let me tell you something about every one of those self-talk messages, which we've all said to ourselves a hundred times if we've said them once: *They are all anti-justification!* Every one of them is a bald-faced lie that Satan rejoices to hear you and me say to ourselves. Why do I say that? Because *every one of them denies the truth about justification!* Let's review those three self-talk messages in light of justification.

First self-talk statement

I'm nothing but worthless scum. I have no right to call myself a Christian! Let me ask, did Jesus die for good people or bad people? The Bible answers that question: "While we were still sinners, Christ died for us" (Romans 5:8). Now, if Jesus died for you while you were still a sinner, then *sinners are of infinite value to God.* That means that all this self-talk about you being worthless because of the sin you just committed is a flat-out denial of the truth that Jesus died for sinners. Guess what: If you just sinned, then you qualify for God's grace. The angels who never sinned don't qualify for grace, but you do precisely *because* of that sin you just committed. And the worse your sin, the more you qualify![11]

So here's what I recommend you say next time you fall into that beset-ting sin: "God, I thank You that even though I just slipped and fell into this sin again, I'm still valuable to You. I thank You that Jesus died for this very sin I just got through committing."

That's how you deal with the self-talk that says *I'm nothing but worth-less scum. I have no right to call myself a Christian!* And you keep repeat-ing it and repeating it, even when you don't feel like it, till it becomes a real part of your daily attitude. Remember Arthur Rubinstein? He had to practice over and over to become a concert pianist. And you'll have to practice over and over to make justification a real part of your thinking and feeling process.[12]

Second self-talk statement

God can never accept me as long as I keep yielding to this tempta-tion! Since when did God's acceptance of Christians depend on their per-formance? I'm sure you've heard the biblical teaching that we're saved by grace through faith and not by our works many times. But when you've just gotten through "doing it" for the hundredth or perhaps the thou-sandth time, your emotions drive all that good theology straight out of your head, and your guilt feelings take charge. Sometimes I think we Christians have the idea that punishing ourselves with guilt will help to atone for our wrongdoing. "If I can just feel guilty enough long enough, then maybe I'll be more acceptable to God," we say. (Well, we don't say it, but that's often what's going on in our subconscious mind.) But guilt feelings will *never* make you more acceptable to God. They only get in the way of your accepting His acceptance. The only atonement for your sin that's of value to God is the one Jesus already provided on the cross.

So how do you deal with those guilt feelings? The first thing, of course, is to tell God you're sorry. But confession doesn't have to take a long time. In fact, it shouldn't, or you may find yourself back into trying to atone for your sin with your guilt. So as soon as you've confessed your sin, then say, "God, I thank You that in spite of what I just did I'm not under condemna-tion. Thank You that Jesus took this guilt away and that it no longer con-trols my mind."

If the guilt still hangs on, repeat the following Bible promises over and over: " 'God did not send his Son into the world to condemn the world, but to save the world through him' " (John 3:17) and, "Therefore, there is now no condemnation for those who are in Christ Jesus" (Romans 8:1). After you've claimed these Bible promises, then say again, "God, I thank You that in spite of what I just did

I am not under condemnation. Thank You that Jesus took this guilt away and *that it no longer controls my mind."*

That's how you deal with the self-talk that says *God can never accept me as long as I keep yielding to this temptation!* And again, you have to keep saying that prayer and claiming those Bible promises over and over.

Third self-talk statement

I'll never gain the victory if I don't try harder! Let's start this time with the prayer that responds to this statement: "God, I praise You that victory over this temptation is already mine in Christ Jesus. I claim it!" You see, you're telling yourself two falsehoods when you say, "I'll never gain the victory if I don't try harder." First, you assume that you have no right to claim victory until you've actually experienced it. And second, you assume that victory depends on your trying harder.

But the justified person has a perfect right to claim victory *even before he or she has experienced it.* A friend taught me to praise God for the victory and claim it even before I've experienced it, and I can tell you that *it works!* It's one of the most powerful strategies for victory that I've ever found.

How about the second assumption in that statement—that victory depends on your trying harder? In a sense it does, but how are you trying harder? Is "trying harder" just exercising your will to stop doing it? That's the problem right there. Your will isn't strong enough to conquer your wrong desires.

Stop a minute!

That last sentence is so important I'm going to repeat it:

Your will isn't strong enough
to conquer your *wrong desires.*

Please look carefully at those italicized words: *wrong desires.* When you yield to a temptation, it's *wrong desires* you're yielding to. Notice these verses:

Therefore do not let sin reign in your mortal body so that you obey its *evil desires* (Romans 6:12, italics added).

Each one is tempted when, by his own *evil desire,* he is dragged away and enticed (James 1:14, italics added).

So next time you're tempted, a good prayer to say is this: "God, I thank You that Jesus has broken the power of (name the desire) over my life. Please remove it, because I can't. And replace it with a desire for what's right." Then say, "I thank You that victory over this temptation is mine in Christ Jesus. *I claim it.*"

That's how you deal with the self-talk that says, *I'll never gain the victory if I don't try harder than this!* And you keep saying that prayer over and over.

Let's talk about sanctification for a moment.

"Good!" you say. "After all this talk about justification, I was wondering when we'd get around to sanctification."

You don't understand. We've been talking about sanctification all along. It's helpful to keep justification and sanctification apart when we talk about them, but in our actual experience they always work together. We can't have one without the other.

What's the point?

Perhaps you're also saying to yourself right now, "I thought this book was about how to think about the end time. Why are we talking about how to deal with the sin in my life today?"

Because nothing is more important, as we face the end time, than putting to the fullest possible use all the tools available for obtaining salvation and developing the Christian-spiritual life now. You see, I do believe, along with the most conservative Adventist, that the trials of the time of trouble and living without a Mediator after the close of probation *will* require a very high level of character development. I just don't find it very helpful to call it "perfection," because focusing too much attention on getting myself perfect leads too easily to an unhealthy perfection*ism.*

Going back now to Brinsmead's theology of the 1960s, even though it's no longer being agitated in Adventist circles, the lesson I learned from studying his theology till I understood it continues to be a blessing to me.[13] The lesson is this: that the preparation to go through the time of trouble won't come from some work beyond justification, conversion, and sanctification that God will perform in your mind and mine just before the close of probation. It comes from applying justification, conversion, and sanctification in our life day-by-day right now.

Remember this: Jesus paid the price of sin for *sinners,* so when you find yourself falling into sin, you qualify. Praise Him for that! And God has a plan for *you* to gain the victory. So thank Him for that too, and claim it!

These are the most important thoughts I can leave with you on

How to Think About the End Time

1. *The Great Controversy*, 620; see also *Patriarchs and Prophets*, 202 for an almost identical statement.

2. *Patriarchs and Prophets*, 358.

3. *Spiritual Gifts*, 3:135.

4. *The Great Controversy*, 593.

5. Ibid., 425.

6. Ibid., 623.

7. Ibid., italics added.

8. "In this life" could be understood to mean prior to our entrance into heaven. Ellen White used the term this way frequently herself, probably most often in that sense. However, the context on page 623 of *The Great Controversy* suggests that in this instance she means prior to the close of probation.

9. *Steps to Christ*, 69.

10. *Selected Messages*, 1:382.

11. Of course, this does *not* mean that sin is a good thing just because it allows God's grace to be demonstrated all the more. The apostle Paul had to deal with that twisted kind of thinking, and he made it clear that we shouldn't keep on sinning so that God will have more opportunities to exhibit His grace! (See Romans 3:7, 8; 6:1, 2.)

12. Because justification is what God does for us outside of us, it's real even if we don't feel like it. But making it real in our *experience* takes time and practice.

13. That's why I am always glad to read ideas that I disagree with. They force me to wrestle mentally and spiritually, and that's one of the ways I grow.

Other books by Marvin Moore include:

How to Prepare for the Coming Global Crisis

A practical plan for spiritual growth and maturity involving insight, grace, transformation, and faith that will help you and those you care about, survive the smaller crises in life as well as the global crisis soon to come. 2001 BOOK FOR SHARING.

0-8163-1798-4. US$2.49, Cdn$3.49. (Quantity pricing available)

The Coming Great Calamity

Marvin Moore calls our attention to startling biblical predictions of coming events that will usher in the new world order. Find out how everything really can change in the twinkling of an eye.

0-8163-1354-7. US$10.99, Cdn$16.49.

The Crisis of the End Time

The best-selling guide that shows how each of us can keep our relationship with Jesus during earth's darkest hour. A forceful, yet easy-to-understand explanation of the vital issues our church and world are about to face.

0-8163-1085-8. US$11.99, Cdn$17.99.

Order from your ABC by calling **1-800-765-6955**, or get online and shop our virtual store at
<www.adventistbookcenter.com>.

• Read a chapter from your favorite book
• Order online
• Sign up for email notices on new products

Prices subject to change without notice.